THE START OF ALL THINGS GOOD

A COMPLETE GUIDE TO BUILDING YOUR BUSINESS

THE START OF ALL THINGS GOOD

A COMPLETE GUIDE TO BUILDING YOUR BUSINESS

DANIELLE BILLETZ-REPPERT

This book is intended to supplement, not replace the advice of trained professionals, such as lawyers and tax advisors. The author and publisher specifically disclaim any liability, loss, or risk, professional or otherwise, that is incurred as a consequence, directly or indirectly, of the use and application of any of the contents of this book.

Copyright © 2024 by Danielle Billetz-Reppert

All rights reserved. No part of this publication may be reproduced, distributed, or transmitted in any form or by any means, including photocopying, recording, or other electronic or mechanical methods, without the prior written permission of the publisher, except in the case of brief quotations embodied in critical reviews and certain other noncommercial uses permitted by copyright law. Thank you for your support of the author's rights. For permission requests, write to the publisher, addressed "Attention: Permissions Coordinator," at the address below.

Dragonfly Farms Publishing
446 East Broad Street
Tamaqua, PA 18252

First Edition: September 2024
10 9 8 7 6 5 4 3 2 1
Printed in the United States

Publishing
Tamaqua, PA

To my family, who have always pushed me to do my best. Without them, and their loving support, this would not have been possible.

TABLE OF CONTENTS

Chapter 1: Introduction to Entrepreneurship 17
1.1: The Entrepreneurial Spirit 19
1.2 Characteristics of Entrepreneurs 24
1.3 Types of entrepreneurs 31
1.4: Exploring Entrepreneurial Mindsets 38
1.5: Types of Entrepreneurs and Enterprises 43
1.6 Innovation and Opportunity Recognition 46
1.7: Building the Entrepreneurial Skill Set 52
1.8: Planning Your Entrepreneurial Journey 60

Chapter 2: Identifying Business Opportunities 65
2.1 Introduction to Opportunity Recognition 68
2.2 Market Research and Analysis 72
2.3 The Role of Creativity and Innovation 77
2.5 Technological Advances and Business Opportunities 87
2.6 Assessing the Competitive Landscape 93
2.7 Evaluating the Feasibility and Profitability 96
2.8 Legal and Ethical Considerations 101
2.9 From Opportunity to Conceptualization 106

Chapter 3: Crafting a Business Concept 112
3.1 Introduction to Business Concepts 113
3.2 Components of a Business Concept 119
3.3 Market Needs and Solutions 125
3.5 Feasibility Studies and Market Validation 136
3.6 Strategic Positioning 141
3.7 Building Business Models 147
3.8 Financial Planning and Projections 152
3.9 Communicating Your Business Concept 158

Chapter 4: Market Research and Analysis 165
4.1 Introduction to Market Research 167
4.2 Designing a Market Research Plan 173
4.3 Data Collection Techniques 177
4.4 Understanding Market Segmentation 184
4.5 Analyzing Consumer Behavior 190
4.6 Competitive Analysis 197
4.7 Industry and Market Trend Analysis 202
4.8 Analyzing Product Demand and Market Size 208
4.9 Data Interpretation and Reporting 213

Chapter 5: Developing Your Business Model 217
5.1 Introduction to Business Models 218
5.2 Core Elements of a Business Model 222
5.3 Analyzing Business Model Archetypes 229
5.4 Designing Your Business Model Canvas 231
5.5 Value Creation and Delivery 236
5.6 Competitive Advantage and Strategy 242
5.7 Financial Aspects of Business Models 246

Chapter 6: Writing a Comprehensive Business Plan 251
6.2 Executive Summary 257
6.3 Business Description 261
6.4 Market Analysis 264
6.5 Organization and Management 266
6.6 Products or Services 271
6.7 Marketing and Sales Strategy 274
6.8 Funding Request 279
6.9 Financial Projections 283
6.10 Refining Your Business Plan 287

6.11 Presenting Your Business Plan 290

Chapter 7: Navigating Legalities: Business Formation and Compliance..... 295
7.1 Introduction to Business Legalities 296
7.2 Choosing the Right Business Structure 301
7.3 Registration and Licenses 308
7.4 Understanding and Managing Taxes 312
7.5 Employment Laws and Regulations 318
7.6 Contracts and Legal Agreements 323
7.7 Regulatory Compliance in Your Industry 327
7.8 Data Protection and Privacy Laws 330
Complying with GDPR, HIPAA, or Other Relevant Laws 332
7.9 Risk Management and Insurance 336
7.10 Corporate Governance and Ethics 341
7.11 Staying Informed and Seeking Legal Assistance 347

Chapter 8: Raising Capital and Financing 350
8.1 Introduction to Raising Capital 352
8.2 Understanding Financing Options 357
8.3 Bootstrapping Your Start-Up 362
8.4 Seeking Loans and Credit 368
8.5 Equity Funding Sources 375
8.6 Crowdfunding and Microfinancing 382
8.7 Preparing for Fundraising 386
8.8 The Fundraising Process 388

Chapter 9: Branding and Marketing Essentials 396
9.1 Understanding the Power of Branding 398
9.2 Creating a Brand Strategy 402
9.3 Designing Your Brand Identity 407
9.4 Building Brand Awareness 411

9.5 Marketing Research and Analysis 417
9.6 Crafting a Marketing Plan 420
9.7 The Marketing Mix: 4 P's and Beyond 426

Chapter 10: Final Word 435

THE START OF ALL THINGS GOOD

A COMPLETE GUIDE TO BUILDING YOUR BUSINESS

DANIELLE BILLETZ-REPPERT

Welcome to *The Start of All Things Good*. In this book, we take an enlightening journey through the complex landscape of entrepreneurship, providing valuable information for prospective business owners on managing and transforming their creative ideas into profitable businesses. It doesn't matter if you are the kind of rookie entrepreneur who is highly determined or one who has been in entrepreneurship for a long time and wants to freshen it up; this guide will always be by your side as it brings out the various easy roads to success.

Our journey starts with an 'Introduction to Entrepreneurship', where we unveil the basic principles and values behind entrepreneurial drive. This chapter acts as a guiding light, showing aspiring entrepreneurs how they can adopt mindsets and attributes necessary for success in a dynamic world of commerce, from having a growth mindset to being resilient under pressure.

Pushing on, we reach 'Identifying Business Opportunities', embarking on a journey across vast markets, on which we find hidden gems. Through practical anecdotes and strategic insights, readers will be shown how best to recognize potential opportunities and market niches and adapt to them quickly enough.

'Crafting a Business Concept' is another crucial stage in our journey, since it involves converting embryonic ideas into fundamental business concepts. From forming compelling value propositions to grasping specificities about target demographics and competitive environments: all these are crucial elements that help innovative sparks become vital business concepts.

'Market Research and Analysis' are two informative pillars of the process, indicating diverse tools for deciphering intricate market dynamics, consumer behaviors, and industry trends. This calls for detailed research and intelligent analysis, so that entrepreneurs become foreseers, moving steadily against waves of uncertainty within markets, towards the shores of success.

'Developing Your Business Model' lays the foundation for any successful venture; here, we analyze what makes different businesspersons' brains. From traditional methods to disruptive innovations, readers can create robust structures to ensure that value is created, revenue is generated, and growth is sustained.

'Writing a Comprehensive Business Plan' is an introspective strategy journey. Through meticulous planning and foresight, entrepreneurs lay the groundwork for tomorrow. They develop a structure with a vision, mission, goals, and strategies that guide them throughout the journey and build confidence in their stakeholders and investors.

The business 'Formation and Compliance' section is a guide to some complex legal nuances, enabling entrepreneurs to move confidently through the regulatory maze. By choosing ideal legal frameworks and obeying regulatory mandates, readers can create legal protections in their efforts to meet their entrepreneurial dreams.

'Raising Capital and Financing' marks another frontier. We will explore different funding sources and investments that drive entrepreneurship. Entrepreneurs use various financing methods, such as bootstrapping or venture capital, which allow them to control funds and attain financial independence.

Lastly, in 'Branding and Marketing Essentials,' I want to share ways to connect strongly with our audience by creating captivating brand stories.

Entrepreneurs tell stories when developing captivating marketing campaigns or crafting the right brands.

As we begin this transformative journey together, let us light up the route that leads to success and open up new doors for the start of good things in your entrepreneurial journey.

Chapter 1

Introduction to Entrepreneurship

Entrepreneurship is a place where dreams become reality, and innovation is king. In this introductory chapter, we will embark on a journey through the tangled web of entrepreneurial activities. Entrepreneurship, at its core, is an abstract but palpable force that makes people refuse conformity and establish their niche in commerce. It is not just about having an entrepreneurial spirit but also a determination to create something different and leave a mark on society. This entrepreneurial fire ignites the kind of creativity, resilience, and persistence that can sustain visionaries during bad times.

The entrepreneurship landscape offers several types of individuals with distinct stories, ambitions, and motives. Entrepreneurial journeys vary from audacious founders disrupting entire industries to seasoned entrepreneurs leading established firms toward growth. This exploration hinges on the defining traits separating successful entrepreneurs from others. These people have a blend of characteristics—a potent mixture of creativity, enthusiasm, resilience, and agility. They perceive uncertainty as an opportunity for growth rather than a challenge that needs to be overcome.

Beyond personality traits lies in an intricate network of the entrepreneurial process—a dynamic model guiding aspiring entrepreneurs from idea generation to implementation. This involves different steps that bring various setbacks every time they proceed; identifying opportunities worth investing in, acquiring resources, or scale up businesses, among many more: all part of the relentless pursuit of innovation as well as growth. We will look into the underlying mindset behind entrepreneurial behavior, characterized by curiosity, risk-taking, and an action bias. Entrepreneurs do not take failure as a deterrent but as part of the path to success; this is because failures are the learning experiences you need before you create outstanding achievements.

In our journey, we will also come across diverse kinds of entrepreneurs and businesses within any given industry. The ecosystem is multifaceted, populated by high-growth startups shaking markets up and lifestyle entrepreneurs focusing on their passions. Understanding these differences will help future entrepreneurs define themselves in the market context and align startups with their personal interests or professional aspirations. Innovation drives progress, growth and prosperity, which are at the heart of entrepreneurship. Successful entrepreneurs are able to spot opportunities where others see challenges, by being creative and insightful. By instilling an innovative culture that embraces change, entrepreneurs are better positioned to remain ahead of the competition as well as cash in on emerging trends and technologies.

Developing entrepreneurial skills is a must when it comes to managing complexities within the entrepreneurial environment, and overcoming various teething problems associated with business startups and development. In order to succeed in today's competitive environment, entrepreneurs should possess a range of skills, from effective communication and strategic planning to financial management and leadership.

In this chapter, we will conclude by discussing the importance of planning one's entrepreneurial journey—a strategic move that aims to convert dreams into reality and ideas into successful ventures. In essence, this chapter serves as a beacon—a guiding light that shows how to become a successful businessperson. It illustrates entrepreneurs' ability to change—through self-discovery, innovation, and growth. Let us begin this expedition together as we unravel entrepreneurship secrets and explore our potential in the business world.

1.1: The Entrepreneurial Spirit

In this chapter, I'll break down entrepreneurship as simply as possible. I'll define it, cover its historical background, and explain its economic value and characteristics. While starting a business is a primary aspect of entrepreneurship, there's so much more to it. Entrepreneurs are risk-takers who think outside the box and create value. One way to describe them is that they see an opportunity in everything and will only stop once they've found the necessary resources to take advantage of it.

There was a time when companies didn't exist, yet entrepreneurs were ubiquitous, causing waves in different industries. That's because these individuals have always been responsible for advances throughout history. Looking at the driving factors behind economies worldwide, entrepreneurs always carry most of their weight on their shoulders. Disruptive technology, new markets, and challenging big names where competition has become stale are just a few examples that have lasting effects on larger economies.

Some might argue that 'entrepreneur' is just another word for 'small business owner.' But there's a distinct difference between the two. A small business owner creates an enterprise and manages it day by day. An entrepreneur will build something from nothing, but with serious growth plans in mind, often leaving profitability and stability out of their initial goals.

You've probably heard people say that, if there's one thing millionaires have in common, other than money, it is how little they care about following rules set by others when trying to make their own wealth. This same appetite for innovation applies to entrepreneurs. They challenge norms wherever possible, take opportunities nobody else dares to, and often make strides where everyone else believed it couldn't be done.

Let's dive more deeply into what entrepreneurship means on a personal level for the individuals who practice it. Of course, I'll also go over what it means for the bigger picture.

Defining Entrepreneurship

Entrepreneurship is a perplexing and dynamic phenomenon that includes finding, making, and exploiting opportunities to create and grow new businesses. At its core, entrepreneurship is all about having the desire and capability to take risks, innovate ideas, and manage resources well enough to create value. Entrepreneurs are:

- people who embody these qualities.
- people who often initiate projects or companies to fulfill unmet needs.
- the pioneers of novel solutions.

- people who capitalize on up-and-coming trends.

This proactive way of doing business and thinking differently to other people sets entrepreneurs apart from traditional business management, which is less focused on the role of creativity, resilience, and adaptability in creating success.

Today's ever-changing world depends on entrepreneurship for economic development, fostering innovation, and facing societal challenges head-on. It helps create jobs, which creates additional job opportunities and contributes to the growth of economies. Entrepreneurs often drive technological advances, as they disrupt industries and reshape markets. It takes a certain mindset to navigate today's global economy, which is so full of uncertainties. You must know when and where you need to change things. You must also cultivate an openness to thinking beyond conventional boundaries, enabling swift learning from failure. You must constantly adapt if you want your company to survive in this cutthroat digital age.

As crucial as it is for financial growth, it's equally essential for social and cultural aspects. Entrepreneurial workers act as agents of change by introducing new perspectives, values, and solutions, thus shaping how things will look in our future cultural landscape.

From a historical perspective:

The idea behind entrepreneurship has existed forever. Its spirit has lived on across centuries and in many cultures across the planet. In this section, I'll examine the evolution of entrepreneurship and how it has impacted societies and economies in different areas over many years.

In ancient cultures such as Mesopotamia, Ancient Greece, and Rome, traders would travel far and wide to exchange goods using complex trade routes. The Greeks were all about mercantile pursuits, while the Romans took it a step further with private initiatives and building large networks for trading purposes.

During the medieval period, guilds emerged in many societies, like England. These were institutions whereby skilled artisans and craftsmen could organize and regulate trade. Although they brought collaboration among workers, they also imposed restrictions on entry, limiting opportunities from an entrepreneur's perspective.

The age of exploration (15th and 16th centuries) was complicated for entrepreneurs. With the rise of invasive exploration came colonialism, which led to many local entrepreneurs losing their businesses due to the stealing and colonizing efforts of other countries. An example worth mentioning is the Spanish Empire, who built colonies throughout Latin America, which ruined local merchants' businesses, once they started using slave labor instead.

European nations sought new trade routes and resources that would change business forever. For instance, the Dutch East India Company was one of many joint-stock companies that reshaped financing models, giving birth to modern corporations.

The Industrial Revolution of the 18th and 19th centuries brought technological advances and the birth of mass production. James Watt and George Stephenson were among the most influential entrepreneurs in this era. Steam power, plus improved inland transport through canals and railways defined a period were crucial

In the 20th century, Henry Ford is one example of an entrepreneur who helped solidify the reputation of 'The American Dream'. In the early 20th century, he revolutionized automobile manufacturing, using assembly lines. The rise of Silicon Valley created another wave of technological entrepreneurship that would eventually give us Apple, Microsoft, Google, Amazon, and Facebook, among others. Venture capital emerged as a new source of financial backing during this time. It fueled innovative projects at a rapid pace.

This period also brought increased globalization—breaking barriers between countries and allowing individuals to start businesses with global reach, thanks to the internet. Social entrepreneurship also became more popular; there was a stronger emphasis on how for-profit companies could make positive changes by addressing social and environmental issues.

The Role of Entrepreneurs in the Economy

Many entrepreneurs make their name in history by being innovators. Most entrepreneurs are known for being the first to invent something and then turning it into a product or service. People like Elon Musk and Mark Zuckerberg have proven time and time again that, if you want success, you need to push boundaries with your ideas.

One thing that all entrepreneurs do well is create jobs. This helps economic growth and lowers unemployment rates nationwide; whether by expanding current businesses or starting new ones, they bring more job opportunities to communities that need them most. Most small and medium-sized enterprises contribute significantly to this job creation process and should be recognized.

Entrepreneurs need wealth to succeed, but many also realize they benefit society by building their empires. As one person gains financial freedom, the rest of society does, too, because now more money can be put towards public services like infrastructure or social programs.

Becoming an entrepreneur takes guts, but these people know better than anyone that it's ultimately worth it. They face high-risk situations every day but always manage to pull through somehow for themselves and the overall economy.

Entrepreneurs also shape communities in ways nobody can replicate without being one themselves. Social entrepreneurship takes on the challenges faced by society head-on, with innovative solutions achieved through business models. By addressing poverty, education, and healthcare issues, their ventures help the world become a better place. They also prioritize environmental sustainability and ethical business practices.

The impact these people have on our economy is hard to measure with words. If one thing can be said about them, it's this: their innovations don't just benefit themselves or their companies; they help you, too.

Policymakers, business leaders, and society should all work together to create an environment that supports entrepreneurs. Emphasizing and incorporating entrepreneurship into our lives will enable us to live in a world where everything fosters growth, not hampers it. Working together will lead us toward sustainable development, increased competitiveness, and a more resilient global economy.

1.2 Characteristics of Entrepreneurs

Entrepreneurship is a dynamic and transformative field. It's propelled by the unique qualities and attributes of individuals who create and manage their ventures. Entrepreneurs are different from ordinary people. This book aims to help future business leaders, current business leaders, policymakers, and academics understand those differences. We'll look at common traits and behaviors that entrepreneurs share, the mindset that makes them different, and the myths surrounding entrepreneurship.

One thing all successful entrepreneurs have in common is a list of specific traits and behaviors. These characteristics equip them with the skills necessary to be good business owners. For example, they're resilient, highly risk-tolerant, and super creative. It makes sense that someone with their own business needs these qualities and the ability to envision opportunities when others can't, while also having strong communication skills.

The unique way entrepreneurs think sets them apart. They're forward thinkers who can see trends before anyone else, which allows them to anticipate market needs before they even exist.

People romanticize the journey as if it involves some magical overnight transformation. Another myth is the idea that some people are born an entrepreneur with risk running through their veins. While successful entrepreneurs take risks; it's only a small part of what sets them apart from others who fail.

A genuine appreciation for hard work and strategic decision-making is necessary to build something valuable. This will give aspiring business owners a more realistic understanding of this world before jumping in too deep, without knowing the reality.

Common Traits and Behaviors of Successful Entrepreneurs

Entrepreneurship is a dynamic and transformative endeavor. The unique qualities and attributes of individuals who embark on this journey allow them to create and manage their ventures. Understanding the characteristics of entrepreneurs is essential for aspiring business leaders, policymakers, and academics looking to unravel the complexities of successful entrepreneurial endeavors. This exploration requires a critical look at the myths and realities surrounding entrepreneurship.

The ability to navigate the challenges of business ownership comes naturally to successful entrepreneurs, as they often exhibit a set of common traits. These traits are resilience, an inclination for risk-taking, and an innate sense of creativity. Even when faced with setbacks, entrepreneurs always maintain their goals. They have an unyielding spirit that constantly drives them toward success. Additional attributes include practical communication skills, adaptability, and the ability to learn from failures. While not all entrepreneurs are cut from the same cloth personality-wise, a closer look at their most common characteristics can help us understand what sets these individuals apart.

Vision and Purpose: Successful entrepreneurs always have a clear vision when starting their ventures. They know exactly what impact they want to make, whether solving a problem or driving societal change. Having a strong vision ensures that they stay on track even through tough times that arise along their journey.

Resilience: Entrepreneurs face daily hardships, but they bounce back quickly after each one. They understand that failure is inevitable but use it as motivation for future success.

Risk-Taking Propensity: Entrepreneurship involves risky decisions—but these risks must be calculated. Entrepreneurs aren't afraid to go out on a limb to achieve greatness. Once they've decided about something, they won't let any 'no's' get in their way.

Adaptability and Flexibility: Entrepreneurs know that the business world is constantly changing. They thus need to be able to pivot their strategies, which allows them to stay ahead of the game and keep up with the times.

Innovative Thinking: Innovation is at the core of entrepreneurship. That's why those who are successful in this space always think outside the box. They're constantly searching for new ways to solve problems, improve processes, or create a unique product or service that'll take off.

Continuous Learning and Curiosity: Entrepreneurs are always hungry for knowledge. They look for opportunities to gain more industry experience wherever they can. Being curious about emerging markets and technological advances keeps them ahead of their competitors.

Results-Driven Focus: Being results-driven is one of the most important characteristics an entrepreneur must have to be successful. Goals are nothing without action and flexibility; entrepreneurs must ensure that every step they take to reach their goals is measurable.

Hustle: The workhorses who succeed in entrepreneurship say it's all thanks to an intense ability to hustle. Their willingness to do the dirty work sets them apart. This grind sets a high bar for their teams and organization, leaving no room for slackers.

Crushing Communication Skills: Talking the talk is as important as walking the walk, if not more so. Clear, concise communication is critical when leading teams, talking with partners, or explaining your idea to stakeholders. Ensuring everyone understands your vision and where they fit in will help foster collaboration, increase trust within your team, and make things run more efficiently overall.

A Customer First Mentality: Make no mistake, customer satisfaction comes first. Understanding how to meet their needs and provide value will allow you to maintain excellent relationships with clients while keeping them around for the long term. This mindset also leads to word-of-mouth referrals, which can be instrumental in growing any business.

Seeing into the Future: At the core of every entrepreneur's mind is a clear vision and an unwavering focus on the future. Those who succeed can envision possibilities beyond their current horizons, identify opportunities, and predict possible outcomes. These thoughts guide their strategic decisions, pushing them further towards long-term goals.

Accountability and Responsibility: The mindset of someone who has started their own business is to take full responsibility for all actions in their venture. They hold themselves accountable and don't rely on others to push them through challenges when they arise.

Networking and Relationship Building: Entrepreneurs see a strong network as a valuable tool; they put a lot of effort into building genuine relationships with others in their field. By doing so, they can gain valuable insights, seek mentorship, and be exposed to growth opportunities.

Successful entrepreneurs share these traits, which have been fostered over years of trial and error. Each journey is unique, but by following this blueprint, you'll be well on your way to creating something great. Embodying these characteristics can ensure that any storm that may come your way won't knock you off course completely.

Myths and Realities of Entrepreneurship

Thanks to many myths and misconceptions built up over the years, entrepreneurship often gets a bad rap. Believing some of these myths can lead entrepreneurs down the wrong path and cause them to make decisions that will hinder their success rather than help it. That's why we're here today: to debunk some of the most common ones to ensure you stay on track.

Is there an 'overnight success' myth? Yes, there is. But anyone whose spent time in the entrepreneurial world knows this is a lie. Building a business takes years in most cases, or even longer. There are people out there who seem to strike gold right away, but you don't see behind the closed doors, to understand all the work they put into getting themselves where they are today.

'Entrepreneurs are born, not made.' How many times have you heard this one? It's sad because plenty of people with great ideas believe it and give up far sooner than they should because they don't think they possess the inherent qualities required for entrepreneurship. This couldn't be further from the truth. Experience is more important than anything else when starting a business.

You'll hear repeatedly how risky starting your venture can be. It's not true that entrepreneurs must take crazy risks to succeed. It sounds counterintuitive; calculated moves are far more effective for avoiding failure rates.

There is also a false belief that entrepreneurship is only for the young—why would young people be better suited to entrepreneurship? We know ageism exists, but experience comes from being in the workforce. Think about everything you've learned while working nine-to-five. Bringing those skills into building your own business would only be common sense.

They say that 'a good idea is enough for success,' but wouldn't everyone be rich if that were the case? The truth is that execution and adaptability are much more important than having a good concept. It's easy to develop ideas; we do it all the time. But putting them profitably into practice is an entirely different beast.

You might think entrepreneurship seems pretty glamorous and would involve a lot of holidays and picking your own hours but let me tell you—that's not reality. I'll never say that being your boss isn't great, because there are plenty of perks, but it requires long hours and dedication to get somewhere. It's nice to think there's a world where you never have to worry about a work-life balance, but that world doesn't exist. For entrepreneurs, separating their personal and business lives is incredibly challenging because everything they do somehow relates to their company.

Think about all the times you've thought, 'If I had money...' Whatever comes after this is usually negative. This myth is partly true —money is significant—but without skills and the ability to adapt to today's constantly changing market, it won't guarantee success. The old joke, especially in the creative industries, is that the best way to make a small fortune is to start with a large fortune. Financial capital helps; don't get me wrong, but would it help if you didn't know how to use it?

Finally, 'Entrepreneurs must fit a stereotype.' I don't even need to explain why this one is bogus. While we have pointed out that there are common traits among entrepreneurs, many of these attitudes can be developed or learned. Anyhow, if it were true, how would any entrepreneur have succeeded?

Knowing the real story behind these myths can prevent you from having false expectations about entrepreneurship or misjudging what you need to succeed on this path. Recognizing that growing your business requires more than just passion gives you the power to handle the journey's complex ups and downs with resilience and adaptability.

1.3 Types of entrepreneurs

Entrepreneurship is a complex concept that takes many forms. Each avenue of innovation and value has its own style and type. This section will discuss the different types of entrepreneurs who have emerged as business landscapes have shifted. I'll examine traditional ventures, social enterprises, and innovative spirits within existing companies. Knowing how these models work, you can better understand your potential in today's climate.

Entrepreneurship isn't one big pile; it works in different flavors. This section opens up those models, looking specifically at startups and high-growth plans. Each model discussed examines what makes it tick, where it struggles, and where it thrives. The goal is for readers to understand why business owners make certain decisions regarding their endeavors.

Many more people are putting purpose before profit, which everyone can agree is good for the world. We will explore social entrepreneurship by investigating its unique characteristics and challenges faced during growth efforts. These businesses play a massive role in keeping our economy green and inclusive.

Thinking outside the box is more comprehensive than starting from scratch; some people need established foundations on which to succeed with innovation. This section also explores those concepts by looking at intrapreneurship within corporate structures. While similar in standard terms, there are some things organizations need that regular folks don't—creativity is usually one of them. I hope readers will learn enough about companies' strategies in this section to know what type of entrepreneurship would suit them.

Different Models of Entrepreneurship

One size does not fit all when starting and running your own business. Traditional small businesses focus on creating products or services for a small community. Startups with scalable potential aim to disrupt entire industries with one product or service they bring to the market.

Lifestyle entrepreneurs are those who refrain from rapid growth to maintain a work-life balance and fulfill personal goals with their business ventures. Serial entrepreneurs repeatedly start startups, before selling them to move on to the next project. Franchise owners purchase rights from another company to open up stores under their brand name, without starting from scratch.

Tech transfer entrepreneurs bring research-driven solutions created by universities and other institutions out of the lab for consumers who need them more than ever.

Green entrepreneurship prioritizes environmentally friendly practices, renewable energy sources, and other green initiatives to make our future brighter rather than darker. Finally, creative entrepreneurs leverage cultural trends in the design and entertainment industries to generate profit and create value through art.

Here are a few other aspects of entrepreneurship we could take into account.

High-Tech Entrepreneurship: With a high-tech mindset, entrepreneurs want to innovate in the most cutting-edge industries. Their businesses are centered around technology, so it's new and will make your head spin.

They'll get innovative with artificial intelligence, biotechnology, and advanced manufacturing.

Niche Entrepreneurship: A niche entrepreneur will go after particular market segments. This specialized approach to business allows those who take it to establish themselves as leaders and experts in their respective fields.

Frugal Entrepreneurship: If you like to save money, this type of entrepreneurship is for you. Frugal entrepreneurs focus on being resourceful and cost-effective in everything they do, in order to create economically viable businesses that don't require much money upfront.

Solo Entrepreneurship: Solopreneurs operate independently without formal teams or partners. They manage all aspects of their ventures, from product development to marketing and administration.

Global Entrepreneurship: Entrepreneurs with a worldwide mindset know there is much more room for growth when they think beyond national boundaries. These business owners navigate international markets and diversities to build cross-border impact

Minority Entrepreneurship: Not everyone has equal business opportunities, but minority entrepreneurs fight against that daily. By focusing on increasing diversity in the entrepreneurial ecosystem, they're creating opportunities for themselves and others.

Cross-Border Entrepreneurship: Cross-border entrepreneurs span multiple countries and must navigate diverse markets, legal frameworks, and cultural norms that vary widely between nations.

Policy and Social Entrepreneurship: Policy and social entrepreneurs seek initiatives like influencing public policies for social good to help society as a whole rather than themselves or other businesses.

The bottom line is that innovation and creation are unlimited across these different models of entrepreneurship. Each one contributes to the rich tapestry of a worldwide economy.

Social Entrepreneurship

Social entrepreneurship is different from your everyday business model. Rather than focusing on profit-making, the entrepreneur addresses societal challenges as profoundly as possible by creating a positive social impact while being financially sustainable. Regular businesses don't prioritize social and environmental goals to better their communities and create long-lasting change like social entrepreneurs do.

It all comes down to this: social entrepreneurs are people who want to make sure their work helps everyone around them who needs it. They view things differently and find ways for businesses to flourish while ending poverty, inequality, healthcare issues, and environmental degradation.

The triple bottom-line concept makes this possible. For these types of ventures to work effectively, the three dimensions—economic (profit), social (people), and environmental (planet)—must all be considered simultaneously.

Their innovative thinking and creative problem-solving abilities set social entrepreneurs apart from others in business. They're always finding new ways to tackle problems and develop more sustainable solutions. Sustainability is critical for these entrepreneurs. They want change that will last much longer than a few years and will last forever, so that generation after generation can benefit from it.

Like many other aspects of life, collaboration is critical here, too. Working with nonprofits, governments, and other businesses allows stakeholders to pool resources and have enough power to overcome any challenge.

There's no use in doing good if no one sees it happening. That's why measuring how much good you're doing matters in this space. These entrepreneurs use metrics and indicators to track their initiatives' effectiveness in achieving positive outcomes.

Figuring out how to fund these businesses can be challenging at times. But it's not all bad. This space is seeing an increase in innovative funding mechanisms such as impact investing and social impact bonds.

TOMS and Grameen Bank are two examples of the many organizations that have successfully found ways to create positive change through their business models. It's clear that, when you dedicate yourself to something bigger than yourself, the world has no choice but to listen.

As with anything, there are pros and cons to this approach. Scalability, resource constraints, and the potential for mission drift are some of the challenges social entrepreneurs face daily.

Despite these issues, there are significant positives with this approach, particularly in trends like using technology for social good and systemic change. Now, more than ever, people realize that small changes made today will eventually turn into big ones—collectively speaking.

Social entrepreneurship does a world of good. It shows that businesses can help society instead of making money. Social entrepreneurs are dedicated to solving real problems with long-lasting solutions. They have shown us that, when profit and responsibility run side by side, it's nothing short of transformative. As the field grows, so will its ability to improve communities, pushing us into a future where businesses care more about purpose than money.

Intrapreneurship: The Role of Entrepreneurial Thinking within Organizations

Intrapreneurship means bringing an entrepreneurial spirit into established organizations. It recognizes that innovation, creativity, and risk-taking aren't things startups can do alone. They sometimes require large corporations and their resources. Intrapreneurship encourages individuals to take on the role of entrepreneurs within the organization, to create new opportunities and innovate competitively for internal growth.

The components of intrapreneurship include autonomy, creativity, and a willingness to challenge the status quo. Being able to explore and implement innovative ideas fosters an environment where calculated risks are encouraged instead of being blocked.

Organizations need to provide a supportive infrastructure in order for intrapreneurship to thrive. This includes dedicated resources, a culture willing to take risks, and ways of recognizing and rewarding innovative attempts. Employees thus be encouraged to embrace their entrepreneurial thinking with this support.

Innovation labs, or incubators, are spaces for employees who want to carry out intrapreneurial activities. These environments are playgrounds for testing experiments and collaborating outside the usual corporate structure.

Because innovation leads to change across industries, intrapreneurship offers many benefits for companies when it comes to innovation strategy. It stimulates innovation, increases employee engagement, attracts top talent, positions organizations as industry leaders, and adapts corporations during market shifts.

Employees become more invested in their work when they can contribute with freedom from innovative ideas, which leads to higher retention rates in these organizations.

Resistance to change may sometimes cause problems in a corporate environment, but a commitment to cultural transformation and embracing uncertainty are needed.

Leadership plays an essential role in fostering intrapreneurship. Leaders need to set up guidelines that support this sort of culture. Employees empowered by top-down commitments can take risks and show their entrepreneurial talents.

To build a corporate entrepreneurial ecosystem, processes, structures, and incentives that support intrapreneurial activities must be established. Pathways for idea generation, mechanisms for resource allocation, and frameworks for recognizing and rewarding them will also be needed. Leaders must also go through leadership development programs that nurture and cultivate intrapreneurial skills.

Intrapreneurship usually involves opening up and collaborating with other organizations. Embracing external partnerships allows external creativity and diversity to flow through the process.

In terms of key performance indicators, the success of these initiatives should be measured by:

- The number of implemented ideas.

- The effect on revenue and profitability.

- The extent of employee satisfaction and engagement.

Intrapreneurial thinking isn't limited to specific roles or hierarchies. Successful intrapreneurship motivates people at every level of a company to think like entrepreneurs, creating a culture where ideas can come from anyone, anywhere.

As companies continue to realize the value of intrapreneurship, future trends indicate widespread adoption of its principles. This includes prioritizing continuous learning, integrating artificial intelligence into innovation processes, and developing adaptable organizational structures that reflect an entrepreneurial spirit.

1.4: Exploring Entrepreneurial Mindsets

An entrepreneur's mindset is critical to success in a constantly changing world. In this section, we diver more deeply into the nooks and crannies of this way of thinking and the personal and professional drivers that push people toward entrepreneurship. You'll fit right in here if you've ever felt driven by a desire for autonomy or innovation.

Entrepreneurs are motivated by all sorts of things when starting their businesses. These might include:

- A desire to solve problems

- A thirst for creative expression

- The yearning to achieve a long-held dream

- Financial independence

- Building a legacy
- Being your own boss

Undoubtedly, taking on an entrepreneurial journey is inherently risky—but so is life, and sometimes risks are worth taking. This section examines the way entrepreneurs balance this delicate game between risk and reward. They often must walk unthinkingly into uncharted territory while praying for success, which requires strategic decision-making they may not even notice themselves doing. I aim to shine some light on these unseen processes, enabling you to fine-tune them yourself.

Entrepreneurs face many obstacles on their journeys—financial hardships barely touch the tip of the iceberg—but it does not stop them. This section investigates their challenges, from market volatility to personal hardship. Every successful entrepreneur has one thing in common, though—resilience. If there's one takeaway from this guide, it is that resilience will become your new best friend.

This section is meant to work like a roadmap for any future business owner looking to take the first steps on their journey and mitigate their risks.

Personal and Professional Drivers for Entrepreneurs

People start a business for many reasons, each unique. You need help pinpointing the exact reason why someone takes that leap into the world of entrepreneurship. It could be a mix of personal goals and professional ambitions, which all shape an idea.

Many entrepreneurs start their journey because they are passionate about solving a problem or delivering something special to people. They believe entirely in their purpose, and money isn't something they even think about much.

For others, being inventive drives them down the entrepreneurial path. They know this journey will let them create whatever they want to create and push past what people say is possible. And that knowledge keeps them going through all the ups and downs. Making your growth personal and taking control are some professional motivators. Charting your course lets you decide where you're going without conforming to others' wants and needs. Plus, learning every day would be nearly impossible with any other occupation.

Some use entrepreneurships as a tool with which to leave a legacy behind or make an impact on society. People like this strive to build businesses that last forever or become well-known worldwide, which acts as fuel when things get tough.

Of course, some want financial independence from big corporations and employers who hold their money over their heads as an incentive until retirement age. This drive pushes them toward alternative careers.

Being your own boss has always sounded nice, but only some achieve it. Entrepreneurs have complete control over everything (and responsibility too), making decisions without interference or backlash from anyone else. Working out how things should be run has saved many startups while causing others to fail.

Innovation is another significant driver for many entrepreneurs today. Breaking old barriers and introducing new products into markets makes them tick. They crave disruption and success in their business's future.

For most people who leap, entrepreneurship isn't about money; it's about a sense of fulfillment. Being able to say that they built something from scratch always gives entrepreneurs a sense of satisfaction unlike any other.

Both personal and professional goals can drive entrepreneurs. This blend of passion, purpose, and financial aspirations keeps them pushing forward in the challenging world of business ownership. When we peel back the layers of these goals, we find that entrepreneurship is not a career choice but a deeply personal journey that offers professional growth opportunities.

Risks and Rewards of Entrepreneurial Ventures

Entrepreneurship is a wild ride, a high-speed rollercoaster with many ups and downs. It's always been about taking risks, striking gold, and moving on to the next big thing. And while that sounds fun and exciting, the path is filled with obstacles that require more than potential future solutions. Let's dive deep into this weird business world and discover why people are drawn to it even though it's a challenging game.

Risks of Entrepreneurial Ventures

One of the most significant risks entrepreneurs' face is financial uncertainty. The beginnings of a venture typically require heavy investments, without any guarantee of a return. Given this, financial losses are to be expected, and success will rely solely on market dynamics, customer reception, and external economic factors.

Constantly moving market trends introduce significant risk for entrepreneurs. Sudden changes in consumer preferences, global economic conditions, and technological advances can bring down an entire business in the blink of an eye. Entrepreneurs face the ongoing challenge of keeping up with market trends while quickly making crucial adjustments.

Entrepreneurs experience many operational challenges, such as disruptions to supply chains or workforce management issues. Careful planning and strategic thinking are required to ensure smooth daily operations, but mistakes can ruin everything.

Competition will always pose a significant risk to entrepreneurial ventures due to their nature. Whether new competitors emerge, customer preferences shift, or industry disruptions happen, complacency can jeopardize an entrepreneur's business at any time.

Rewards of Entrepreneurial Ventures

The potential for a big payday motivates many entrepreneurs. The ability to create something out of nothing—and wealth along with it—is an irresistible lure. Even if money isn't the primary goal, many people enjoy seeing their ideas manifest in reality and impact the world. Inventing something new or improving something that already exists is satisfying in its own right.

Entrepreneurship involves such high stakes that personal development is inevitable. With countless opportunities to fail, learn, and grow, each setback can become a steppingstone toward success. And even though new business ventures are risky endeavors, they offer immense opportunities for building something lasting and meaningful.

The control an entrepreneur has over their destiny is unparalleled. They have a blank canvas on which to paint their masterpiece on and a life's work that will be worth leaving behind once they're gone.

Entrepreneurship has many risks that can take time to manage. While ambition, resilience, and vision are great, you might also need luck. Success as an entrepreneur requires overcoming complex, nightmarish obstacles at every turn.

Overcoming Obstacles and the Resilience Factor

Entrepreneurship is the journey of a lifetime. Faced with many obstacles and challenges, the ability to overcome difficulties separates a successful entrepreneur from the rest. We will look at the types of hurdles entrepreneurs face and how they can maintain optimism despite them.

These issues come from all sides and angles, whether financial problems or not having time for work and play. The trials thrown at these people can lead to burnout; so, again, resilience is critical.

Resilience has different levels, too. These range from adapting to failure to developing emotional intelligence so that you don't take every setback personally; there's no shortage of situations in which you will need to stay determined.

Mindfulness, self-care practices, and a constant drive for learning will help you overcome these challenges. When times get tough, you need to keep the right goal in mind to continue pushing forward.

1.5: Types of Entrepreneurs and Enterprises

Solo Entrepreneurs and Freelancers

An unconventional assortment of people has emerged in the dynamic realm of entrepreneurship. Challenging traditional ownership models and employment structures, solo entrepreneurs and freelancers blaze their trails in the business world. By doing things their way, we can see what it's like to be free from bosses and corporate ladders.

Entrepreneurship is a path that many solo entrepreneurs take alone. They use their skills, vision, and tenacity to carve out a niche for themselves, all with no help at all. By contrast, freelancers have similar specializations but offer them on a contractual basis. While they are different in practice, they both appreciate autonomy. They keep going, even without any safety net or structure accompanying regular employment.

Making decisions is much easier when you're not beholden to anyone else's interests but your own. Freelancers find this especially helpful when choosing projects that align with their skills and passions. Adapting quickly also allows them to build a portfolio of experience across multiple industries.

Despite all the good things about being your boss, some downsides exist. One major challenge is financial uncertainty when demand for your services wanes—as it inevitably will sometimes—and nobody else picks up the slack for you. Building up a strong network and personal brand becomes especially important here, because past clients or fellow professionals in the industry can vouch for the quality of work these entrepreneurs produce.

By now, you probably know that solo entrepreneurs and freelancers value their independence above anything else. But what does it allow them to do? The answer is simple: work whenever they want on whatever they want. Sure, the road can be challenging and the work frustrating sometimes, but, for them, it's all worth it to do what they love most.

Many are hesitant to embark on solo entrepreneurs' and freelancers' journeys to build their businesses. But when it comes down to it, their stories represent a changing landscape in entrepreneurship. When you mix independence with interdependence, you get some powerful results. Over time, we'll see more and more people choosing this route over traditional employment opportunities.

Startup Founders and Innovative Ventures

Deep in the core of the startup ethos lies innovation. Founders take those first steps into entrepreneurship, hoping to break away from the pack and do something no one has seen before, and often end up as employers themselves in the process. The risk-taking culture helps foster this spirit, as people learn to embrace uncertainty when they have an idea of how to change the game. Those risky decisions can lead to excellent rewards; entrepreneurs push boundaries, experiment with new ideas, and envision possibilities that most people can't even fathom.

When bringing an idea to life, founders must master multitasking. At any moment, they could be pitching investors for some cash or answering questions on why their business even exists. It's a balance few people can handle alone, so you need to allocate resources wisely while carefully planning your next move. You'll hit speed bumps along this journey, probably more than you'd like. It would help if you focused on pushing past them toward your ultimate goal.

Running a startup is more than making a product or offering a service; many moving parts need masterful orchestration if founders want it all to work out. One of those things is building a damn good team—one that sees your vision and will do whatever it takes to make it happen. Hiring people who bring creative minds and practical problem-solving skills sets a startup for success from day one. And trust me, you'll need a hands-on deck when market feedback starts rolling in, demanding changes left and right.

Going up against other businesses is challenging, especially when you are trying to gain attention in such a loud world. Startups must be different, in every sense of the word, if they hope to make it out of their niche and into the mainstream market. Marketing, branding, and customer acquisition all play a role here, as companies need to work hard to get noticed and build a loyal customer base.

It's no secret that running a startup is an uphill battle, but there are victories along the way that make it all worth it. As we've said, failures don't exist in this landscape; only lessons to help founders grow and improve for what's next. A pivot here, an iteration there—these small moves keep businesses moving forward when everything seems to be falling apart.

As with anything else, once you've reached some stability, you must keep pushing forward or risk stagnation, which is the last thing startups want. Pursuing sustainable growth never stops; founders will continue looking for new ways to extend their reach while keeping operations as efficient as possible. This often requires forging strategic partnerships and securing more funding—both vital cogs in the startup machine.

The stories behind startups and their founders paint a beautiful picture of entrepreneurship's transformative power. In this ecosystem, dreamers turn ideas into reality by challenging norms and breaking molds that have existed forever. It's not easy, by any means, but those who dare take on the challenge find fulfillment far beyond traditional success metrics like money and power—they have the satisfaction of knowing they made industries better while leaving an everlasting mark on the world.

1.6 Innovation and Opportunity Recognition

Let's look at why innovation is essential in the entrepreneurial space, what opportunities exist in real-time, and how to craft and sort through many different ideas. When it comes to success, innovation is critical. Innovation isn't some fancy word we throw around; it is the thing that gives a company its edge. Setting yourself apart from others can make or break you in such a competitive market. The market is constantly changing, and understanding this is crucial for anyone trying to keep their wits about them when they're hit by sudden jolts of technological advances or market expectations shifting overnight.

They say you should always look ahead to what's next, but how do you do that? I will show you how entrepreneurs sense these changes coming on. You might even learn a thing or two about predicting them yourself. We'll explore idea generation and screening techniques. Being an entrepreneur means constantly coming up with new ways of doing things, some good and some bad. How does an entrepreneur sift through all the noise? There are strategies for that, from brainstorming sessions to formal ideation processes.

Throughout this section, it will become apparent that innovation and opportunity recognition go hand-in-hand. Entrepreneurs need all the help they can get when navigating through uncharted territory, and this section of the guide is here to give it to them. By understanding innovation's importance, mastering trendspotting, and learning the art of generating and sorting through ideas, entrepreneurs will be ready for anything they encounter.

The Importance of Innovation in Entrepreneurship

Innovation is essential in the world of business. It keeps companies alive and growing by allowing them to break free from tradition and establish a solid foundation for success. This section takes an in-depth look at entrepreneurship and the role that innovation plays within it.

While starting a company is about creating a business, much more goes into it. Solutions must be crafted, needs must be met, and adapting to change is crucial. Entrepreneurs must consider these things when considering the following steps, but they must also focus on innovation.

The heartbeat of any entrepreneurial venture has always been its ability to think outside the box. Those who can envision possibilities where others don't see potential have consistently found success through creative problem-solving.

Innovation differentiates companies in an oversaturated marketplace. With competition fiercer than ever and consumers constantly expecting something new, businesses need help. Entrepreneurs who innovate survive this brutal environment and thrive because they can offer something nobody else can. This could be a new product, service, or business model. Whatever it is, customers love novelty.

When used correctly, innovation becomes a potent catalyst for growth. No one has ever thrived by staying stagnant and complacent about how things are going; they instead, thrived when they've continually evolved their offerings with market trends in mind—everything from fashion lines to food chains.

In addition, fostering creativity and encouraging employees' curiosity helps build better communities around brands and drives economic development. The core concept of entrepreneurship means you'll be creating jobs regardless. Innovative thinkers find ways for those jobs to make more money at their highest potential.

Those in charge need to reward creativity rather than overlooking it. Employees should feel like they have the power to think outside of their everyday tasks, even if it doesn't involve working on what they were assigned to do. Innovation starts with leadership, vision, and an inherent curiosity that individuals within this ecosystem all share.

The role innovation plays in entrepreneurship is much larger than most people think. Ventures that prioritize it shape their trajectory and help build communities by creating jobs along the way, which boosts economic development.

Spotting Trends and Capitalizing on Opportunities

Getting ahead in the dynamic business world has a lot to do with your vision and seizing opportunities. Finding trends is like reading between the lines of change in the entrepreneurial space. It mixes good observation, market research, and knowing where society is headed. The best businesspeople are always aware of their industry. They can see when consumers change their habits, technology evolves, or global economics shifts.

One way to stay ahead is to stay informed. By reading up on your market, going to conferences, and networking with other businesses, you put yourself in a position to think ahead. Sometimes, all it takes is one idea to inspire a new approach.

Another thing to keep an eye on is consumer behavior. Entrepreneurs who are great at spotting trends know precisely what people want before they even ask for it. They'll analyze data sets, survey groups of people, and browse through social media comments to get an idea of what's on people's minds.

Technological advances are also significant indicators of future trends. If someone is serious about entrepreneurship, then there's no doubt they've already embraced existing technology in their business model, but still may need to adapt.

International trends also matter. Entrepreneurs who have succeeded abroad can bring new perspectives home, giving them a competitive advantage over domestic competition. Developing strategies that work well globally will give any entrepreneur the upper hand.

Once someone spots emerging shifts, acting fast becomes critical. Timing matters because, if the first person isn't ready, someone else will surely be just behind them. Seeing an opportunity coming and striking before everyone else keeps companies unique while helping them grow sustainably.

Spotting trends and creating a successful business takes time and hard work. The best businesspeople are always well-informed, know how to read between the lines, and can act quickly. By doing this, they've positioned themselves for success by making calculated moves others didn't have time to prepare for.

Techniques for Generating and Screening New Ideas

Coming up with new ideas is necessary for finding solutions and innovating. Everything from business to science to art relies on new ideas for progress. Brainstorming is an oldie but a goodie; it was named in the 1940s but has been around forever. The process involves individuals collectively generating ideas without criticizing them. The goal is to get as many ideas as possible; quantity is more important than quality here, though the final output does need to be high quality. By doing this, participants have the freedom to think outside of conventional boundaries and explore unconventional concepts.

Mind mapping allows for visual representations of ideas and their interconnections, which can be helpful when looking at the big picture of an idea or concept. This technique starts with one main idea, topic, or theme and then branches leading to other related issues and concepts. Journaling and freewriting are both individual methods that lean towards introspection. Writing your thoughts down regularly allows for a bank of raw material that could become something great later on. At the same time, freewriting gets your brain charged by creating a continuous flow of thought on paper.

With technology booming, platforms are now available that make brainstorming with millions of contributors easier than ever before. Crowdsourcing uses online communities and forums to generate ideas or solve problems without everyone being in the same room.

Screening techniques come in handy once you already have a pool of potential winners; you must figure out which will work best for you. A SWOT analysis assesses each idea's strengths, weaknesses, opportunities, and threats, giving you a better understanding of what will work best. Prototyping serves as a trial run, where you create tangible representations of your concept. You'll see how well it functions when real people give feedback.

Cost-benefit analysis is as simple as it sounds. By assessing the financial implications of your idea against the potential returns, you can make a more rational decision about what's worth pursuing and what isn't. With all these techniques at your disposal, there's no excuse not to develop something extraordinary. These methods are easy for everyone and anyone to do. At the same time, screening techniques are meant to help weed out bad ideas before they take too much time or money.

1.7: Building the Entrepreneurial Skill Set

Entrepreneurs will find that the business world is full of skills that must be mastered. A firm grip on these abilities is a requirement to succeed in business. The first thing an entrepreneur must do is understand how to navigate uncharted waters, understanding that this skill set includes diverse points such as effective communication and networking, financial expertise, and strategic thinking. This skill set allows them to overcome problems in the business world and seize those opportunities.

Gaining leadership experience is one essential part of their journey. The ability to inspire others and guide a team towards one common goal instead of multiple different ones is crucial for any successful venture. They must also create a positive work environment for everyone involved, understand team dynamics, and lead by example. Then, when it comes to management skills, they must have the tools necessary to coordinate utilities, make educated decisions, and ensure operational efficiency throughout the entire process. These two areas can make or break an entrepreneurial journey.

Once entrepreneurs begin their ventures, finding a balance between taking risks and making smart choices is vital. Knowing when to take calculated risks rather than always playing it safe helps businesses grow immensely. Adapting your company based on what customers want at the time is vital for progress in all fields of entrepreneurship. Industries change daily, and entrepreneurs who cannot change with them will quickly fall behind their competitors. Adapting willingly by learning new things, being innovative in products or services, and adjusting strategies according to current market trends is good practice.

Learning from failure is something every entrepreneur must face at some point along their journey. Successful people don't view failed attempts as roadblocks but more as ways of refining their strategies for future trials or companies alike. Though it may not seem like there's much value in failure at times, a significant amount of opportunity is hidden within. These four main points help entrepreneurs better understand what they need to focus on. This, in turn, gives them a more in-depth perspective on business, leading to sustainable success.

Essential Skills for New Entrepreneurs

Entrepreneurship is an arduous journey. It's a high-demand, high-stress environment that constantly requires you to think on your feet. And that's just the start. A great idea isn't enough—you need to know more about how a business works, in order to start and grow from there. New entrepreneurs will want to develop many skills to recognize success in their future endeavors, and some of the most important ones might surprise you.

First things first, entrepreneurs have to be able to communicate effectively. That means being able to speak clearly and articulate your thoughts well for presentations and making sure you can get your message across to potential investors and other team members. It's all about finding the right way of expressing yourself, so you resonate with people.

Next up is adaptability. The business world is unpredictable, and things change at an astronomical pace sometimes. Successful entrepreneurs must be able to roll with the punches and make quick changes when necessary—whether due to customer feedback or something else entirely out of left field.

As much as we'd all like business success without it, financial literacy is also critical. Knowing how money works so you can plan investments properly and set prices accordingly may require some clarification. It's worth doing the research.

Taking this one step further, how good are you at managing time? Entrepreneurs juggle many tasks at once, which could make heads spin, if we're being honest. Prioritizing work takes skill, especially when everything seems equally important.

Building the right team around you also makes all the difference in ensuring your success. Only some have every quality needed for entrepreneurship on their shoulders; sometimes, finding partners who fill those gaps will propel a new business ahead faster than solo founders ever could.

Risk-taking scares many potential business owners away from pursuing their dreams before they even get started. After all, no one likes to lose money or see their hard work fail. But if you want to make it in this world, you'll need to learn how to assess risks well and make educated gambles here and there.

The classic phrase 'It's not what you know but who you know' still rings true in today's business world. Building a solid network is essential for everyone. Entrepreneurs should always remember that it could be the difference between sinking and swimming later.

Always continue learning. Business changes every day, and anyone who stops adapting will be left behind. If they want to succeed, they must commit to staying abreast of trends and technology.

Being an entrepreneur is about taking risks. It takes a unique mindset and a set of skills most people don't naturally have—but that's why we're attracted to this field in the first place. Effective communication, adaptability, financial literacy, time management, team building, risk-taking, and networking are vital skills new business owners should develop so they can see their ideas turn into something tangible.

Developing Strong Leadership and Management Skills

Developing leadership and management skills is crucial for individuals who want to excel in any professional field. Leadership and management are vital in running teams, overseeing projects, shaping organizational culture, and achieving success. Although many things contribute to effective leadership and management, let's start with some foundational points.

One significant aspect of being a good leader is communicating persuasively and authentically. A good leader should be able to pitch their vision to someone in 30 seconds, if necessary, to gain confidence and create an environment where the team feels comfortable talking. Proficient communication also means being good at active listening, so you hear what your team needs or wants. This creates an environment in which everyone respects each other's opinions.

Strategic thinking is another cornerstone of solid leadership and management skills. Leaders have greater visions than most; but they need to know how they will get there. Leaders must think critically about situations to make informed decisions when needed. They also must adopt strategies as circumstances change or devise new ones altogether.

A leader's effectiveness is often measured by their ability to motivate and inspire those under them. This includes recognizing individual contributions, fostering positive working relationships between coworkers, and cultivating a shared sense of purpose within the team, allowing you to reach goals more quickly than ever.

Influential leaders possess elevated emotional intelligence, allowing them to navigate interpersonal dynamics while maintaining healthy boundaries. It also helps managers build strong relationships with employees, making the work environment more enjoyable for everyone involved.

In parallel with these skills, managers need practical management skills to ensure daily operation. Managers should be able to organize tasks effectively, delegate others as necessary, and monitor everyone's progress.

Managers should pay close attention to financials, especially budgets, because they need to make significant resource allocation and cost-effectiveness decisions. This skill allows the company to grow.

Adaptability is another trait that great leaders and managers share because, in business, you never know what will happen or how fast things will change. It takes a lot of energy, but when it is done right, it can keep your organization competitive by staying ahead of industry trends.

Unsurprisingly, ethical leadership is necessary in order to establish trust and credibility within an organization. When employees trust their leaders, they're more interested in providing feedback, which can be used to make informed changes later.

Cultivating strong leadership skills is essential for both personal and corporate growth. As individuals continue to work on these skills, they'll be more likely to propel themselves further professionally while helping their teams along the way.

Balancing Risk with Opportunity

Juggling between risks and opportunities is crucial to decision-making in various fields, including business and personal finance.

One thing to consider when balancing these two is knowing the consequences of every choice. Risk comes with uncertainties and the possibility of adverse outcomes, while opportunity, on the other hand, indicates positive results and rewards. To find a balance between risks and rewards, you need to carefully evaluate what could go wrong or right with every choice involved.

In entrepreneurship, risk-taking is usually seen as necessary for growth and innovation. It's common for entrepreneurs to venture into uncertain things because success follows those who know how to weigh the potential benefits against the possible downsides. On the flip side, people fail when they make decisions without considering the dangers that lie ahead.

Regarding investment strategies in finance, people often seek opportunities to help grow their wealth; this often means putting their money at risk, because financial markets are unpredictable. Diversification is one of many strategies that investors use; it involves spreading investments across different assets to shield them from huge losses while optimizing their chances of return. Striking a good balance between tolerance for risk and alignment with investment objectives can help achieve financial success.

Everyone faces individual decisions where risks must be weighed against opportunities. For example, choosing a career involves some levels of risk. And choosing between pursuing a new job or making a career change can bring good fortune or ruin everything thoroughly, if not well thought through.

Leaders also juggle risk-taking decisions to improve organizations' performance. Yet, they ought to consider all ethical aspects of a situation before implementing such plans. Expanding into new markets may sound great, but sometimes it could cost a lot in terms of reputation if it is not done right. Innovative leaders evaluate these two factors and make informed decisions to achieve sustainable success.

In addition, balancing risks with opportunities highlights the importance of being adaptable. Different fields, such as business, finance, or personal life, have dynamics that keep changing; therefore, people need to adjust their strategies when responding to these changes. Flexibility and the ability to recalibrate the risk-opportunity equation are always essential for long-term accomplishment.

Always remember that working within ethical principles and striking a balance ensures both short-term success and the sustainability of good results in the future. Unethical practices could give you immediate gains, but eventually they will haunt you and cost you even more.

Balancing risk with opportunity requires thoughtful decision-making and strategic approaches. It requires familiarity with specific contexts, thorough analysis of potential outcomes, and the courage to make decisions that align with overarching goals. Whether it's entrepreneurship or personal finance, learning how to navigate between these two is a skill that separates prudent and reckless individuals.

The Importance of Adaptability and Learning from Failure

Adaptability and learning from failure are crucial for personal and professional growth. In a constantly changing world, individuals and organizations need to be able to adapt. Rather than seeing failure as something negative, viewing it as a way to gain valuable experience is much healthier.

Adaptability means being able to change and thrive when things get complicated. This skill helps people navigate challenges, understand opportunities, and maintain strength through times of uncertainty. Being adaptable separates those who can succeed in dynamic environments from those who cannot.

In the business world, organizations with a culture of adaptability will be better at responding to market changes and unexpected challenges. Having an open mindset will lead to quicker decisions that are more effective, fostering innovation, which will set your company apart from the competition. Such teams are also more likely to embrace change, leading them toward success in their day-to-day work lives.

Learning through failure is also crucial for personal and professional development. As we've seen, failure isn't the opposite of success; it's part of it. People who view these failures as chances to learn will often refine strategies and become more resilient in future endeavors, helping them reach their goals more easily next time.

Failure should always be expected when starting a business. Many entrepreneurs say that's precisely why they eventually succeeded, after all was said and done. They took their losses along the way and learned critical lessons from them. These failures set entrepreneurs up for innovation and, eventually, success.

Learning from failure also has the added benefit of improving problem-solving skills. It helps us break down setbacks and understand where we went wrong. This way, when we rebuild, we will know exactly which parts need to be improved. We then implement these changes, and, as a result, our personal growth will benefit.

Creating an environment in your organization that encourages employees to take risks without fearing the consequences is also necessary. The culture here needs to be one where people feel safe trying new things because they know there won't be any outrageous punishment if they fail. Encouraging experimentation in this way can lead to breakthrough innovations that contribute to the employee's long-term success and the company's overall betterment.

Adaptability and learning through failure are critical for personal and professional growth. Being adaptable allows you to succeed in changing environments, while learning from mistakes. These qualities make up a strong foundation for success for individuals and organizations in this ever-changing world.

1.8: Planning Your Entrepreneurial Journey

Embarking on the entrepreneurial journey is a rollercoaster, requiring meticulous planning and strategic foresight. This section delves into crucial aspects that pave the way for a successful venture. Defining your entrepreneurial goals sets your foundation; it involves clarifying what you want to achieve in your new business. Setting precise and achievable goals provides a clear direction. It serves as a guiding force throughout your journey, steering decisions and actions toward your desired outcomes.

When it comes to research and preparation, learning from others is more than research—it's about understanding other people's experiences. By learning from the successes and failures of other entrepreneurs, you can take those valuable insights with you into your business. This way, you can avoid common mistakes while adding new tricks to your entrepreneurial toolkit.

The journey towards entrepreneurial success continues with creating a roadmap. Here, we'll explore how to plan meticulously and make strategic decisions while formulating a roadmap that charts the course of your venture. A well-structured plan not only provides a blueprint for execution but also serves as a dynamic tool that can be adjusted in response to the evolving landscape of entrepreneurship.

Next, I'll guide you through these complex processes—defining goals and strategically planning your future business ventures. I hope this exploration will equip ambitious people like yourself with the insights and tools needed for an impactful journey into entrepreneurship.

Defining Your Entrepreneurial Goals

Getting your entrepreneurial start can be daunting. There is so much to do and think about; knowing where to start is hard. That said, defining goals from the get-go is one of the best things you can do for yourself as a business owner. It lays down the tracks for all future moves and decisions, establishes an overall direction for your establishment, and aids in resource management.

At its core, goal setting is about drawing up a clear vision of what you want from your company. This vision should include smaller short-term objectives and long-term aspirations, which comprise the bigger picture. Clear-cut goals like this align you and your team during work hours, giving everyone something tangible to work towards together.

Being precise during the goal-setting process is critical. If you need more clarity about what you want, it will be easier for those around you to help develop plans or measure progress.

Successful entrepreneurs always come up with SMART goals—ones that are specific, measurable, attainable, relevant, and time-bound, that is. Following these guidelines creates a great frame of reference for later communication within the company.

While developing your goals, you'll also have to pay attention to market trends and customer needs. Unfortunately, they won't all fit into this package deal, but businesses would be far more accessible if they did. Realistic expectations will help ensure they align with market possibilities rather than wishful thinking.

And remember yourself, too. How often do we get to sit down and consider our precise motivations? While figuring out which direction you want your company to take, make sure it aligns with the reason why you wanted to start it in the first place. Money is good, but it's not everything.

That being said, money is still essential. We all have bills to pay while focusing on our personal goals and remembering milestones and scalability aspirations. A company that isn't built for growth won't grow.

Finally, communication is critical. You need to channel your inner middle school soccer coach here and ensure everyone on your team understands the goal. Building a motivated and cohesive group starts with everyone being on the same page about their work.

And remember: Goals aren't written in stone. They can change and evolve with time, just as we do. Remain flexible during this process because things will shift around at least once or twice throughout the lifetime of a business.

It's clear that defining entrepreneurial goals will take time, thought, and effort—but I promise it's worth it.

Research and Preparation: Learning from Others

The process of defining your goals includes comprehensive research and careful planning to clearly understand what you are getting into. This means learning from others' experiences. The chances are that you'll encounter plenty of obstacles on your entrepreneurial journey, and there are always uncertainties. This is why the insights people in similar situations can provide are invaluable.

The practical knowledge that comes with first-hand experience of success and failure can't be taught through a textbook or a lecture in school. Experience gives us insight into how business works and teaches valuable lessons about entrepreneurship—lessons that only real-life scenarios can teach.

One way to learn from other people's experiences is to be mentored by someone who's experienced them. Established entrepreneurs can offer invaluable advice to those just starting out. They can also warn about pitfalls along the way and help give a broader perspective on the challenges that may arise in the future. Mentorships help spread wisdom throughout an entrepreneurial community while providing newbies with a sense of community and support within the startup ecosystem.

Case studies and success stories are another excellent resource for learning from others' experiences. Studying how companies overcame their hurdles, capitalized on opportunities, and adapted to market changes can give budding entrepreneurs an understanding of which strategies work and best, and which don't when it comes to business decisions.

Networking events, conferences specific to an industry, and even ordinary entrepreneur communities are hubs for knowledge-sharing between like-minded individuals. Engaging in conversations with peers and leaders lets ideas flow freely challenging each participant to think differently and solve problems makes everyone better at what they do.

On top of all these things you need humility—the willingness to listen to successes and failures. No one likes thinking about their ideas failing—that's human nature. But by embracing that mindset, you are opening your eyes to new possibilities and opportunities for improvement.

By understanding the pitfalls others have encountered before starting their businesses, entrepreneurs can set up a plan of action to mitigate these risks. Knowing what could go wrong can prevent it from happening. All this research and preparation will enhance your decision-making skills. It will allow you to better adapt to unforeseen circumstances, ultimately increasing your venture's likelihood of success.

Chapter 2

Identifying Business Opportunities

Creating a roadmap for entrepreneurial success is a careful, thoughtful process involving detailed planning, setting goals, and directing the path ahead. This phase is essential, as it helps transition entrepreneurial aspirations into actionable steps and provides a framework with which to navigate opportunities and challenges.

Establishing clear and achievable goals is at the core of creating a roadmap. These objectives are guiding beacons that help steer both the entrepreneur and the team toward their collective vision. Objectives must be specific because they help create focused strategies, monitor allocate progress and sources effectively.

Strategic decision-making is critical when creating an entrepreneurial success roadmap. Entrepreneurs should carefully evaluate market dynamics, customer needs, and competitive landscapes, among other factors, to create an effective business strategy aligned with the primary goals. Decision-making should consist of product development plans, marketing approaches, and resource allocation, which can lay a strong foundation for growth.

A comprehensive understanding of target markets is also essential in creating successful roadmaps. Market research assists in identifying potential customers, determining what customers analyze and competitors to see how best to dominate your niche. A well-informed roadmap based on these insights improves the chances of meeting consumer needs while staying ahead of industry trends.

The financial aspect must be addressed when creating a roadmap; entrepreneurs should develop realistic financial plans covering all initial investments, operational expenses, and revenue projections. This will enable budgeting activities like resource allocation and allow for an assessment of the venture's financial viability.

Parallel to these processes mentioned above comes talent acquisition—not simply talent. Passionate individuals who share common goals and have skills that complement each other are perfect candidates to join any team building an entrepreneurial roadmap. Building such teams will boost productivity and retain long-term success for your venture.

One thing about businesses is that success takes work; to create a roadmap, one must be adaptable and flexible. Entrepreneurs should anticipate unforeseen challenges, since the business landscape and evolves, opportunities unfold. Expecting this will enable entrepreneurs to adjust strategies, embrace emerging trends, and pivot wherever necessary.

Communicating your vision, goals, and strategies effectively is critical when building an entrepreneurial roadmap—with team members, stakeholders, and potential investors. Doing this creates shared understanding and aligns everyone's efforts towards common objectives. Transparency is also vital, because it helps build trust within the team and with external partners.

Creating a roadmap for entrepreneurial success is a tall order and requires careful consideration of many factors. But when entrepreneurs take the time to build it, they'll find it easier to weather storms and see their vision through in the long run. This guide is instrumental for everyone's journey, steering them in the right direction with a clear purpose and flexibility to overcome inevitable obstacles.

Embarking on an entrepreneurial journey is as exciting as it is scary. It's all about exploration, innovation, and seeing into the future. We open this chapter with opportunity recognition. We will explore the forces that drive business success from several perspectives.

Opportunity recognition is what gets things rolling. Aspiring business leaders become unstoppable when they are given this lens through which to see potential avenues more clearly. This chapter dives into recognizing, evaluating, and seizing the opportunities that promise transformative growth and sustainability.

This skill goes far beyond developing ideas—it involves understanding market dynamics like consumer behaviors and emerging trends. As you progress through these pages, we will unwrap how businesses are built from scratch by defining their opportunities first.

We will also examine how opportunity recognition shapes strategic decision-making and risk management for future ventures.

The last leg of our trip through opportunity recognition introduces creativity, market analysis, and innovation. You will discover how these elements combine to build innovative business models that thrive in existing markets. This chapter challenges you to think differently, pushing you toward new ways of thinking about entrepreneurship while promoting an understanding that action is necessary for innovative solutions to come to fruition.

2.1 Introduction to Opportunity Recognition

The path of an entrepreneur can be compared to that of a sailor. The values are nearly identical: exploration and innovation are necessary, as are taking advantage of opportunities and making strategic moves when it counts. In this world, opportunity recognition is a compass for you as you delve deeper into your business and identify the paths to success.

This chapter begins by exploring and defining business opportunities. By understanding the fundamentals here, you will have a solid base of knowledge of the entrepreneurial landscape you will be traversing in your journey.

Opportunities are about more than knowing how to recognize a good opportunity; they are a necessity if you want your business to grow and succeed in today's economy.

My aim here is to excite you about diving into your creative side while keeping business in mind. The goal is for individuals like yourself to hone in on the skills required to identify opportunities that will become second nature when making big decisions down the line.

Defining Business Opportunities

Opportunities are crucial to success in the ever-changing world of business. These can range from identifying gaps in the market to predicting future trends or technological breakthroughs. Understanding and defining these opportunities is crucial if you want your company to thrive in a competitive environment.

At its core, an opportunity is a set of circumstances that will help entrepreneurs introduce new products or services. Any factor might benefit a business's growth in some way. Spotting one often depends on market awareness and the ability to combine unrelated issues to create potential paths for success.

Knowing where consumers aren't being served and creating solutions is pivotal when defining business opportunities. Successful entrepreneurs have a solid grasp of customers' needs and offer ways to satisfy those desires. This could mean researching markets, analyzing customer feedback, or understanding why people buy certain products.

Being aware of industry trends and keeping up with technological advances is also necessary for spotting these opportunities. Markets change constantly, so you can stay ahead of the curve by keeping track of emerging patterns and technologies. Anticipating these shifts might be difficult, but those who do this are more likely to take advantage of them.

Risks are another part of seizing business opportunities—calculated risks. You must evaluate potential pitfalls before taking any next steps, while remembering that innovation requires stepping outside your comfort zone. The rewards must be worth the risks.

Opportunities sometimes come knocking, so engaging with peers, establishing partnerships, or joining forums can be wise. Gathering insights from others can lead you down paths you would've never thought about otherwise—ones that might benefit both parties involved.

We live in an age where businesses span continents, so you should never limit yourself geographically when trying to seize an opportunity. People worldwide think differently, meaning ideas will always differ; try embracing this diversity and opening yourself up to new possibilities you wouldn't have found inside your bubble.

Overall, defining business opportunities is a complex and ever-changing process, but it's something every entrepreneur must master. They need to be able to read market dynamics, understand consumer desires, and spot new trends if they're going to hit those big growth numbers. By embracing innovation, staying on top of current trends, and working with others, you will put yourself in the best position possible for sustained growth and success in an unpredictable business environment.

The Importance of Opportunity Recognition in Entrepreneurship

Opportunity recognition is key in entrepreneurship. It dramatically affects the success and sustainability of business ventures. Entrepreneurs are specialists who can spot openings others miss, and this skill is crucial.

At its core, opportunity recognition is about finding circumstances or gaps in the market that can be used to make money. Navigating this process requires knowledge, intuition, and awareness of how markets work. Successful entrepreneurs uncover trends yet to happen and identify untapped areas before anyone else can act on them.

This skill becomes important when starting a venture since it lays an essential foundation for all future steps.

The ability to recognize opportunities also leads to innovation. Entrepreneurs who understand what is missing from current systems can develop creative new solutions. These thinkers lead industries by creating new products or services that disrupt how things have always been done.

Networking plays a role, too; those who engage with industry peers gain access to new perspectives and ideas they never would've thought of alone.

You must maintain this skill. It is essential to business endeavors if you want them to succeed long-term through value creation and sustainable growth.

Sources of New Business Opportunities

Discovering and exploiting new business opportunities is a never-ending pursuit for entrepreneurs. To navigate the ever-changing landscape, they must be well versed in the several sources of these opportunities. The speed at which the market changes, paired with the dynamism of businesses, makes it crucial to understand how entrepreneurs can innovate and grow their businesses.

New technology opens doors entrepreneurs can take advantage of, especially when rapid advances are being made. Those who keep up with these advances can create solutions by leveraging emerging technologies.

Collaborations or partnerships are another way to expose yourself to potential business opportunities. By interacting with other businesses, industry stakeholders, or research institutions, you may learn something valuable about their ventures that you hadn't known before. It could also lead to identifying unseen synergies that allow for co-created solutions or access to untapped markets through strategic alliances.

Market research and data analysis are vital for knowing your audience and what they want, and discovering new segments or markets you still need to notice. Learning more about how consumers behave will empower you with knowledge about specific niches that may succeed if strategic interventions are correctly executed.

Regulatory changes also happen constantly; you must notice them and adapt your ventures accordingly. Staying up to date with regulations will give them insight into where compliance or innovation is required, and this is a chance for businesses to create solutions to meet newly set standards or solve emerging challenges.

Environmental and societal shifts are also good indicators of what people want. By watching for changing social values, sustainability concerns, or cultural shifts, you can adjust your focus to things that resonate better with these evolving dynamics. Doing this will also make a business socially responsible, something many customers value today.

All in all, several sources of business opportunities are waiting for you to find them. The ones who do will position themselves to allow for continued success as they grow with the evolution of the market around them.

2.2 Market Research and Analysis

Market analysis and research are crucial to strategic decisions in an ever-changing business landscape. Market research allows businesses to dive deep into consumer needs and find gaps in the market. This gives companies a global understanding of consumer trends, what they're not getting, and what they need. With this knowledge, you can align your products or services with the market's demands from the start.

After laying down this initial foundation, businesses must then go on to analyze market trends and consumer behaviors in greater depth. By examining market trends, companies can observe how a strategy will play out over time by identifying changes in consumer preferences and emerging technology threats. On the other hand, observing consumer behavior offers insights into purchasing patterns and brand loyalty, which could determine whether or not your company is successful. This information grants decision-makers foresight, allowing them to optimize their ventures before it's too late.

In addition to these forms of research, using data science methods can take your brand one step further than the basics. Whenever more data exists than people know what to do with, there's always an opportunity for success waiting in plain sight; all you have to do is search for it. By extracting meaningful patterns from databases, you can thus identify growth opportunities, optimize operational efficiency, and anticipate changing consumer demands before they happen. While this may sound like a lot of hard work for one company, data analytics is here to stay, and for a good reason. When implemented adequately in any specific business sector, it streamlines operations, improving accuracy and precision across all teams.

While conducting market research helps you get off your feet, analyzing trends, behaviors, and tools will help you retain momentum. Finally, utilizing data completes the trifecta required for every successful business decision. As long as you remain adaptable, businesses can be agile and responsive to an ever-changing market. In other words, who knows where it might take you?

Conducting Market Research to Identify Needs and Gaps

Conducting market research is one of the most important aspects of a business attempting for success. The process requires systematic exploration of the market, with the primary goal being to understand the customer's needs and find gaps in existing products or services. Successful businesses know and understand which step is crucial to making something resonate with their customers.

Market research serves as a window through which businesses can see what their customers want. By employing different methods, such as surveys or focus groups, enterprises can interact with consumers directly, helping them figure out what they might need. This approach provides a comprehensive understanding of customer expectations, which helps foster relationships between the business and the people who buy from it, setting the business up for future success when providing solutions to consumer problems.

Finding gaps within an industry is as critical as everything else in this process. This part involves analyzing what competitors are doing well and poorly. Identifying gaps helps you lock down a unique value proposition to help set you apart.

This process is ongoing and must be updated constantly as industries evolve. Moreover, as industries change, so do consumer expectations, making it paramount for businesses to stay on top of them if they wish to remain relevant within their respective spaces.

Conducting market research is how you create a roadmap for success, nothing more or less. Enterprises use these findings to personalize their products or services directly toward what consumers want most. Focusing on this research and using it to establish any business's foundation will ensure they meet what their target audience expects from them and then exceed it.

Analyzing Market Trends and Consumer Behaviors

Studying how the market behaves and how consumers react to certain things is vital for businesses today. Making good decisions based on accurate information about what people will do or want next is a reliable way of staying ahead of the game.

At the core of this process is analyzing market trends. This means discovering what happens in an industry that makes it go up or down. Businesses want to be able to do yesterday's thing when they need to do tomorrow's thing. Even if changes happen due to technology, new mass opinions, or even international developments, understanding these changes gives companies a chance to position themselves for success before anyone else.

Analyzing consumer behavior is also crucial here. By doing this, businesses can get into the minds of individuals and understand why they do certain things with the brands they choose. It may appear intrusive, but figuring out these behaviors tells companies why someone would buy from them, rather than their competitors. By dissecting these actions, companies can create strategies explicitly catered to each individual.

This is all about grasping the connection between external influences and personal choices. For example, online stores have popped up like mushrooms over the past few years because people find them convenient and easy to use, especially given our current reliance on social media platforms like Instagram, where you can scroll through shops while waiting in line without ever having to leave your phone's screen. Companies can adapt accordingly with equal agility by examining how online shopping has changed buyer habits.

There isn't one final answer as to why all these steps work together well. After studying one company from every angle possible, executives should be able to conclude what they need to change or keep doing to survive another year in business.

At least, that's the idea...

Utilizing Data to Discover Business Opportunities

Using numbers to inform business opportunities has become a critical part of the decision-making process in business. We all know that information and data are everywhere. It's about how companies use these data analytics to perfect their strategies.

To start with, businesses must collect as much useful information from various sources as possible. This can be transaction histories, website interactions, or other customer interactions on social media, for example. Once you gather all the information, a company can grasp what consumers like or don't like, market trends, and how to operate more efficiently.

The next phase is where it gets fascinating =. You'll listen to people talk about correlations, patterns, and trends that may sound like gibberish if you haven't familiarized yourself with analyzing data. What all this means, though, is that they are identifying stuff about their customers and markets that would've gone unnoticed by traditional methods. This helps businesses improve on their flaws, grow more extensively in the right direction, and find new ways of changing the game entirely.

One of the advantages of using data is its ability to help create predictive models. By looking at historical data, businesses can see if there's any pattern or trend worth capitalizing on for future success or anticipating any sudden changes in consumer preferences or market dynamics.

Data-driven decision-making is not merely used to understand consumers; throughout every aspect of a company's supply chain—from beginning to end—businesses will optimize their strategy based solely on the insights from data collection analysis.

The last advantage of utilizing data is the degree to which it catalyzes innovation. Big data lets a company find trends, gaps, and unmet needs in its market. With this knowledge, we'll be able to create products or services that align perfectly with the demands of consumers and ultimately stay relevant.

When companies integrate artificial intelligence and other machine-learning algorithms into their operations, the sky is the limit. These technologies can analyze data in real-time. This capability alone allows businesses to make quick decisions and take advantage of all opportunities. It's like having a super-efficient solution when things get tough.

With all these potential ways of using data for business opportunities, it's easy to see how dynamic and transformative data has become. By using insights from their customers and respective markets, companies will refine strategies more efficiently than anyone else today. The dynamic nature of businesses requires adaptability these days, and data-driven approaches help make it possible right now.

2.3 The Role of Creativity and Innovation

There's something magical that happens when creativity and innovation collide. The two have the power to change the way we think and transform businesses into unicorns. Let's break this down by looking at the significance of creativity as an opportunity identifier and how fostering an environment for innovation can lead to success.

Creativity is what lights the spark under every good idea. When businesses cultivate an environment where creativity can thrive, they give themselves a chance to discover what other companies might miss. This means welcoming new ideas, encouraging experimentation, and embracing problems as chances for mind-blowing solutions. By viewing things from this perspective, entities are also opening their eyes to untapped markets and finding unconventional ways to grow—without following in the footsteps of traditional competition.

Innovation is about more than developing game-changing products or services; it's about implementing them effectively. And no, I don't mean throwing out all your old stuff yet. To innovate within existing markets, companies must find a way to redefine industry standards while not alienating customers who already enjoy their products. It's like finding the perfect balance between sweet and sour flavors—they are both great on their own but better together. To do this successfully, it requires an understanding of consumer expectations and future trends. With this knowledge, entities can take baby steps toward revolutionizing how business gets done.

Don't exclude real-world examples. Sometimes, people need tangible proof before they believe anything, like my allergic reaction to seafood. By dissecting case studies where creativity has led to disruptive outcomes, you'll get the inspiration to navigate challenges, use your imagination as a compass for opportunities… and maybe even eat a lobster again someday.

Fostering Creativity to Identify Unique Opportunities

When your natural creativity comes to life, a unique aspect of business strategy transcends traditional paradigms. Creativity is often heralded as the key to innovation, and for good reason; when businesses break new ground and take hold of untapped potential in the market, they can achieve tremendous things.

Fostering creativity starts with cultivating an organizational culture that not only nurtures imaginative thinking but also values diverse perspectives.

When a workplace encourages experimentation, appreciates unconventional ideas, and promotes flexibility, it creates a breeding ground for innovative ideas. This ethos should touch every corner of the company's structure, so each person feels empowered to contribute their innovative insight.

The primary benefit of fostering creativity is the ability to identify unique opportunities. Conventional approaches won't prompt people to question the status quo or challenge assumptions about what they think they know. This mindset shift opens doors for recognizing unmet needs, discovering market gaps, and staying ahead of emerging trends.

Fostering creativity also relies heavily on divergent thinking—combining multiple perspectives to generate unique ideas. Creative individuals often excel at making unlikely connections between elements that don't appear related at first glance. They're great at finding patterns where no one else does.

Putting these concepts into practice requires strategic alignment across an organization's values, leadership commitment, and supportive structures like resources and cross-functional collaboration platforms. Leaders play a pivotal role in setting standards for risk-taking tolerance, including failure.

Businesses prioritizing the cultivation of creativity are more likely to succeed in evolving environments, because imaginative ideas naturally follow suit when such a culture is cultivated.

Innovating Within Existing Markets

Unlike starting anew in another market, innovating within existing ones requires familiarity. It adds new elements with which to gain traction, interest consumers, and establish the business as more competitive than others.

Innovation within markets ranges from minor adjustments to groundbreaking model changes. Each endeavor aims to improve what's already been established or completely disrupt the norm by introducing something new. While both have their strengths, innovating with what you already have is sometimes more accessible because of its familiarity.

Strategic growth begins with understanding who your customers are and how they expect your company to perform. By knowing the subtle differences between preferences, businesses can see when an opportunity arises for a change customers will adore, and when they won't even notice it is implemented at all.

A big part of innovating within established industries starts with understanding markets outside your own. It is about becoming familiar with emerging trends while keeping up with technological advances as time progresses. This approach allows those who follow it to stay ahead of competitors by providing customers with products they didn't even know they wanted.

Employing individuals who crave change sets up organizations for success by stepping outside their comfort zones and challenging any idea that may become stagnant over time. When employees feel like they need to be held back by old conventions, they are less likely to be able to think creatively when it matters most.

The phrase 'if it isn't broken, don't fix it' undoubtedly carries value. Minor improvements are still beneficial whenever possible, as long as they stay within what makes a product unique in the marketplace. These minor tweaks allow businesses to remain relevant and meet customer expectations. Those who can spot consumer trends before they become mainstream often profit from them the most.

Learn from those who have done it before you. Many case studies show established companies undergoing rebranding to keep up with changing market demands, introducing upgraded features, or leveraging technology to breathe new life into their offerings. Each example highlights businesses' adaptive strategies and how they could fend off competitors while staying alive amid their ever-changing landscapes.

Innovation is critical for companies trying to stay successful. The more familiar you get with this fact, the better your chances of being one step ahead of your competitors become.

Case Studies of Innovative Business Models

Exploring case studies of innovative business models allows us to examine companies' strategies for adapting and thriving while disrupting traditional norms. These examples show us how creative thinking can reshape industries and redefine what makes them successful.

One great example is Netflix. They became one of the world's most extensive streaming services by transforming how we view television. Their subscription-based model was perfect for modern consumers who wanted things on demand, and it made binge-watching ubiquitous. This created a win-win scenario for consumers and companies alike, giving businesses a consistent source of income while offering users the flexibility they wanted.

Spotify is another shining example of an out-of-the-box approach that paid off. They took the freemium model, which offers essential services for free with premium options available at a cost, to new heights with their music streaming platform. By giving away part of their product for free, Spotify could attract millions more users than if they had asked for money upfront creating as many opportunities as possible to convert listeners into paying customers.

Airbnb disrupted the hotel industry by offering travelers unique accommodations through its sharing economy platform. They leveraged technology to deliver personalized experiences hotels couldn't offer, tapping into a growing hunger among travelers who craved more than a typical hotel stay. This shows that reimagining old industries leads to new economic opportunities that would have been unimaginable before.

Warby Parker's direct-to-consumer model allowed them to cut costs significantly for eyewear consumers by eliminating intermediaries and selling directly online, a strategy exploited by Tesla, as they also bypassed dealerships with direct sales of electric vehicles. Both companies could maintain control over customer experiences and quality through these new models—leading customers toward sustainability without sacrificing style or choice.

These case studies highlight how strategic business models can lead to innovative success. They show us that, if we want to keep up with an ever-changing world, we must challenge what we know as 'normal' and embrace new forms of technology.

Networking and Leveraging Relationships

Jumping into the extensive networking world and using relationships reveals a dynamic and interconnected landscape that plays a big part in shaping professional lives. Networking profoundly impacts opportunities, so interpersonal connections are seen as gateways to unforeseen possibilities. Not only do people share knowledge and insights through these connections, but they also access an array of opportunities that would otherwise remain hidden.

Creating connections beyond basic acquaintanceships builds a solid pipeline, often transcending industries and disciplines. When professionals view their network as more than just another contact list, they can open doors to collaboration, sharing knowledge, and mutual support, which could be the game changer they need. With many perspectives readily available, new ideas, innovative solutions, and collaborative ventures will follow suit.

Synergy drives all partnerships between individuals, organizations, or industries by combining unique strengths for a more significant outcome. Strategic partnerships involve substantial, long-term alliances designed to ensure every party involved gets sustained value from the deal. When objectives align with resources like this, each entity enhances its capabilities and opens up extra lanes for shared growth and success.

The Impact of Networking on Opportunity Discovery

The profound influence of networking on opportunity discovery is an aspect of professional development involving connecting with people, allowing you to unlock new possibilities. It's not just about business cards and casual chats. Networking creates paths by which individuals can find opportunities by accident. As the world of professional growth becomes more complex, the connections built through networking play a significant role in helping others discover options they wouldn't have seen before. Formal events and informal gatherings facilitate information exchanges between everyone involved, including insights, market trends, and opportunities that could make or break someone's career.

In entrepreneurial endeavors, networking catalyzes opportunity creation rather than discovery alone. With it, ideas are exchanged at rates never thought possible before, and collaboration fosters partnerships that surprise even people like me. Entrepreneurs often find their most promising opportunities emerge from the intersection of diverse perspectives and skill sets, facilitated by a robust professional network.

Interacting with others who've led different lives to you broadens your worldview and can help push you forward. Through mentorship provided by those who've been where you're trying to go, individuals can refine their goals for growth.

The impact of networking on opportunity discovery is both immediate and enduring. When two minds work together and connect creatively, the chances are that something unique will happen. Networking creates an environment where unlikely events occur organically.

As individuals cultivate and expand their networks, they grow alongside them. This gives them not only chance encounters but also collaborative initiatives with others at times when they need them.

Building and Utilizing Professional Networks

Building professional relationships is a vital part of any career. It is far more valuable than short interactions or one-time meetups.

Building relationships is more than exchanging business cards or connecting with others online. It's about actively connecting with individuals outside your current circle. The more extensive the network, the better, but what's even more important is the range of mentors to peers; a broad range can create an atmosphere perfect for personal and collective growth.

There are many ways to grow your network. You might contribute to an association, join online communities, attend conferences, or even join forums. All these things allow you to expand yourself as an individual while also giving you opportunities to connect with others who share your interests.

Getting started on building a network is half the battle. You will need to work overtime to continue cultivating the connections you've made. Meeting up for coffee, talking on the phone, or collaborating on projects are all great ways to strengthen relationships, and eventually become close friends.

Building up and then utilizing this professional network goes beyond having those connections. Think of how much value you could offer someone else if they came seeking advice from you—now think of how valuable someone else's advice would be if you needed help deciding. Sharing resources creates an environment where everyone can prosper through collaboration, learn together, and ultimately advance in their respective professions.

Entrepreneurship also thrives on networks like these, where entrepreneurs gain access to funding opportunities, partnership options, and insights into market trends. Having this many experienced individuals in one place will always lead to great things, like developing new projects and ideas, since everyone brings a different skill set.

Building a professional network is essential for success; there's no other way to put it. Carefully developing connections, active engagement, and a mutual mindset create an environment that allows each individual to adapt quickly and bounce back from failure. When professional relationships are nurtured, everything comes full circle for those who work together, making their goals easily attainable as long as they remain dedicated to achieving them.

Collaborations and Strategic Partnerships

Exploring how companies and entities can collaborate for collective success is always complex. The business world is full of opportunities to grow and bond with others, but only if you know where to look.

When working with other businesses, a lot can go wrong. But one thing is sure: no matter how well your operation runs, we are stronger together than apart. Business owners face countless daily challenges, which can only be tackled with help. This is why it's essential to find alliances in your industry that make sense for both sides.

For starters, collaboration works best when your strengths are complementary rather than similar. It may sound strange initially but think about it carefully for a second. With different skill sets from each side at the table, problems will be approached in ways neither might have thought of on their own. This level of diversity goes even further when you talk about exploring new avenues or trying out fresh ideas.

Conversely, strategic partnerships can change a company's course forever. These collaborations happen when two groups implement long-term plans while focusing on shared values and goals.

In a competitive market like today's entrepreneurial landscape, finding success as a startup is hard work. Trying to break through in an industry dominated by more prominent players sometimes feels like an impossible goal. But it is still possible if you foster these unique partnerships, offering access to established customers or distribution channels, something tech companies looking for faster growth have grown to rely on themselves.

Resilience should always be encouraged within your team, no matter what line of work you're in. A team that can adapt and pivot in a split second isn't just valuable; it's indispensable. Joint ventures often embody this synergy at their most potent, as startups and global companies come together to create new solutions or ideas.

These relationships may be a dime a dozen, but they all share one thing: They are a way to reshape industries while making life easier for everyone involved. It's easy to feel like you're moving backward when you are trying something that seems risky but trust me when I say it—you'll be okay.

2.5 Technological Advances and Business Opportunities

The intersection of business and technology is a fascinating place. They're like two puzzle pieces that fit perfectly together. Technology gives birth to new ideas and innovation, while business shapes those ideas into something tangible. But the connection isn't one-way. As companies grow, so does technology.

It's truly a transformative relationship.

One side of this relationship is the notion of technology as fuel for new startups. Innovation profoundly impacts our world, allowing us to tear down old systems and build better ones in their place. When entrepreneurs get access to these advances, it helps them craft groundbreaking ideas and services that change everything we know about how business works. Creativity mixes with technology to form a force so powerful that there are few barriers it can't overcome.

Strategic adaptation within established companies is on the other side of this technological coin. The world is changing at an ever-increasing pace.

We must keep up or risk being left behind by more forward-thinking competitors, who see progress as an opportunity rather than an obstacle.

Technological advances pave the way for efficiency improvements, better customer experiences, and more impactful operations.

But you'll be left behind if you don't keep moving forward.

Emerging tech markets are growth opportunities. Entrepreneurs who keep their fingers on the pulse of cutting-edge technology can spot new trends before they explode into prominence.

AI, blockchain, biotech, and renewable energy are all growing at breakneck speed right now. Companies positioned well enough to ride these waves will undoubtedly witness incredible growth firsthand—both economically speaking and from an industry standpoint—as they help steer the world towards more innovative solutions.

The narrative is straightforward: technology makes us better, faster, and more vital if we use it in the right ways.

Technology as a Catalyst for New Business Ideas

Exploring the idea of technology as a catalyst in business unveils an exciting story full of transformative possibilities. Technology has changed our world and has become far more than a tool. It drives the conception, development, and realization of new ideas.

Technology plays its part by giving you room to flex your creative muscles. The endless possibilities offered by AI advances or data analytics lay the perfect foundation for people to reimagine outdated systems, while creating new business ways. Entrepreneurs have started to see technology as more than a means to an end but as a medium through which to explore uncharted territories, identify gaps in specific markets, and create innovative ways to meet growing consumer needs.

Thanks to its widespread accessibility, technology is now instrumental in allowing anyone with a great idea and an internet connection to turn their vision into reality. Because of this, 7we see people from all walks of life joining the entrepreneurial ecosystem, creating this massive pool of unique ideas, as they come from diverse backgrounds.

Tech also forces businesses to adopt adaptive strategies that help them keep up with ever-changing market dynamics. Those who want to stay ahead understand the importance of integrating these new trends into their business models early on. With cutting-edge communication tools readily available, we have no excuses for not having top-notch customer service and support. We have everything we need to make accurate, data-driven decisions that will help us remain agile even when everything else appears to be falling apart.

It takes a bit of convincing for entrepreneurs today to realize how much of an edge they would be giving up if they didn't learn to use technology effectively. Everyone knows you should use the internet to understand your customers and reach new ones. Those with a good grip on this will be able to understand their customer's behaviors better than others, and they'll get there faster. They'll be able to adjust their business model at the drop of a hat when trends change.

You can find many examples of technology being a catalyst; as I said, the fintech platforms reshaping finance as we know it or e-commerce giants like Amazon are perfect examples of how tech can push industries forward while creating fresh ideas. It won't stop here, either. Tech is constantly growing and evolving, and there are sure to be plenty more mind-blowing advances coming our way. All we need now are entrepreneurs with the vision to take advantage of them.

Tech wouldn't be anything if it didn't make things easier, especially in business. It gives us access to virtually unlimited information and tools, but, more importantly, it helps turn entrepreneurial visions into reality.

Adapting to Technological Changes and Innovations

All individuals, businesses, and societies must adapt to thrive in this age of rapid technological change. What's current today may be obsolete tomorrow. As these advances take on different forms across industries and sectors, the challenges—and opportunities—they bring will change shape.

In such an environment, adaptability is synonymous with survival. You must learn to roll with the punches at every level to come out on top in this brave new world.

This means more than adopting fancy new gadgets or software systems. While those can help, real success starts with building a culture that values innovation and learning. You need everyone, from your newest intern to your oldest employee, to embrace the digital age and reap the rewards.

Governments, too, must shift their focus to keep up with innovation driven by technological advances. You can't regulate something to death—especially when it's been changing as fast as tech has been lately—but you also can't ignore its potential dangers. It's going to be a tightrope walk for future regulation.

But even those not interested in making money from these changes have a lot at stake personally. Learning about technology is now crucial for career advancement across all industries. There's no telling what'll happen tomorrow if you don't at least try to keep up today.

Tech involvement doesn't stop mattering after work hours either; social media and smartphones are already drastically changing human behavior, whether we like it or not. While understanding these things is essential, knowing their downsides is also important. Many only learn of the dangers they pose once it's too late.

Of course, adapting to such a rapidly moving world can be challenging. There are always concerns over losing jobs or finding out your last purchase is now leaking your social security number on the dark web. And as we keep advancing, who knows what other ethical and moral dilemmas we'll face? But if we pull together as individuals, businesses, and nations, we can ensure we get the best outcomes.

Opportunities in Emerging Tech Markets

Within the dynamic crossroads of technology and markets, emerging sectors like artificial intelligence, blockchain, biotechnology, and renewable energy serve as more than agents of change. Instead, they present rich opportunities for visionary entrepreneurs and forward-thinking businesses to nurture fresh paths of growth and development.

The swift advance of artificial intelligence has become a transformative influence, reshaping the operational landscape of businesses and providing unparalleled capabilities. In emerging tech markets, opportunities abound for those who harness AI to enhance decision-making processes, automate tasks, and unlock novel solutions to complex problems. Entrepreneurs venturing into AI-driven applications, from predictive analytics to natural language processing, find themselves at the forefront of innovation, poised to reshape industries and pave the way for unseen advances.

Blockchain, a decentralized ledger technology, has emerged as a disruptor with the potential to revolutionize various sectors. Its inherent features—

transparency, security, and immutability—make it a cornerstone for innovative finance, supply chain, and healthcare solutions. Entrepreneurs exploring opportunities in blockchain tech markets can unlock new realms of efficiency, traceability, and trust within business processes, creating decentralized ecosystems that redefine traditional paradigms.

Biotechnology, where biology meets technology, presents an opportunity for groundbreaking innovations. From genetic engineering to personalized medicine, entrepreneurs in emerging biotech markets can solve pressing human health, agriculture, and environmental sustainability challenges. The convergence between technological advances and biological sciences opens doors to transformative solutions that enable businesses to contribute to improving the human health environment.

Renewable energy is a focal point of the global sustainability challenge, which is also a burgeoning market with vast potential. Integrating technological advances in solar, wind, and other renewable sources offers entrepreneurs opportunities to contribute to a more sustainable future, foster environmental stewardship, and drive economic growth. Businesses venturing into emerging tech markets for renewable energy will be pivotal in accelerating the shift towards cleaner, more efficient energy solutions.

Navigating these emerging tech markets requires more than technological prowess; it demands a strategic understanding of market dynamics, regulatory landscapes, and consumer needs. Entrepreneurs deciphering the intricate interplay between technology and the market will position themselves to seize untapped opportunities. The collaborative nature of emerging tech markets encourages partnerships, knowledge sharing, and cross-industry collaborations, amplifying the potential for innovation and growth.

The global landscape of emerging tech markets is marked by diversity and dynamism. It extends beyond the traditional boundaries of industries, inviting creative minds and forward-looking businesses to explore uncharted territories. Entrepreneurs in emerging tech markets serve as catalysts for change, whether they are utilizing artificial intelligence to redefine efficiency, implementing blockchain for transparent and secure transactions, pioneering innovations in biotechnology for health and sustainability, or spearheading advances in renewable energy. They play a crucial role in molding a future where technology is utilized to improve human lives and the planet. In this dynamic tapestry of opportunities, those who navigate the intersection of technology and markets with vision and agility are poised to shape the future of industries and contribute to a more technologically advanced and sustainable world.

2.6 Assessing the Competitive Landscape

Exploring the ebb and flow of the competition is a must for businesses that want to thrive in these fast-paced markets. This starts with evaluating rivals through their strategies to identify profitable market sectors and competitors' advantages. With this scrutiny, businesses will have a wealth of knowledge beyond simple rivalry, giving them an edge over their opponents.

Analyzing a competitor is far more complex than examining what they do. To understand where your business can gain the upper hand in certain places, you need to know where competitors are missing out on filling gaps or unmet customer needs. Once identified, you can put yourself in a position to grow and differentiate yourself from others, who may be too focused on one thing.

At the same time, knowing what makes your competitors good at what they do also helps you understand how to improve while compensating for areas they are weak in. Keep up with industry trends and observe how other businesses set themselves apart; this way, you will always catch up on everything, including innovation or sustainability.

This kind of evaluation isn't a one-off process; it should be constantly monitored as long as you run a company.

Analyzing Competitors to Find Market Niches

Knowing how to create a distinctive position in the marketplace is crucial. Any exploration of potential market niches involves learning about competitors' strengths, weaknesses, and strategies; by doing this, you can uncover your niche's untapped spots and opportunities.

Competitor analysis begins with examining rival products and services. You'll want to observe their features, pricing strategy, and overall value proposition. By understanding what competitors bring to the market, you can identify gaps or areas where innovation and differentiation are needed.

For this analysis, you also want to examine your rivals' target audience and customer base. Learn about them, including demographics, consumer behavior, and preferences. This will help you identify segments that may be underserved or overlooked by your competition, further helping you create your unique market niche.

Now, let's get into the nitty-gritty of marketing and distribution channels. You'll want to examine your competition's every move here, since it will provide insights into potential gaps or inefficiencies in the market.

The next step is to understand how your competition operates daily. Please familiarize yourself with their supply chain efficiencies, production capabilities, and distribution networks, so you can compare them with yours. This will allow you to identify areas where they lack efficiency, allowing you to swoop in on an opportunity.

Always stay vigilant. The business landscape is always evolving; constantly monitoring changes in competitors' strategies and customer feedback will be beneficial for finding those initial market niches. Only then can you adjust and enhance your strategy, keeping up with the ever-changing business landscape.

Understanding the Competitive Advantages

Understanding competitive advantages is crucial for businesses in a highly contested market. To do this, you must examine what makes your company unique among the competition and how this gives you an advantage in the market.

One way to do this is to examine your business value proposition. Find out about how your products or services most benefit customers. Once you know what sets you apart, get ahead of your competitors. It could, for instance, be superior quality, innovative features, or exceptional customer service.

Looking deeper into your operational processes can also lead to advantages over competitors. Review if there are any internal processes where you could save money or make things more efficient throughout the supply chain. These tactics will help lower costs and increase efficiency.

By partnering with other companies, businesses can access new markets and resources they wouldn't otherwise have had. When used correctly, these partnerships can give a business the boost it needs to stay ahead in its respective marketplace.

Awareness of consumer behaviors and trends is also critical when understanding how to get ahead of the competition. A company needs to keep its finger on the pulse of emerging technologies and changes within the economy to adjust accordingly.

A positive image is crucial for success when marketing and branding a product or service. Building up brand loyalty gives customers no choice but to choose your business over others, even if it costs more than going with another option would.

Competitive advantage stems from understanding why people choose one thing over another, whether it is product differentiation, operational efficiencies, strategic partnerships, market awareness, or branding efforts. By putting effort into these areas, businesses set themselves up for success, as long as they also work hard to create resilience for future obstacles.

2.7 Evaluating the Feasibility and Profitability

Are you looking to embark on a risky, creative business venture? The first step is determining whether it's even feasible. Don't worry; there are ways to do this without overcommitting. By examining the many factors that play into this decision from different angles, you can decide whether or not you should continue with your expensive pipe dream.

A business needs to examine opportunities in the market by researching how they're trending. If consumers need what you're selling, and these needs are emerging market opportunities, your idea has potential. Poking holes in all aspects of your concept will allow you to make more informed decisions before investing time and resources.

It also helps if you know people may already be interested in buying what you are planning to sell, and it'd is crucial to set a price that makes sense for both parties involved. Assessing risks and barriers to entry adds a layer of depth to the evaluation process. Entrepreneurs have to navigate threats like competition, regulations, economic turndowns, and other negative possibilities. The better they understand these risks, the better prepared they'll be when threats come along.

Evaluating feasibility and profitability is a challenging task. It's essential to determine whether something could work out financially. By identifying potential risks at the start, entrepreneurs prepare themselves mentally for anything terrible that may come their way and devise preemptive plans for countering problems. It's also necessary to poke around at barriers because one might think an idea is unique, only for others in their industry to come along doing something similar. Remember, as we dive deeper into this, there's no such thing as being too prepared.

Techniques for Preliminary Business Opportunity Evaluation

Evaluating a business's potential can be confusing. The process requires a subtle, strategic approach, to ensure you know what you're getting into. One part of this is the preliminary evaluation of business opportunities, which helps us navigate all the possibilities and choices we'll have to make as we start our ventures.

One technique involves a thorough analysis of market trends. You must examine consumer preferences, industry dynamics, and emerging technologies. By understanding how the market works, people can identify gaps or areas ripe for innovation, laying the groundwork for an idea that fits todays and tomorrow's worlds.

Consumer needs also play a significant role. You must listen and research what sparks a person's interest in their target demographic. Once they find out what makes them tick, they'll have to tailor their offerings around these key points while also providing value elsewhere, in order to stand out.

To ensure you stay ahead and blend in with everyone else, you will want to evaluate current competitors and pinpoint possible ways to stand out. Doing something others have yet to think of can go a long way, whether it is distinctive features or services, higher-quality products, or innovative approaches.

Moreover, if you plan on running your business, you still need money coming in at the end of the day. This is why financial feasibility studies are critical in evaluating business opportunities. Before making any final moves, potential costs like initial investment projections and operational expenses must be carefully considered. Otherwise, you might find yourself going bankrupt before even getting started.

This part of starting your gig is about scalability, or the potential for growth and expansion over time. It's only sometimes possible, but if there are opportunities to capitalize on things like increasing demand, they should be considered. There are many different parts to running a business, which can be overwhelming. However, you can set yourself up nicely by navigating consumer wants and needs, market trends, competitive landscapes, financial feasibility, and scalability.

Market Demand Estimation and Profit Potential

Comprehending market demand and determining profit potential are critical when strategizing for business and guiding you through a complex marketplace. This evaluation involves assessing many factors that influence consumer behavior, financial viability, and market dynamics.

Estimating market demand is fundamental to measuring how successful a business venture will be. You analyze what makes consumers tick, what they want, their preferences (which usually change), and purchase patterns to identify the target audience's expectations and pain points. By understanding market demand, businesses can tailor their offerings to the people they're designed for; they can make things that resonate with customers.

Assessing profit potential goes hand in hand with understanding cost structures to ensure a company's financial sustainability. You must forecast potential revenue streams, considering pricing strategies, sales volumes, and overall market share.

Market demand estimation has a lot to do with profit potential, as these two things work together, shaping the core of a business's success. To remain ahead of your rivals, you'll need to keep innovating your products or services to allow them to stay the number one go-to for customers year in and year out.

External factors like economic conditions also play a role in estimating these two aspects of business—stay vigilant. You don't want any surprises down the road because, more than ever today, companies must be able to adapt at any given moment if they want to survive this wild marketplace.

Estimating market demand and profit potential before taking on any venture is essential. With these two pieces of information, your business is likely to succeed. Make sure you understand consumer behaviors, forecast revenue streams, and keep up with market dynamics to guide your business to the best course of action for success.

Assessing Risks and Barriers to Entry

Comprehending market demand and gauging profit potential play immense roles in business strategy. For you and others looking to succeed, these two factors serve as guiding lights through the ever-changing market.

By analyzing consumer behavior, preferences, and trends, businesses can identify opportunities yet to be capitalized on. They can also gain an understanding of where existing solutions may be lacking. This allows companies to align their products or services with what consumers want.

Estimating a company's profit potential is as important as knowing its sales potential. You need to dive deep into your company's financial aspects, such as forecasting revenue, cost structures, and pricing strategies.

Market demand and profit potential work together. For a business to succeed, it must answer all current demands while simultaneously predicting consumers' future wants and needs. Responding to these trends positions businesses as innovative leaders, leading them toward long-term sustainability.

External factors such as economic conditions, technological advances, and societal trends directly shape market demand and profit potential. Companies that stay vigilant about these forces can adapt accordingly, thus putting themselves ahead of their competition.

One good way to ensure long-term profitability is to stay at the forefront of innovation within a specific industry. By continuously evolving and introducing new things, businesses can differentiate themselves from others in the market, which will, in turn, attract customers.

Only some moves you make have high stakes, but estimating market demand or analyzing profit potential is crucial for success. Those who take the extra step and thoroughly examine consumer behavior and external influences will always come out on top because they know exactly what customers want.

2.8 Legal and Ethical Considerations

Knowing what's legal and ethical is crucial in the business world. Businessmen and women need to walk this tightrope in every new venture they embark upon. This complex dance contains many elements, such as legal requirements for new opportunities, the intricacies of intellectual property law, and ethical decision-making.

Understanding legal requirements is fundamental to your journey, starting with the fundamentals. You must know how to register a business, get a license, and understand specific industry regulations if you want your venture to succeed. Of course, if you fail to meet these requirements, you might face financial consequences or even ruin your own company.

Intellectual property laws add another layer of complexity to this already difficult task. Many entrepreneurs constantly ask themselves, 'How do I make my idea better than everyone else and then retain it?' For some, it may be patents, trademarks, or copyright law to protect their ideas from others who might try to steal them. But before you jump headfirst into a patent application, you'll need to do your homework first and properly search for any existing patents that could prove problematic down the road. Playing by these rules will keep your idea safe while giving you the necessary ammunition if someone tries to steal it from you.

While legality often takes precedent in business operations, ethics should never be pushed aside. By considering right and wrong when deciding about potential projects, entrepreneurs can keep themselves accountable for any harm they might later cause stakeholders or society. Ethical guidelines include being transparent with customers, staying honest with yourself, and treating everyone with decency no matter who they are, especially when profit is involved.

Aspiring businessmen and women must remember how complicated navigating this system is. Even the most successful entrepreneurs will fail to find a balance between everything at one point or another. But if you can walk all these lines, your business will be well on its way to success.

Legal Requirements for New Business Opportunities

The road to new business opportunities is layered with legal complexities. You must be vigilant and ensure complications of your own making do not arise. The legal requirements for new business opportunities lay the groundwork for future operations; so proper care must be taken.

One of the main things an entrepreneur should register as soon as possible is their business. This is necessary to comply with jurisdictional laws that govern their geographical location. An example would be registering a sole proprietorship, partnership, or corporation. If you don't take this step, you could suffer severe consequences like monetary fines, lawsuits, or even being forced to close. We will delve further into legal business structures in Chapter 7.

Licensing is another legal necessity when forming a new business opportunity. You will have to meet all the licensing parameters, depending on the field of your new venture. Some examples are health permits, environmental permits, or industry-specific licenses. For this part, you will need to research your specific business type. Failure to do this could result in getting shut down by the authorities.

Adhering to industry-specific regulations can feel like a burden, but they're there for a reason. Different sectors have different rules and requirements, and, if you want their businesses taken seriously, you need to be familiar with them all.

Knowing employment law is another legal requirement for new business opportunities. Because minimum wage, working hours, and employee rights change from place to place, you must have enough knowledge and understanding about each place you plan on operating in; otherwise, there will be some big problems down the line. Another benefit of knowing these laws is that they help you stay safe from potential legal disputes and liabilities.

As dull as it sounds, taxes are legally necessary. Entrepreneurs must understand what they must do when paying their share of taxes. You must know when the deadlines are and how much you will owe; You must get those numbers right. Failure to comply may lead to penalties, which could put your business at risk.

Navigating Intellectual Property and Patent Exploration

When you have an idea that you think will change the world, it's essential to take a moment to try to protect it. Many people come up with great ideas, but if they don't go through the proper steps, they might never become what they could have been. Intellectual property is a giant topic; patents are one part of the puzzle. Having a patent on your idea can give you some peace of mind.

How does someone go about getting a patent? First things first: you need to do your research. You wouldn't want to spend all the time and effort developing something, only to realize it already exists. Do yourself a favor and take the time to examine existing patents similar to yours to save time later.

If everything checks out after your search is complete, then congratulations. You're ready for step two: drafting your application. At this point, I recommend reaching out for professional help, because this process can take a lot of work for someone inexperienced in law. You need to ensure it's done right, because, once again, if there are any errors, you might find yourself stuck with an invalid patent.

Patent laws vary worldwide, so understand how things work where you live before diving too deep into these waters. Regardless of what laws exist, I recommend speaking with a professional on this matter, as there is little room for error.

Trademarks and copyrights are also essential when protecting intellectual property. A trademark protects things like company names and logos, while copyrights protect your more artistic creations. Compared to patents, these are easy to get; it's worth the time and money invested here.

Ethics in Business Opportunity Recognition

Ethics is the foundation of business opportunity recognition.

When searching for opportunities, you must prioritize transparency and honesty. This means you must run an honest operation and give people truthful information about what you're selling. This will help build trust among stakeholders, and when a potential partner or investor comes along, they'll already know this is someone who isn't afraid to say it like it is.

Respecting rights is another ethical obligation when recognizing business opportunities. You can't steal someone else's idea and claim it as your own; it ruins the level playing field needed for fair competition. Instead, people who take ethics seriously respect intellectual property rights and refuse to engage in deceptive practices that might harm other businesses' assets.

Environmental sustainability and community welfare should also be considered when seeking a business opportunity. People who are mindful of this tend to make better choices, because they weigh out all potential outcomes before making decisions that impact others around them.

When considering business opportunities, a great entrepreneur considers everything from reducing harm to animal life to green practices and overall ecological conservation goals.

In addition, fair treatment is also something entrepreneurs must consider when spotting a good business opportunity. The people in charge must guarantee equitable wages, secure working environments, and equal opportunities for everyone involved in their venture. This extends beyond employees to suppliers and partners, too.

Another ethical imperative is integrity in ads and marketing campaigns for your product or service. It's important to refrain from playing with words to fool customers into buying your product; this usually leads to bad reviews and a harmful reputation. Make sure not to create unrealistic expectations. Be honest about what you're offering; people will buy it if it's good.

Ethics go beyond the basic rules and regulations set down by law. People who understand this know they must build their business with honesty, transparency, respect for intellectual property rights, social responsibility, environmental sustainability, fair treatment of stakeholders, and integrity in marketing.

2.9 From Opportunity to Conceptualization

What's the worst part of running a business? Making decisions. What's the most important part? Making decisions, again. You can see where I'm going with this: making solid and quick decisions is crucial for success.

This also means that some business elements are easier than others. One such piece is transforming opportunity recognition into conceptualization. Let's discuss how entrepreneurs refine their ideas from raw concepts and focus them into something cohesive yet actionable. The goal here isn't just to make something that consumers want, but also something that resonates with them.

Building a valuable proposition is another step in this journey. It's essential to craft a story around your product or service by highlighting their best attributes and describing why people should care about them. Remember when you were little and had a new toy cooler than any of your friends? Why was yours so much better? How would you explain its greatness?

But let's say you've made it this far. Now what? Now comes the scary part—testing and validating your new idea(s). Getting ahead of these problems early on can be super helpful in preventing your ideas from failing down the line.

At the end of the day, if there's one thing you take away from this chapter, it's creativity, which needs a strategy. A solid understanding of market dynamics and customer behavior goes hand in hand with imagination. With those two in hand, nothing can stop you from creating an affordable business concept that people will love to buy.

Developing a Business Concept from an Opportunity

An entrepreneur's first step is spotting where there might be untapped potential in the market. They need to find gaps they know how to fill or problems that still need to be solved. When they find them, it's their job to act. This takes intuition, industry knowledge, and awareness of emerging trends.

Once they know what they want to pursue, entrepreneurs must start making sense of their abstract ideas so others can understand them, too. They'll ask themselves if their concept is possible, unique enough, and likely to make any money in such an overcrowded space. This means assessing the competition and ensuring there are not too many obstacles in their way.

During this part of the process, creativity meets practicality. Entrepreneurs must think big with their ideas and be mindful of budgeting and investment requirements. They must consider who their marketing is aimed at and how their brand will stand out from competitors.

Entrepreneurs continue refining their concepts until they are as polished as possible. This means listening intently to feedback from professionals outside of their inner circle and studying similar businesses' successes before them. By incorporating other people's ideas into their own, they hope to create something completely fresh.

Communication skills are crucial throughout every step of building a business concept, because one tiny miscommunication could cause everything to crumble at any point in the journey. Entrepreneurs need everyone involved on the same page—investors, stakeholders, and employees—so everyone knows what role they play moving forward.

Throughout this wild ride toward a functioning business concept, you must be okay with taking risks and dealing with the consequences later. You'll make decisions based on some degree of concrete information, your gut instinct, and things you've picked up.

Building a Value Proposition

Stepping into entrepreneurship means making a firm offer and positioning yourself as a critical factor for success. This section will cover the details of creating an appealing offer and help untangle entrepreneurs' complex considerations and strategies to establish their identity with their target audience.

Now, what is a value proposition? It's the unique thing your business does better than anyone else. It goes beyond product features or services; it taps into tangible benefits and solutions to address specific market needs or challenges. To get started on this journey, you need to have a deep understanding of their target audience. You need to know what's happening in the market and who your competitors are.

Creating a compelling value proposition requires one crucial step: daily identification of your target customers' pain points or challenges. Once you figure this out, you can shape your value proposition around their desires. It would help if you showed people how your product can better meet demanding requirements than any other option available.

It would help if you also spoke in plain English. Simple communication is more critical than ever, because it helps people quickly grasp what makes you unique and why they should care about your product.

Another essential factor is differentiation. When you are pitching to potential customers, competitors may be standing right next to you. This alone should tell you that you will need something special to stand out, so people will choose you instead of them.

But only make promises if you know your team can keep them. Your brand promise must align well with customer experience to build trust.

This may go without saying, but always be ready for customer feedback. Listen and adapt accordingly to keep your offer relevant.

To wrap things up, building an attractive offer is about something other than telling people how great you are. It's about addressing the pain points of your target audience, showing how you stack up against competitors, and ensuring your internal operations align with what you want to deliver on paper. You might think it's just words on a page, but it could be the core of success in the competitive landscape of your industry.

Testing and Validating Business Concepts

Validation is an essential part of entrepreneurship. It's where the rubber meets the road, and you get honest feedback on your idea. We examine what validation means, how it's done, and what you should expect when you embark on this essential process.

Testing a business concept always starts with market research. By examining what already exists in the space and understanding consumer behavior, startups can refine their ideas to better suit customer needs. This step helps form a solid foundation for further testing.

Prototyping and experimentation are critical next steps, because they allow you to bring your concepts to life so people can observe them working. Prototypes help clarify strengths and weaknesses, so product developers know exactly what to improve before launch.

Asking potential customers directly is another crucial aspect of testing a business concept. Surveys and interviews help gauge interest, identify pain points, and give startups an idea of whether or not users would be happy with their product or service offerings. Feedback loops like these ensure businesses hit the mark before sending anything out into the world.

Pilot testing allows companies to deploy their ideas on a smaller scale and gather honest user feedback. With pilot tests, all these improvements can be made in time for full-scale implementation.

Market acceptance is how businesses know if all their hard work has paid off. Tracking sales metrics and customer satisfaction indices will give you complex numbers showing how well your products are being received.

Sometimes, all this trial and error isn't even necessary: The first iteration of your product might sell millions right out of the gate. But often—especially in today's ever-changing market—you must constantly pivot as new challenges arise or customers present changing demands.

But no matter how many enhancements need to be made, one thing remains constant: testing your idea early on paves the way toward future success. Once you have a solid concept, validating your business with investors and partners becomes more feasible. Support can help streamline market entry and reduce the risk of fatal missteps during the early stages.

Testing and validating business concepts requires patience, resilience, and adaptability. But in a world where startups fail every day, this iterative process is well worth the effort.

We have learned in this chapter that creating a roadmap for entrepreneurial success is a detailed process requiring intricate planning, goal establishment, and strategic choice. This is when an idea begins to be put into action, and it marks the beginning of moving from one point to another.

At the heart of this roadmap is setting clear and achievable goals that act as the guiding lights for you and your team. These objectives must meet the SMART criteria: specific, measurable, attainable, relevant, and time bound. Hence, they must enable focused strategies as well as effective resource allocation.

To build an efficient business plan, strategic decision-making requires analyzing market dynamics, customer needs, and the competitive landscape. If it is informed by deep market research, a comprehensive understanding of target markets enhances product development processes, marketing approaches, and resource allocation in roadmaps. Even more critical are financial plans covering initial investments, operational expenses, and revenue projections to ensure the business venture's viability. Passionate individuals with common goals but diverse skills contribute tremendously towards increased productivity levels within the organization.

Although its creation may seem daunting, it is indispensable in weathering storms, sailing through tempests, and realizing long-term visions. Through exploration, innovation, and forward-thinking, you can experience transformative growth, thereby achieving sustainable development.

Chapter 3

Crafting a Business Concept

Crafting a business concept is like creating the foundation of a great enterprise. Understanding and forming the essential parts of business ideas is critical to entrepreneurial success in the ever-changing world of commerce. Navigating market needs, developing, and finding your spot will all be necessary.

A business concept begins when you have a clear vision of what will set your venture apart from others. This vision goes beyond products or services; it must consider what innovative ideas are viable. In-depth risk analysis is also essential during these early stages.

Feasibility studies determine whether your idea can handle market demands and still be relevant. They gauge the market demand for a product or service and the larger financial landscape.

Strategic positioning is crucial for founders who want to avoid getting lost among competitors in the same space. Every company should strive for a unique selling point, which can only be achieved after analyzing trends and preferences.

Building a business model involves delving into how revenue streams work, how costs compare to them, and which resources need to be allocated where. It's all about constructing an operational framework that can withstand whatever is thrown at it once it is implemented.

After the first steps have been taken to ensure things make sense financially, budgetary considerations will take over. Securing investment opportunities through forecasting will help you understand whether or not you're on track with your goals.

Entrepreneurs must communicate their plans to investors, customers, and collaborators before implementing their concepts. Investing time in good communication will promote trust and keep things running smoothly throughout development.

There are many ways ideas can go wrong or right when translated into real-world businesses; some aspects of concept creation require creative thinking, while others require strategic planning. Either way, this process contributes to economic innovation, so keep pushing forward.

3.1 Introduction to Business Concepts

Starting your own business requires a firm grasp on its concept. This is what determines how it performs. When stripped down to its core, a business concept acts as the entire foundation for an enterprise, embodying the base layer of an idea and defining how it brings value to the market.

A clear understanding of a business concept is essential when breaking into entrepreneurship. It includes more than describing what product or service you're offering. A business concept is a potential company's vision and mission, setting it apart from competitors. It stretches beyond physical offerings, including the intangible parts that make it unique.

There's no overstating the importance of business concepts when starting in the entrepreneurial world. They're guiding lights that illuminate uncertain market dynamics and provide clarity. A well-defined one attracts potential investors and partners as it resonates with target consumers and establishes solid groundwork for sustainable growth.

Knowing how concepts and planning work together is crucial for anyone wanting to be their own boss. A robustly defined business concept creates space for strategic planning by influencing every part of your business model. It guides informed decision-making and resource allocation and helps you position yourself in the market where everything aligns with your goals.

The road to creating a successful business concept is long, but it can be done. You need to know how ideas transform into strategic maps that handle problems, take advantage of opportunities, and ultimately shape your future success story. Enterprises understand these key concepts and are better equipped to deal with any curveballs thrown at them in such a highly competitive market landscape.

Definition of a Business Concept

A business blueprint is more significant than an idea. It's a comprehensive plan that combines a business's purpose, offerings, and value. To understand the full extent of what it means to develop and realize a business concept, the definition of a business concept must be broken down into its many layers.

It's more than a product description. Your vision and mission distinguish you from your competitors. Therefore, when defining your business concept, you must consider what you offer, the values you embody, and the problems you aim to solve in the market.

For your business to work as well as it should, consumers must also be able to see some unique feature or set of features that differentiate your business from others. This sets up everything else within your business concept and gives it its foundation. This answer alone will highlight why consumers should choose your product over others.

The final two pieces are crucial for any long-lasting success in such a dynamic industry: adaptability and internal coherence. Because it evolves alongside market conditions, consumer preferences, and technological advances, there will be constant refinement and adaptation.

During the solution sessions, the group recognized the importance of improving the enterprise's co-worker and customer experience. Once aligned with market needs, this connection enhances the likelihood of acceptance and overall success.

All these words sound nice on paper or on a screen, but action is needed. That's where this blueprint comes from: making decisions, fostering innovation, and eventually shaping what this whole venture is destined for.

The Importance of a Solid Business Concept in Entrepreneurship

It's impossible to overstate the importance of a clear, focused business concept in entrepreneurship. It's the key to success in today's fast-paced and competitive world. A strong and clearly defined business concept is the driving force that shapes an entrepreneurial venture from start to finish, guiding everything from brainstorming ideas to long-term sustainability. To truly understand how vital a solid business concept is, one must deeply dive into how it influences and defines the entrepreneurial journey.

A clearly defined business concept offers a practical roadmap for entrepreneurs navigating the complexities of running a business. It provides a sturdy foundation to build their entire venture, offering a comprehensive vision outlining what their company does, its purpose, and its unique value proposition. Clarity like these aids in decision-making, but it also serves as a powerful unifying force among team members by giving them all something tangible to work toward.

Attracting potential investors and partners is often crucial for entrepreneurs when it comes to getting their ideas off the ground; this is another area where a solid business concept proves invaluable. Investors look for ventures with clear and exciting business concepts, because that clarity instills confidence in that enterprise's feasibility and long-term viability. A well-crafted concept communicates the financial return potential along with strategic foresight and market understanding from entrepreneurs themselves.

A strong business concept will immediately resonate with its target audience, providing those behind the venture with a sturdy foundation for market acceptance. Nowadays, consumers are saturated with options across every product or service they can think of. What draws them to one brand over another? The answer lies in businesses offering something different while directly addressing consumer pain points. When companies have these elements baked into their DNA, customers make connections much more readily. This connection isn't about purchasing, but resonating with a target audience ultimately leads to customer loyalty, drives brand recognition, and establishes an all-important competitive edge vital for long-term growth. A solid business concept is also crucial for strategic planning and resource allocation. With clear business concepts, entrepreneurs are better equipped to make informed decisions about how their products should be developed, which marketing strategies they should employ, and how their business processes can be streamlined. This forward-thinking approach maximizes efficiency and minimizes risk—positioning any venture with a distinct advantage over less-prepared competitors.

Adaptability is everything in the world of entrepreneurship. Things move at lightning speed, and if you can keep up with the times, your business will stay caught up. That's why having a rock-solid business concept that allows you to pivot quickly is important. When market trends shift, new technology emerges, or consumer preferences change on a dime, you need to have something solid to fall back on if you want your company to survive.

The importance of a strong business concept goes without saying at this point. It influences strategic decisions, attracts financial support, resonates with consumers, and provides direction for long-term success. In other words, building one is non-negotiable.

The Relationship between Business Concepts and Business Planning

Business planning and business concepts go together like a horse and carriage. One cannot exist without the other. It's that simple. These two aspects are the strategic development and operational execution of any entrepreneurial venture. They are crucial in helping entrepreneurs navigate the complex business world and achieve growth.

At its core, a business concept is a framework with which an entrepreneur can build effective business plans. It details the entrepreneur's venture idea, purpose, offerings, and unique value proposition. This base is then used to create strategies, objectives, and decisions for the business plan in later phases.

The next step is turning abstract ideas into actionable steps through business planning. This means setting marketing, finance, resources, and risk management goals. The entrepreneur takes those initial conceptual frameworks from the first phase to create a roadmap to guide day-to-day operations and long-term strategies.

Strategic development relies heavily on alignment between these two elements. A solid business concept gives entrepreneurs insight into their target market, allowing them to identify what sets them apart from competitors and establish benchmarks for success in future stages.

Then there's resource allocation, which impacts this relationship. When entrepreneurs have a concrete understanding of what their venture is trying to accomplish, thanks to its concept, they can quickly figure out what areas need focus most urgently or how much money certain aspects will require.

Through risk mitigation, entrepreneurs prepare for uncertainties by anticipating potential risks using information they learned when constructing their concept, with contingency planning strategies developed after building their plan.

You must remember that this iterative process is essential for growth in today's ever-changing world markets. Business plans should be treated as constantly evolving documents because growth relies on continuously improving them. Hence, they align with changes happening inside and outside your company.

Overall, it all comes down to this: business concepts provide the vision needed for effective planning, while business planning turns ideas into tangible strategies. This relationship is the cornerstone of any entrepreneurial venture's strategic development, resource allocation, risk mitigation, and growth.

3.2 Components of a Business Concept

Developing a business concept involves a nuanced exploration of its essential components. Each part is a critical building block for constructing a viable and successful enterprise. By considering the elements that define purpose, relevance, and potential in the market, you can ensure your business is on the right track.

Core products or services are the essence of every business venture. They set it apart from competitors and form the basis of its existence. Entrepreneurs consider market needs, consumer demands, and industry trends to choose which specific products or services they'll offer. In doing this, they get to their vision and identity.

Understanding your target markets comes next. A profound knowledge of your intended customer base is crucial for success in any industry. Entrepreneurs conduct comprehensive research to discern a target audience's characteristics and behaviors, ensuring their business concept aligns seamlessly with them.

Crafting a unique value proposition allows businesses to differentiate themselves from their peers in saturated markets. The unique value offered becomes the foundation of the entire concept. It goes beyond communicating product benefits; it also taps into emotions and aspirations.

Above all, revenue models ensure long-term profitability through consistent income generation. Putting all these parts together is not easy by any standard, but once you do achieve that feat, you're one step closer to building something resilient and thriving.

Identifying Core Products or Services

Defining a core product or service forms the pivotal foundation for any business model. This process lets you see what a business offers and then build upon that. Entrepreneurs must be able to identify these things to make strategic decisions about their venture. Doing this will allow them to comprehend how their products work with the market.

This deep dive involves finding market gaps, trends you may not have noticed, and opportunities that align with your vision. If you need to know where to start with this process, it is simple: ask yourself what current market demands consumers have and how they could change in the future. By asking yourself these questions, you can ensure your business has products or services ready to fill those holes.

Understanding your audience also plays an essential role in identifying your business's core offerings. People want what they want, and understanding their desires, challenges, and needs is necessary to know precisely what they want from a product or service. If you need help finding out who your intended consumer base is, conduct some research. Find out how people interact with similar businesses on social media or through surveys.

Differentiation in any industry is becoming rare since most products serve the same purpose, but in different ways. Take Coca-Cola vs. Pepsi, for example. Both are carbonated beverages but differ highly in taste due to their recipe differences. The point here is that consumers need choices, which means they need different options within the same niche area. While defining your offerings, ask yourself how yours will stand out from competitors.

When starting a company, your goals are everything; it makes sense for all other aspects of your business to align with them. By doing this, you can ensure that the core products or services will help you work towards those goals by fulfilling market demands and narratives. Once your offerings align with the company's purpose, it becomes much easier for potential customers and stakeholders to resonate with them.

Identifying these things is what will make or break a business model. Failure to do so would result in a product that nobody wants, ultimately leading to the downfall of any new company. It may seem like another 'checklist' item, but it can lead to success when done correctly.

Target Market Identification

Figuring out who the target audience is an essential part of starting a business. It takes time and effort to do it right, and a deep dive into market analysis, consumer understanding, and industry know-how is needed.

A complete market analysis is essential for identifying our target audience. You need to understand the ins and outs of the market where your business will operate. This means examining industry trends and competitors' actions, and identifying niches where we can differentiate ourselves. This helps us understand consumer behavior and determine who will become our competition.

The next step is figuring out who we're trying to sell to—acquiring data on demographics, psychographics, and socio-economic factors for our intended customer base. We need to know their age, gender, income levels, lifestyle preferences, and purchasing behavior to create detailed profiles. This way, we'll observe what makes them tick.

Figures alone won't give us enough insight into customers; we must also look at psychographics. We need to find out what they value, their interests, and their lifestyle choices, so that we can connect with them on a deeper level in our marketing efforts and tailor products or services to these beliefs.

Some consumers may be more than one segment within your target audience; in these cases, it's good practice for businesses to consider niches within niches that could present specialized opportunities. By customizing offerings for these segments, you can establish yourself as unique within certain pockets of customers.

Identifying a target market involves many steps, and it's far from an exact science. But by combining data, empathy, and adaptability, we'll be able to figure out who our customers are and get to know them on a deeper level. That way, we can ensure our offerings resonate with them long-term.

Unique Value Proposition

Strategizing a business concept involves crafting a unique value proposition. What sets a venture apart from the competition and embodies it? A UVP represents the distinctive value that a business promises to deliver to its customers. It is a compelling narrative that differentiates the venture and profoundly connects with the intended audience.

Understanding one's target market and consumers helps one craft a unique value proposition. It isn't about highlighting any product or service features; it's about communicating the benefits and outcomes customers should expect from your business's products or services. Business VPs go past functional attributes, tapping into consumers' emotional aspirations and behaviors.

The ultimate goal is to address both the rational and emotional dimensions. Hence, your messaging establishes a profound connection with your target audience. The idea is to resonate with customer motivation. Therefore, you need to catch their attention and foster alignment between them and your brand, thus coaxing them into supporting you.

The UVP also requires entrepreneurs to evaluate what competitors are offering. By discerning gaps in rival marketing strategies, entrepreneurs can emphasize their business's advantages.

A successful UVP must be clear, concise, and easily transferable from person to person. Its presentation must successfully encapsulate everything that makes the business stand out in a way that is digestible by target audiences, who may need more time for lengthy readings. Whether through taglines or visual representation, people should observe businesses' core values.

A good, unique value proposition resonates with, but is never detached from the more comprehensive brand identity of the venture it represents. The UVP must fit within a broader narrative that defines the venture in a way that consumers can resonate. This alignment helps maintain authenticity and credibility, building trust between audience members and the venture.

The unique value proposition is a strategic tool that summarizes a business's differentiation and relevance in the market. It's a dynamic expression of what a company uniquely offers to its customers by addressing their needs, in an appealing way. Crafting one requires entrepreneurs to blend market insight, consumer empathy, competitive analysis, and brand alignment. Successful businesses leverage the power of their unique value proposition to build strong customer loyalty, enabling them to achieve sustainable success overall in the marketplace.

Revenue Model Foundations

Setting up a business is indeed a work of art. And, like all great works of art, it needs a solid and robust foundation to stand on. That's why creating a revenue model is important when it comes to sustainable business ideas. This framework will establish how your business makes money, allocates resources, and, most importantly, stays profitable over time. Doing this right requires you to analyze countless factors in-depth—pricing strategies, cost structures, and even your business's adaptability to market dynamics.

One key aspect of creating such foundations is determining the best pricing strategy for your products or services. There are many routes you can take when devising the perfect plan; make sure you do some research before settling on one. Some businesses prefer setting low, attractive customer prices, while others have a higher margin but fewer customers. There isn't any wrong way of doing it, as long as it aligns with your overall goals and positioning.

Another critical component is identifying all possible revenue streams supporting your venture's growth. By doing this, your venture will generate income through different channels, thus reducing dependency on one source. Your revenue streams include direct sales, subscription models, or licensing fees.

We have cost structures that dictate how expenses will work within the business model. To ensure optimal resource allocation and operational efficiency, entrepreneurs must also consider fixed and variable production marketing efforts.

Businesses must consider what adaptations they may introduce to better suit their customers' wants and needs.

Integrating financial goals with overarching objectives is also crucial if you want everything to be perfectly aligned with one another.

Let's remember to stay customer centered. Focusing on precisely what customers perceive as value allows organizations to nurture customer retention and loyalty; fundamental for maintaining sustained long-term revenue growth.

Revenue model foundations provide the solid base a business needs to stand on. You'll need to lay the groundwork for a solid one, fully considering pricing strategies, diversifying revenue streams, optimizing cost structures, fostering adaptability, and customer satisfaction.

3.3 Market Needs and Solutions

Developing a business concept is about understanding what makes it tick. That's because at the core of your venture are customer pain points, solutions that people will use, and meeting those expectations. They're the building blocks you need to build a solid business.

Understanding customer pain points is crucial when creating your business concept. Successful entrepreneurs deeply understand their audience's problems and unmet needs and develop innovative solutions. This puts companies in a strong position to tackle real-world issues head-on, showing customers they care about facilitating positive change.

Crafting solutions comes next. Once you know your target audience's needs, you can start developing products or services that directly cater to them. You want your solutions to stand out from the crowd; focus on making them practical but original enough that people will choose them over others.

Your final step is aligning your product with consumer expectations. Going above and beyond immediate needs shows customers that you understand and care about their broader values. By exceeding expectations, businesses can earn respect and loyalty while putting themselves firmly ahead of competitors.

Everything has its place in this multifaceted puzzle of a business concept. Understand customer pain points, craft solutions based on market demand, and exceed consumer expectations. By putting these pieces together correctly, entrepreneurs can ensure they're on track for success.

Understanding Customer Pain Points

The foundation of any successful business concept is deeply rooted in a nuanced understanding of customer pain points. This crucial aspect of entrepreneurial exploration involves a comprehensive and empathetic examination of the challenges, frustrations, and unmet needs of the target audience. By delving into the intricacies of customer pain points, entrepreneurs can uncover invaluable insights that pave the way for developing innovative solutions and a business concept that resonates authentically with the intended market.

Understanding customer pain points requires a genuine commitment to empathy and an open-minded approach to listening. Successful entrepreneurs recognize the importance of putting themselves in their customers' shoes and immersing the customers in the experiences and perspectives of the target audience. Empathetic comprehension surpasses superficial observations and delves into customer challenges, in both emotional and practical dimensions.

One fundamental aspect of exploring customer pain points is identifying explicit and implicit needs. Detailed needs are those that customers explicitly express or articulate. In contrast, unstated needs may be subtle but can be inferred through careful observation and in-depth conversations. Uncovering these implicit needs requires a keen awareness of the subtleties and nuances within customer interactions, enabling entrepreneurs to address not only what customers say they need, but also what they may not articulate, but actually do desire.

Customer pain points are dynamic and vary across demographics, industries, and contexts. Gaining a comprehensive understanding requires segmenting the target audience and identifying the unique challenges faced by different customer groups. By acknowledging the unique pain points of distinct segments, entrepreneurs can tailor their solutions to meet the specific needs of each subgroup, enhancing the overall relevance and impact of the business concept.

In understanding customer pain points, entrepreneurs often engage in active dialogue with their target audience. Surveys, interviews, and focus groups are invaluable tools for soliciting direct feedback and gaining firsthand insights into the challenges faced by customers. This direct engagement fosters a collaborative relationship, positioning customers as co-creators in developing solutions. The feedback loop between entrepreneurs and customers becomes dynamic and iterative, driving continuous improvement and innovation.

Successful businesses leverage the insights from understanding customer pain points to drive product or service development. Empathetic comprehension of customer challenges empowers entrepreneurs to craft solutions that meet immediate needs and deeply connect with the emotions and aspirations of the target audience. This alignment creates a sense of authenticity and trust, essential elements for building enduring customer relationships.

Understanding customer pain points is a foundational step in the entrepreneurial journey, guiding the development of a business concept that is not only market-responsive but genuinely empathetic. Entrepreneurs who embrace this facet of customer-centered exploration position themselves to create solutions beyond mere functionality, addressing their audience's core challenges and desires. With this understanding, businesses foster a meaningful connection with their customers, laying the groundwork for sustained success.

Crafting Solutions that Meet Market Demand

Entrepreneurial success depends on crafting solutions for your target audience that answer the market's current needs. But you also must keep an eye on what's coming next. Entrepreneurs want a deep dive into researching their intended customers to understand consumer behavior and emerging trends. What specific needs is someone else meeting? By answering this question now, you can position yourself later as the industry leader.

Being innovative will help you get ahead when finding ideas for products or services that satisfy market demand. This means constantly looking forward to and encouraging new ways of thinking from your employees, so they stay energized while technology surrounds them. Keeping up with industry advancements will enable your business to create offerings that stand out from the competition and attract consumers seeking something new.

The business landscape shifts constantly, in terms of trends, consumer preferences, or external factors; 'adapt or die,' some might say. Those entrepreneurs who navigate change best can quickly switch gears and adapt offerings based on these changes to stay relevant. That can mean small things like adding new features, or completely changing how the company operates its day-to-day functions. Regardless of how large-scale those changes may be, adapting ensures businesses remain resilient even when things don't go as planned.

A forward-thinking entrepreneur can leverage their knowledge of industry trends to anticipate people's needs or wants. Being on the leading edge of innovation allows you to outpace the competition and keep your company ahead.

Businesses also need to consider scalability when crafting their solutions. As demand grows, these businesses must be ready for larger markets. This could mean establishing more robust supply chains, optimizing production processes, or considering potential logistical issues that may arise later.

Creating marketable solutions isn't easy work; it requires deep thought about the current state of things and what's coming next. By staying agile and using market insights, creative thinking, customer engagement, and strategic foresight, entrepreneurs can align their solutions with consumers' current and future wants.

Aligning Solutions with Consumer Expectations

Matching solutions with what consumers can make or break a business. That's why it's essential to understand in-depth consumer preferences, behaviors, and aspirations when crafting offerings. The objective isn't to meet their expectations but to go beyond them. Products and services that find this sweet spot are bound to be successful because they'll build a base of loyal customers.

At the core of this strategy is an understanding of your target audience. Successful people put time and resources into studying what makes consumers tick—but not at a surface level. They get deep into the details, so they know their needs and desires like the back of their hands. By doing this, businesses can tailor their solutions accordingly, which helps form strong connections with customers.

Companies also need to recognize how diverse their customer base is if they're going to match up with them. Every person has different needs, wants, income levels, and cultural influences that shape what they expect as a consumer. Entrepreneurs should embrace these differences and create custom-tailored solutions for each group, so they resonate directly with them.

Business owners must never forget how customer opinions can help improve their company even further. They should actively seek feedback through surveys, reviews, and any other means possible to know where something might need tweaking to better align with demand.

Another thing that should be on your radar when considering satisfying consumers' expectations is delivering an overall pleasant experience from start to finish. From first contact to post-purchase support, there should always be a bright moment for consumers interacting with your company.

People are more transparent than ever today, especially now that social media plays a significant role in everyone's life. With all eyes on everyone around the clock, businesses need to be aware of this and ensure they're promoting a good image. Consumers are yearning for brands that show corporate social responsibility, and entrepreneurs who can deliver on that will strengthen their brand reputation.

Aligning solutions with consumer expectations sounds easy, but it's much more complicated than you'd think. Committing to diversity, being open to feedback, and being aware of broader societal trends all take time.

Setting off on the idea and concept development path can be an exciting and transformative time for entrepreneurs. This phase is a crucible where simple notions become tangible. At its core, idea and concept development requires creativity, critical thinking, and relentless refinement, to give nascent concepts legs.

In the landscape of idea and concept development, entrepreneurs have no choice but to explore myriad strategies for creative thinking. That means cultivating an atmosphere conducive to brainstorming sessions, embracing a spectrum of perspectives, and using methodologies that inspire innovative thought processes. In short, it's about pushing the boundaries of conventional thinking to uncover groundbreaking ideas.

But take your time in the introduction phase because this is one part of what entrepreneurs must do. The thinking stops once you've got something viable after refining your initial ideas through market feedback and trying them out with consumers in real life. Concept testing comes next, as businesses subject their refined concepts to rigorous scrutiny to determine whether their idea will succeed or fail once it hits the open market.

As the entrepreneurial landscape evolves in response to dynamic market forces, geopolitics, and technology, idea and concept development becomes even more critical. Entrepreneurs who can navigate these uncertainties while adapting their visions stand a better chance at success. Keep pushing forward with your vision.

Techniques for Idea and Creative Thinking

The vibrant energy of innovative ideas and creative thinking fuels entrepreneurialism. It ignites the sparks of growth ventures that redefine industries and meet society's constantly evolving needs. Society's dynamic landscape requires entrepreneurs to keep their minds elastic as they explore a rich tapestry of techniques for idea generation.

Brainstorming is a fundamental technique. Participants are encouraged to share ideas freely and without judgment. By unleashing collective thinking power, diverse thought perspectives intersect with each other and generate many ideas. This helps create a space that liberates everyone from the fear of criticism, leading to an environment perfect for uninhibited creativity.

Then there's mind mapping—another powerful technique that allows entrepreneurs to visualize their ideas' interconnectedness. By visualizing concepts together, people can see how a main idea branches off into related thoughts and associations. Not only does this help with creating new ideas, but it also reveals connections between surprising things, too.

The SCAMPER technique pushes people to think even more creatively by prodding them to question and manipulate existing ideas. The acronym stands for substitute, combine, adapt, modify, put to another use, eliminate, and reverse. If you need fresh perspectives or potential innovations on your current concept, apply these prompts one after another until something sticks. You never know what might come out. By doing this, entrepreneurs will stimulate their creativity by completely dismantling established mental frameworks. Only then will they be able to explore uncharted territories of possibility.

Analogies and metaphors are also critical. They help foster creative thinking by allowing you to link unrelated concepts. Sometimes, expressing one thought in terms of another can offer fresh lenses for exploring and interpreting complex things.

The provocation technique exists to disrupt traditional thinking patterns with challenging or provocative statements. As soon as individuals get jolted out of their comfort zones, that's when they begin questioning and reconsidering assumptions we've held for far too long. We stimulate creative thinking by pushing past conventional boundaries and embracing more unconventional possibilities.

And that's a natural innovation right there. Entrepreneurs who become masters of these different techniques will unlock limitless possibilities. Inside these doors, a culture fueled by creativity lives on, strongly pushing any venture towards pioneering achievements with transformative impacts on society.

Refining and Iterating Business Ideas

Finding success in the business world is a complex task. Entrepreneurs must be ready to work long hours and endure trial after trial. Refining an idea until it succeeds is a vital part of the process. Any entrepreneur will tell you that their journey was full of ups and downs, but they'll all agree that this part of the process is vital.

Refining and iterating your ideas forces you to dig deep into every aspect of your business concept. If you want it to work, you must fully understand what makes it tick. The whole point of refining is to see if there are any areas for improvement within your venture, so that you can take advantage of them right away before it's too late.

Once a refined idea exists, getting feedback from people familiar with your industry can only help improve things. It'll give you valuable data and help improve various aspects of your project—whether it be market appeal or customer satisfaction. At the end of this road, there should be a product that satisfies customers and solves their problems.

This goes beyond making something that works; entrepreneurs must also fully believe in what they're selling. Most successful businesses have an identity that aligns with their goals and objectives, which must be seen through each aspect of the venture. Only then will everyone involved genuinely feel like they're working towards something.

The first iteration of an idea might show promise. Nobody should declare success immediately because they would be lying if they did. Those who can adapt their plan based on feedback will position themselves properly to take advantage of new opportunities.

When times get rough, innovation should never come last on the list—instead, it should always be the number one priority. As I said earlier, things change quickly in this field, which means those slow on their feet will be swallowed up. The belief that there is always room for improvement keeps the world turning.

To see a change, you need to get out of your head and take advice from others who may not think as you do. Family, friends, or a team of people with unique skills will bring different perspectives to the table, which, in turn, means more ideas can be thrown around. Sometimes, groups like these have a hard time getting along, but they're vital to growth in business.

Entrepreneurs should be bold when using data to make informed decisions quickly. These tools allow you to gather and interpret information more profoundly, giving you the best chance to make moves without hesitation.

Concept Testing

Concept testing is an essential process that entrepreneurs must go through when starting a business. You can't come up with an idea one day and expect it to work the next. The testing phase of developing a concept is there to make sure everything aligns. For example, if you've got a burger place in mind, you must ensure people like your burgers before investing thousands of dollars into opening a shop.

To determine whether or not your idea will succeed, you need to expose it to potential customers and people representing your target audience. This will allow you to see how well the idea resonates with them and their preferences. If something's wrong, you can spot it here and fix it for better market fit.

Entrepreneurs must also get feedback from those who will use their products or services most often. For example, someone who enjoys eating at burger places could give great insight into what works and what doesn't.

For someone other than yourself to understand your vision, they need something physical they can interact with—a prototype. Taking this step clarifies things for everyone involved. Hence, you don't waste time or money.

You might think concept testing means finding out what makes an idea strong, but sometimes it's the opposite. Entrepreneurs are trying to identify how their venture could fail; then they will know how to prevent those problems from happening when they scale up.

Seeing how well your idea fits into current market dynamics is crucial for determining whether or not it can last in the long term against growing competition. Understanding what makes yours stand out will help you discover a niche that resonates with customers.

I know this is all a lot to take in, and it is overwhelming, but trust me when I say: it's better to be safe than sorry.

3.5 Feasibility Studies and Market Validation

Taking the plunge into entrepreneurship means examining a business concept to see if it can hold up in the market. This phase is critical to bridging the gap between ideas and real-life business execution. To turn an idea into an enterprise, entrepreneurs perform detailed feasibility studies with tools to validate the market's acceptance and resonance of their product or service offerings.

At its core, this analysis involves picking apart multiple facets of a business concept. It goes beyond seeing how much money it can make, accounting for technical feasibility, operational viability, and legal compliance. By looking at challenges through this lens, entrepreneurs can strategize accordingly identifying opportunities, threats, and weaknesses that will allow them to more clearly assess what could help or harm their success.

Entrepreneurs employ various methodologies for market validation to ensure the real-world potential and acceptance of a business concept. Surveying pilot programs and prototype testing are methods used to gauge their target audience. With this empirical approach, they can validate demand for what they're proposing while gathering specific insights about consumer preferences that align with industry trends.

The iterative feedback-gathering process is crucial for the synergistic feedback loop between feasibility studies and market validation. Entrepreneurs actively seek input from stakeholders like industry experts and potential customers, creating a continuous loop that informs the development of their business concept on every level. Those who follow this engagement model position themselves best by staying aligned with evolving customer needs and adapting to meet other expectations within the industry.

To minimize the risks that come with jumping headfirst into full-scale implementation, entrepreneurs need an ongoing commitment toward adaptability when conducting feasibility studies and validating markets. They need deep dives into the real world to help them make more informed decisions. Doing this will ultimately enhance their concepts of resilience and sustainability.

Blending feasibility studies with market validation creates what entrepreneurs need when heading from idea to market entry—this provides a 360-degree view of the concept, and its acceptance in the market, responsiveness, and alignment with consumer expectations. Through active involvement in these analyses, future business owners can dodge unnecessary risks by arming themselves with data-driven choices that will enhance their concept—even if they haven't realized it yet.

Conducting Feasibility Analysis

Launching a new business is complex and, at times, extremely risky. Before diving in, it makes sense to run the idea through a feasibility analysis. By doing this, entrepreneurs can ensure they've considered all the potential challenges and opportunities that could arise as they push their ideas forward. It's a way of stress-testing the concept, seeing what might break before it's built.

Of course, financials are critical, but this sort of analysis is even more important than numbers. Entrepreneurs must consider whether the product or service could be made with current technology. They should also look for legal and regulatory roadblocks that could keep them from realizing their business concept.

Beyond these sorts of practical considerations, market feasibility comes into play. Will there be enough demand for the product or service? Who will you be competing against? And is there something about your proposed offering that would give you an edge over others?

Feasibility analysis is never done—instead, it becomes a guiding light for entrepreneurs as they navigate challenges and find new opportunities. As things change around them—new competitors enter markets, regulations get updated, and technologies advance—entrepreneurs should regularly reevaluate their ideas using this framework. How do things stand now? Should anything change? What are we missing?

Tools for Market Validation

Market validation is the way that entrepreneurs determine if their business concept is viable and if the general public will accept it. They use various tools to explore consumer reactions, assess market demand, and adjust business concepts for optimal fit.

One tool is surveys, which are well-designed questionnaires that help gather quantitative data on customer preferences and buying behavior. Surveys provide an organized approach to understanding how a target audience operates. They can also reveal potential issues, enabling entrepreneurs to refine their ideas.

Another tool is focus groups, where a few representative individuals gather to discuss qualitative information about consumer perceptions. Here, they can talk more deeply about the business idea and discover nuances that quantitative methods couldn't identify alone. Focus groups present unique opinions that are useful in finding areas for improvement.

Prototyping is a tangible method for testing a concept's durability. Entrepreneurs create physical representations of what they want to offer customers. By allowing potential users to interact with prototypes before full-scale production, entrepreneurs gain insight into things that need fixing or enhancing and validate overall appeal and usability. Prototyping refines the user experience based on real-world interactions.

Pilot programs offer a way to test ideas in a controlled environment by launching mini versions of products or services. This helps gauge market interest and exposes operational challenges early on, while not putting too much money or at risk. Work hours

Social media engagement allows entrepreneurs to stay updated on changing consumer sentiments, address concerns quickly, and build anticipation around offerings using real-time interactions.

Crowdfunding platforms give marketers access to both market validation and fundraising simultaneously. When entrepreneurs showcase their concepts this way, people can financially support them, depending on whether they think their idea will be successful and valuable or not.

Early adopter programs are another handy method for testing new ideas before wider adoption. Knowing how the first customers feel about a product or service is invaluable in refining it, creating word-of-mouth marketing, and building momentum for later launches.

These tools work together to make market validation easier for entrepreneurs. By employing quantitative and qualitative methods alongside prototyping, pilot programs, social media engagement, crowdfunding initiatives, and early adopter targeting techniques, entrepreneurs can validate their business ideas more effectively.

Gathering Feedback and Incorporating Insights

Entrepreneurs' journeys require constant feedback and insight. This continuous dialogue occurs between the entrepreneur and stakeholders, like customers and industry experts, who shape the business concept.

Entrepreneurs can seek this feedback from many sources, such as potential customers, focus groups, industry peers, or mentors. This wide range of information ensures that they understand the perspectives surrounding their idea. Interviews, surveys, and direct interactions allow for qualitative data collection about consumer preferences and pain points.

As crucial as gatherings may be, there needs to be an environment in which people are comfortable sharing their thoughts. Constructive criticism is vital in creating a space for people to share diverse opinions about your idea, beyond mere validation. A culture of encouragement helps foster innovation through improvement.

Entrepreneurs frequently get instant feedback via digital platforms on anything related to their venture, such as social media channels or engaging with online communities or forums. These platforms give them immediate access to consumers' concerns, so they can adapt quickly when trends change.

Once they have all this information, successful entrepreneurs know how to analyze it effectively and make strategic decisions based on patterns in consumer responses.

Prototyping gives entrepreneurs something tangible to refer back to during the improvement process, by iterating on initial prototypes based on user insights gathered. These tangible models guarantee that enhanced offerings are not forced down consumers' throats but fit smoothly into their expected experiences.

Customers who see changes made based on their observations will also begin trusting you more. Loyalty develops when customers see first-hand proof of your dedication to satisfying them.

Feedback is helpful in product development, but also in other areas, including marketing strategies and operational efficiency. Taking advice from everyday individuals is critical to achieving sustainable success with any venture.

3.6 Strategic Positioning

Navigating the business ecosystem demands informed strategic positioning. Organizations seek to discover an identity and establish a market share by analyzing competitors. This complex task entails evaluating current landscapes, analyzing rivals, and formulating a strategy that aligns with their goals and resources.

Assessing market position and competitor analysis lays the groundwork for organizations in the strategic positioning landscape. Companies look at factors like customer perception to see where they stand within the market. Concurrently, a strength-weakness analysis of rivals can be used to identify gaps, capitalize on strengths, and navigate potential challenges.

Developing a competitive strategy involves using analyses from market assessments and competitor evaluations. This blueprint shows how businesses can compete while staying true to their goals. Competitive strategies define objectives, help allocate resources strategically, and help create structures that support them.

Differentiation tactics are vital in standing out among the competition, while implementation helps properly communicate value propositions to target audiences. Organizations emphasizing unique offerings or innovative approaches will resonate most with customers. On the other hand, positioning tactics involve marketing efforts that reflect the desired perception in the marketplace. These include branding, messaging, and promotional activities.

Organizations must keep up with constantly changing consumer preferences if they want a chance to differentiate themselves from the competition. Achieving successful strategic positioning extends beyond any fixed plan. It involves continually refining, iterating, and responding to evolving circumstances.

Organizations that nail down strategic positioning succeed where others fail—especially when every decision plays a vital role in shaping their future. By creating this foundation, companies gain an edge against rivals as they adapt to today's ever-evolving marketplace.

Assessing Market Position and Competitor Analysis

Certain practices need to be implemented for long-term business success. One of these is assessing a market position and conducting competitor analysis. These allow for effective decision-making and put businesses on the right path towards their goals.

The initial step involves examining an organization's standing within the market and competing forces. By understanding both, businesses gain insight into their next moves.

Discovering how you stand next to your competition is a great first move to make when trying to figure out what direction you want to lead your company in. It gives you a starting point from which strategies can flow and ultimately turn into goals achieved.

There is also an aspect of competitor analysis, where organizations operating within the same industry dissect strengths and weaknesses. This is extremely valuable because it allows them to see where they stand against similar companies regarding their products or services. The perks continue; organizations will learn how much market share other entities hold, how much they charge for things, and what distribution tactics they use.

"SWOT" (strengths, weaknesses, opportunities, threats) is another tool that businesses employ when more precision is needed during evaluations. Internal factors like unique capabilities and operational efficiency are compared with external ones such as emerging market trends and competitors' potential threats. A systematic analysis such as this provides invaluable knowledge about your surrounding landscape.

As we all know by now, technology matters. That's why modern assessments like these have become reliant on it. Data analytics allows for the analysis of vast amounts of information about customer behaviors and competitor performance at once, giving companies the upper hand when making informed decisions.

Through assessing a market position and conducting competitor analysis, organizations can craft business strategies that will withstand the test of time. They will go through stages that identify trends customers are moving towards and a plan to set a company apart. With each step these companies take, they inch closer to success in a world where failure is possible at any given time.

All of this may seem like a lot to keep on top of, and it is. Investing the time and resources into evaluations like these is one way to ensure your business stays ahead of its competitors. It's no secret how quickly the world moves nowadays; it only makes sense that organizations should do everything they can to keep up with it.

Crafting a Competitive Strategy

In business, crafting a competitive strategy is a complex process that forms the foundation of an organization's ability to gain an advantage in the market. It involves aligning resources, capabilities, and positioning to navigate the competitive landscape.

At its core, crafting a competitive strategy requires organizations to fully understand their internal dynamics and external market forces. They must evaluate their unique strengths, capabilities, and core competencies as they prepare to face competition head-on. This self-awareness gives them an edge in the market, because they know what makes them stand out.

It's also essential to gauge outside forces when crafting a competitive strategy. Organizations should assess market trends, customer behavior patterns, regulatory changes, and technological advances that may impact their industry. Doing this allows them to identify opportunities and potential threats, which helps determine whether or not certain business decisions are worth pursuing.

It would help to answer some questions when building your organization's strategies. Whether you're aiming to become a low-cost producer or offering unique products or services that stand out in the market, you have choices about where and how you want to compete with competitors.

Once you've identified your focus, it is essential to establish your business scope within the marketplace. Will your company operate within a broad market or focus on a specific segment?

The dynamics of cost vs. differentiation are also at play when crafting your competitive strategies. Achieving lower costs involves streamlining operations, while differentiation focuses on innovation and providing exceptional value for customers.

After decisions are made throughout this process, they are implemented into actionable plans. This could involve restructuring, resource allocation, and daily operations based on your chosen competitive strategy.

Once it is implemented and efforts start rolling out, it does not mean stopping monitoring or adapting. Market conditions change continually, including technological advances and competitor movements. Regularly reassessing the strategy is an excellent way to keep up with these changes.

Crafting competitive strategies requires many moving parts that must be synched together. It is a blueprint roadmap that helps organizations navigate business challenges, seize opportunities, and build competitive advantages in the long run.

Differentiation and Positioning Tactics

In the intricate world of competitiveness, many words, such as differentiation and positioning, are thrown around. While they may seem trivial initially, these two ideas can be essential to separating yourself from the pack. It's all about presenting yourself and creating customer value.

Differentiation essentially means being unique. You want your product to be different from everyone else's in some way, so customers will choose yours over theirs. Apple has built a reputation for its sleek design and user-friendly interfaces, which sets it apart from its competitors.

Service differentiation takes that idea one step further. Sure, it is good for your product to be unique, but how is it sold? How do customers feel when they use your service? Companies like Zappos have built themselves around exceptional customer service; this means their customers keep returning.

Positioning tactics are all about how customers perceive you in comparison to others. Depending on your goals, there are different ways to achieve them.

One tactic focuses on targeting specific groups or niches. By tailoring their product or service to meet the needs of a particular demographic, organizations can become relevant to their target audience. A luxury brand like Rolex positions itself as exclusive by only targeting people who care about high-end watches.

People often think about price positioning without fully grasping it. They gravitate toward whatever price point fits their budget without considering why. Some companies price their products low because they're trying to reach as many consumers as possible, while others make things expensive because people associate cost with quality.

The final tactic makes you the solution people need for problems they realize exist. If you address these hidden issues effectively, people will recognize that and reward you with their business.

When it comes to strategic planning for a business, tactics like differentiation and positioning are integral. Companies that manage to stand out in the competitive world do this by offering something truly unique. Their product or service may have special features or provide excellent service to their customers. Some use pricing strategies as their means of distinction. Meanwhile, effective positioning tactics ensure that these organizations' uniqueness is communicated in a way their customer base can relate to and trust. All this helps shape perceptions and foster long-term brand loyalty. In an environment as complex as the marketplace, it is crucial that companies have strategies for differentiating themselves from others, while staying connected with their target audience. That's how brands make an unforgettable impression on consumers and ultimately take over their industry.

3.7 Building Business Models

Next, we will discuss the dynamics of creating companies from the ground up. We will dive into the strategic framework, operations, revenue, and overall architecture. As entrepreneurs face the challenge of making their ideas a reality, we will show how to build resilient models that can withstand anything.

Explaining some popular models is a good start when founding a business. These traditional models will help you understand how others have found success in different industries. Some companies still use these strategies today, and some use innovative new ones like sharing economies or platform-based ones. Whichever you choose, you should know what's out there to better understand what works best with your concept.

Once you narrow it down to something more specific, building around core products and services comes next. This process mirrors finding target audiences and value propositions. The trick here is ensuring everything lines up correctly and that every piece of the puzzle fits together perfectly while optimizing operations and improving customer satisfaction.

Moving onto sustainability and scalability, any entrepreneur wants to create something that lasts longer than other trends today. We explore how to do that using changing market conditions and technological advances to survive consumer preferences that change over time. When thinking about scaling things up after creating a decent foundation, entrepreneurs must envision future demands while considering geographic aspects, if need be. These factors all come into play when creating something scalable. This serves as a compass for those who may need direction while trying to figure out the complexities behind their creation.

Overview of Popular Business Models

Business models are the structures that companies use to make money and maintain operations; hence, they vary greatly. To be successful in commerce, you need to understand the ins and outs of these models.

A traditional example of a model is the retail model, whereby businesses can purchase goods at wholesale prices and then sell them to customers at a higher price than they bought them for. It's been the foundation of business for centuries and it's effective. But with new technology come new ways of doing things.

Enter e-commerce, which has given birth to direct-to-consumer, an innovative way for brands to connect with their audience without intermediaries like wholesalers or retailers. This tech-enhanced approach enhances customer engagement through data collected when customers interact with sites and services, which businesses will use to tailor products and services in a way that suits them better. Since this method helps digitally native companies build strong online communities, it makes sense that their customer base would have such a strong relationship with their brand.

Subscription-based models work by providing customers with ongoing access to products or services. Instead of paying once, you pay a recurring fee, like those seen in meal delivery programs or streaming services. This fosters customer loyalty through continuous value updates and improvements while keeping your pockets full of all those recurring payments.

The freemium model combines free premium offerings into one hybrid option. The service's essential parts are free, but advanced features require a paid membership. Think about software applications or gaming platforms, which give us only so much until we want more and pull out our wallets.

Platform-based business models have become increasingly dominant, because they act as intermediaries between two groups via online interactions, reducing overall company risk. These platforms leverage network effects where everyone benefits from joining, creating a self-reinforcing cycle.

The sharing economy business model connects people willing to share things like transportation or skills. Companies use this model because it saves them money and promotes sustainability, which customers will be more inclined to support in today's shopping-friendly world.

The gig economy focuses on connecting freelancers with short-term work opportunities, in the way Uber, Fiverr, and Doordash do. This approach provides flexibility for both businesses and individuals. Businesses save money because they don't have to hire full-time employees. At the same time, individuals can take on as many jobs as their schedule permits.

The way businesses work is constantly changing. Technology, what people like, and how the market works shape how a company makes money. Business owners and people need to learn the subtleties of different business models to use their strengths, understand challenges, and create a custom approach that lets them meet their goals in the best way possible.

Tailoring Business Models to Fit Your Concept

Building a business is more complex than developing a concept. Many factors must be carefully considered when creating a tailored business model. You must consider the product or service, target audience, market dynamics, and competitive landscape.

Every product operates differently, from pricing to distribution requirements. You focus on manufacturing costs, supply chain logistics, and inventory management for tangible goods. At the same time, service-oriented businesses concentrate on customer retention and delivering excellent service.

Another critical factor is understanding your target audience. You need to know what they like and how they act, in order to better tailor your business model for them. Certain features of your model will resonate with certain people differently; it's essential to find what aligns best with your market.

Maintaining current market dynamics is crucial when molding your business model. It's no secret that markets change constantly. They're influenced by technology and trends; predicting these changes can give you a significant advantage. Regarding scalability, if growth is part of the plan, it is wise to ensure that your chosen model can handle increased demand without needing significant reconstructions. Focusing on financial sustainability may seem like common sense, but some entrepreneurs overlook this step when crafting their business model; balancing revenue and cost structures is critical.

Sustainability and Scalability Considerations

No matter what the industry is, sustainability and scalability are two things that play a big part in determining whether a business will be successful in the long run. These interconnected aspects have a lot to say when it comes to shaping an organization's strategies, influencing decision-making processes, and determining whether a company can handle whatever life throws at it.

When people think of sustainability, they usually think about recycling and renewable energy. But in business terms, it means something different. In this context, sustainability has more to do with longevity over extended periods of time. A sustainable business model includes responsible practices that balance economic, social, and ecological considerations. Nowadays, we observe companies trying their best to reduce waste and minimize their footprint on the world by embracing renewable resources. On top of all that environmental stuff, companies should also focus on providing value to stakeholders and ensuring employees are taken care of both financially and emotionally. Nobody likes feeling like another cog in the machine.

Regardless of how solid your foundation is, there will always be room for growth. Scalability is crucial if you want your business model to last longer than a few years. Flexibility allows organizations to accommodate increased consumer demands without sacrificing too much performance or spending too many resources. It also makes it easier for businesses wishing to expand into new markets to capitalize on emerging opportunities.

You are right if you think these two concepts conflict. Balancing sustainability with scalability requires excellent insight into how economies work and general business smarts. There must be some equilibrium between what's good for the environment and what could attract thousands more new customers. Leadership is vital in deciding which direction the company should move in.

Sustainability and scalability are the two things all the other aspects of the business will evolve around. Get them right, and you'll have an organization ready to take on the world and leave it in a better place than when it started.

3.8 Financial Planning and Projections

Here we will explore financial planning and projections, which explore vital elements that affect a business's economic health and trajectory. This comprehensive dive covers three essential topics: estimating costs and forecasting revenue, creating financial models specific to your business concept, and identifying funding sources based on your financial needs.

Estimating costs and forecasting revenue might not be the most exciting part of running a business, but they're essential. Accurate cost estimation allows you to set realistic pricing strategies with which you can turn a profit. It also helps determine where resources should be allocated for maximum efficiency. Forecasts related to revenue require some forward thinking as you consider market trends, consumer behavior, and the competitive landscape. Both of these elements are crucial for making sound financial decisions that lead to sustainable growth.

Building financial models for your business concept lets you break your entrepreneurial vision down into something quantifiable. These models help identify what kind of impact strategic choices or operational decisions will have on your bottom line, acting as a snapshot of your finances in the future—which is handy. By zeroing in on revenue streams, cost structures, and other financial metrics, businesses can assess their overall health while pinpointing improvement areas. Learning how to create these models takes time because they must be explicitly tailored to your unique concept, the market space it fills, and other intricacies surrounding money matters.

Identifying funding sources and financial requirements is one of the more practical aspects of planning finances for a venture of any size. You can only run a company with money. Whether looking into traditional options such as loans or investors or exploring more modern routes like crowdfunding or grants—knowing all possible avenues can only empower you when making important decisions about cash flow. Determining the necessary financial requirements involves calculating startup costs, overhead expenses, like rent and utilities, employee salaries, and growth potential. This kind of well-rounded understanding ensures businesses are prepared to secure the capital they need for their journey.

The topics covered in this section are just the beginning. As we progress through financial planning and projections, we will cover even more information. While there may be more gripping subjects, having a solid grasp of these fundamentals will ultimately guide your business in the long term. Whether you're just starting, or you've been around for a while, keep an open mind as we dive into these concepts together. The knowledge you acquire will help you make confident choices when faced with financial obstacles—allowing your company to grow and succeed well into the future.

Estimating Costs and Forecasting Revenue

Estimating costs and forecasting revenue is a major part of financial planning. It requires the utmost attention and a deep understanding of how every single factor can affect a business's economic situation.

Estimating costs involves examining all the expenses related to making, distributing, and promoting goods or services. These can include raw materials, production expenses, marketing, and overheads. Businesses can benefit from a thorough cost analysis by setting realistic pricing strategies and identifying areas where they can save on costs for a higher profit margin.

Forecasting revenue is as significant as estimating costs regarding financial planning. It would help if you always looked ahead and analyzed upcoming trends in your market. By evaluating trends, consumer behavior, and competition, then predicting future sales, you give yourself a financial guide that you can use to make decisions about things like operations or marketing efforts.

Cost estimation and revenue forecasting work together to keep your finances balanced. Knowing your costs helps you set competitive and profitable prices, while knowing your revenue enables you to utilize resources efficiently for growth strategies that will ultimately pay off.

Many external factors could change everything about your cost or revenue models at any time, such as economic conditions or new technological advances. Continuously monitoring these two elements based on market insights contributes to an active approach to mitigating risks before they become problems, and pouncing on opportunities before they pass by.

Technology plays a significant role in optimizing this process for us. Advanced financial modeling tools and data analytics allow businesses to perform scenario analyses, which help identify trends. Hence, we will know what to do next time something similar comes up—which it inevitably will. The truth is, there's no finish line here for this skill set because the whole business landscape changes constantly.

Honing your skills to estimate costs and forecast revenue is an ongoing effort. It requires attention to detail and a deep understanding of business in general. Thankfully, with these two things, we can navigate anything that comes our way, as long as we keep adapting to change.

Building Financial Models for Your Business Concept

Creating financial models that fit your business is a strategic act. It's about taking a complicated concept and putting it into concrete numbers so that you can navigate it in the future. A financial model is like a blueprint. It gives you a clear image of your economic landscape's elements. The essential things it covers are costs, revenue streams, and key financial metrics. They're fluid enough to keep updating as the market changes and its behavior shifts.

Before working on your model, you must understand what you're selling and who will buy it. Beyond that, you should also understand everything that comes with making that product or service a reality. You'll also want to break down all the production costs, operating expenses, marketing expenditures, and anything else finance-related that will come up when managing this new venture.

Being flexible isn't an option when building models like these. Scenarios and sensitivity analyses are designed for those who want to see how different circumstances would impact their business.

Technology has made creating complex financial models easy for non-finance people by providing some user-friendly tools. When integrated into daily practices, these tools could provide serious efficiency boosts in accuracy and speed.

Internally, they help management make better resource decisions by accurately representing what's happening now and predicting how it could shape the future. Externally, investors feel more comfortable knowing their money is being put into something realistic.

Models should constantly evolve alongside your business as it grows or adjusts strategies. Updates with new data ensure they stay accurate with market trends over time. Beware; these trends will often change. Being stuck in the past will make these projections less valuable, or even useless.

At first glance, this process may seem daunting, but once it is broken down into pieces, we can see that it's all about understanding the different numbers that make up our business. By the time you build your model, you should have a solid grasp of everything going on inside and outside of your company.

Identifying Funding Sources and Financial Requirements

Finding where the money is and understanding what you need to do to get it is crucial for all businesses looking to start and grow. Many potential sources exist. They all have unique characteristics and requirements. Traditional options include loans and lines of credit, which usually follow a repayment plan that works for both parties involved. This option often requires a financial history before anyone will give you a second glance. On the other hand, equity financing is based on investments made by individuals or venture capital firms, who are then given partial ownership over your business. This method is commonly sought by startups hoping for an influx of cash in exchange for some control in decision-making.

Crowdfunding platforms have also risen exponentially in popularity over recent years, because they can effectively raise funds with little to no strings attached. By allowing people from across the globe to donate as much or as little as they want, his has fostered incredible projects funded by everyday people rather than billion-dollar corporations or entities. Government grants and subsidies are another non-repayable option to help fund research, development, or other initiatives aligned with governmental goals.

It doesn't matter where you plan on getting your money from if you need help understanding what kind of budget you'll need first. Consider every aspect of your venture and determine how much it will cost from the beginning until eternity. Think about startup costs, marketing campaigns or materials, expansions… Anything that could cost money should be considered here, so that you know exactly how much debt you're getting into before signing on any dotted line.

Knowing when and where the money will come from is just as important. Typically speaking, entrepreneurs will know roughly when they'll need funding, depending on their stage of development: Starting up? Growing? This will play a crucial role in which funding option you choose, and could even have a drastic impact on the trajectory of your enterprise.

Businesses must be aware of all the terms and conditions surrounding the debt they're about to take on. Interest rates, repayment terms, and ownership implications can differ significantly between lenders; evaluate them before signing any checks. This extra step is essential in finding the right lender who works for your specific goals and needs.

Understanding how much money you need, where it will come from, when, and how much it will cost you in the long run takes practice and patience. Once mastered, this strategic phase can set a business up for exponential growth as it confidently pursues its targets while adapting to market changes when necessary.

3.9 Communicating Your Business Concept

Let's consider critical aspects of communicating your business concept, like developing a solid pitch and storytelling, creating a business plan and executive summary, and establishing effective communication with stakeholders and investors.

Building up the skill of crafting a persuasive story is crucial to pitching an idea effectively. It's more than being able to sell ice to an Eskimo; it's about capturing people's attention and keeping them engaged in what you're saying. I'll show you how to condense complex ideas into simple yet intriguing ones. You'll be able to connect with your audience at a much deeper level that goes beyond wanting them to buy from you.

While a good pitch can attract potential customers, a proper business plan will ensure sustainability. A good one provides direction through market challenges, allowing better decision-making for your company, and it doesn't collapse under pressure; we'll go over how to paint an accurate picture of your business by covering your vision mission, and operational intricacies. We'll also cover the importance of having an executive summary—a shortened version that busy people can understand quickly.

Among all these skills lies one that most entrepreneurs overlook: effective communication with others who aren't their clients. The list includes internal stakeholders like employees and potential investors who may not have heard of you before but are now curious. Being transparent with everyone involved will build peer trust while leaving no room for error or miscommunication. Trust me when I say that credibility means everything in this field.

You may get overwhelmed by everything I have listed but don't worry. This part was made specifically for those who need help communicating their business. You can grow your company sustainably and successfully with a bit of practice, reading, and understanding.

Developing a Strong Pitch and Storytelling

Creating a compelling pitch and telling a good story are skills people can apply to many aspects of their lives. They're useful in anything from making business presentations to having personal interactions, and they'll help you persuade stakeholders, open doors, and make yourself memorable.

Before you build your pitch, it is essential to know who will be consuming it. Who is your audience? What do they care about? What are their needs? By making sure your presentation aligns with those concerns, you'll start building rapport with them and making them more receptive. Whether pitching a business idea or sharing something personal, this step is crucial for getting where you want to go.

A strong pitch starts with a clear message that gets straight to the point. Refine your ideas until only one remains at the core of everything else: one concept anyone can understand. Outline the problem you're addressing and present your solution in an easy-to-understand way. There's no need for jargon or convoluted language—simplicity often wins when it comes to communication. Make sure your message is authentic and compelling enough that passion shines through in every word.

Storytelling has captivated audiences for centuries because it is effective at memorably conveying information. Weave your pitch into a narrative that will engage emotions and resonate with others' experiences as humans. Share anecdotes that people can easily relate to, paint vivid imagery whenever appropriate, and use metaphors if you need to explain something complex in simpler terms. Doing all this will ensure that people pay attention while you talk and remember what was said long after you're in their presence.

There's a pattern within most compelling stories. Apply this to your pitch by identifying challenges or obstacles in your narrative. This will pique interest and build suspense in your audience. Then, when it's time to reveal the resolution, they'll be itching to hear what you have to say and more likely to remember how meaningful it was.

Incorporating visuals and metaphors into your pitch will have an even more significant impact after you've caught their attention with a good story. Visual aids like graphs or charts can help show people exactly what you're talking about instead of having them take your word for it. It would help if you aim for a balanced mix of words and pictures so that all audience members can understand everything perfectly.

Engagement goes two ways: if you want someone to interact with you, you must first invite them into your world. Pose questions, encourage discussions, or whip out something interactive during your pitch so that everyone stays on their toes while listening. Not only does this keep people attentive, but it also gives them a sense of involvement in your presentation. Try not to forget that engaging an audience involves more than words, though—maintain eye contact, vary your tone, and use body language as much as possible so that others are convinced by more than what's coming out of your mouth.

A polished pitch comes from endless practice and revising until success is reached. There are many ways that people practice speaking in front of others: Some stand in front of a mirror, making sure they hit every mark, while others record themselves talking so that they can go back later and critique each part one by one. The most effective route for improvement is usually relying on trusted colleagues or mentors. They'll give honest feedback on pacing issues, clarity problems, and emotional impact levels. As you become more comfortable with your pitch and have it memorized, you can focus on putting personal flair into the presentation. Once that's done, people will believe what you're saying and truly see why they should buy it.

Knowing how to craft a solid pitch and tell a compelling story can put anyone ahead of the game, whether trying to sell an idea at work or getting someone emotionally invested in something personal. By understanding your audience, defining messages clearly, creating narratives that captivate emotions, using visuals and metaphors, engaging everyone with questions or interactive elements, and practicing repeatedly until it's perfect, you'll be set up for success every time.

Creating a Business Plan and Executive Summary

Starting a business requires a comprehensive business plan. It's like a strategic roadmap that helps you get your idea to the finish line. At its core, it conveys your venture's vision, mission, and objectives—serving as an essential tool for attracting investors and providing clarity and direction internally.

The executive summary—typically found at the beginning of a business plan—is essential because it encapsulates everything about your venture. In summary form, it becomes your first point of contact with stakeholders, giving them a quick look into what makes your business unique and profitable.

Here are some elements you should include in your executive summary:

Start by clearly stating your mission: This will help you define precisely what problem you're trying to solve with this new venture. And how can you stand out from existing solutions?

Take time to analyze the market. Your team needs to sincerely understand who they are serving. That means knowing key trends, demographics, and even competitors in that market.

Emphasize the unique value proposition: What are the main benefits customers will derive from using your product or service? How can you distinguish yourself from your competitors?

Detail how money flows in and out. In other words, build an effective revenue model that covers pricing strategies, sales channels, and potential partnerships that will contribute to the business's sustainability.

Map out operational efficiency: This section should highlight your business structure and explain the key processes involved in making it happen. Financial projections tell a story; answer questions like, 'How much do we expect to make this year?' Provide estimates for expenses, too, so readers know you understand where money is going.

Effective Communication with Stakeholders and Investors

Communication is the lifeblood of a successful business. It connects the entrepreneur with stakeholders and investors to turn dreams into reality. A good communication strategy is not an option; it's a must-have if entrepreneurs want to share their vision, build trust, and foster long-term relationships with those who will benefit from their success.

Navigating stakeholder and investor communication requires understanding and empathy. People all have different needs, expectations, and perspectives that need to be considered.

Stakeholders include customers, employees, suppliers, regulatory bodies, and the community. Recognizing this helps entrepreneurs create unique strategies that resonate with each group since they have different interests. Everyone wants something else out of it; customization is critical.

Transparency is also vital. Trust is gained by being open and honest about the company's activities. That means providing clear and accurate information about its performance and any challenges or plans ahead. This kind of transparency bridges entrepreneurs and stakeholders beyond financial figures.

Entrepreneurs must tell a better story than their competitors to connect with investors and stakeholders. Facts are great, but feelings are better than communication alone when building lasting connections.

Different stakeholders engage with information differently. Understanding how to foster engagement makes a big difference. For example, some prefer traditional reports, while others scroll through social media pages for updates or watch webinars instead of reading about changes in other formats.

Maintaining a regular schedule of meaningful communication shows them you care enough about their support or interest to make time for it, even after your project has taken off. Communication isn't one-size-fits-all; adapting it over time keeps things fresh and exciting.

When it comes to business, effective communication is as important as the product itself. It is required to harmonize relationships and build trust with stakeholders and investors. And with a little bit of effort, entrepreneurs can build an empire. Messages from the company should be clear and concise, but sometimes they need to be tailored toward specific ears. Meanwhile, listening to feedback is vital for growth and improving services. When something goes wrong, entrepreneurs need to be open and honest about what happens. Not only does this help in damage control, but it also shows everyone they're not afraid of confrontation. Diverse communication channels are necessary when running a successful business; so use them.

Chapter 4

Market Research and Analysis

In chapter 3 we discussed crafting a business concept. While a business concept and market plan outline a strategic approach that will allow you to achieve its marketing objectives, market research and analysis become the basis of the information necessary for informing and supporting the development of such a plan. Market research and analysis also enable you to identify the target market, competitive landscape, and industry trends.

Understanding market dynamics is critical to any successful business strategy. In an ever-changing business world, market research and analysis serve as the organization's compass, guiding it through consumer preferences, industry trends, and competitive landscapes. This chapter holistically explores the ins and outs of market research so that you can make informed decisions and enable growth in your business.

Market research isn't just a process—it's also strategic planning's heartbeat. To begin this journey together, let's start with a basic introduction to market research. This will help us understand what drives consumers' choices, where opportunities lie, and how to manage associated risks.

It is good to have a great plan, but it is insufficient. Designing a market research plan should be our next step from here. This part emphasizes the need to approach objectives systematically while identifying resources correctly. It also stresses adaptability and flexibility when dealing with changeable scenarios in corporate backgrounds—which are inevitable.

Data collection techniques separate theory from authentic insights. Traditional surveys and interviews, along with modern data analytics and artificial intelligence applications, bridge that gap. Businesses must effectively specify how they approach different issues relating to their customers' needs.

Markets are not homogenous; so, understanding market segmentation helps unlock your complete marketing potential. By breaking them down demographically, psychologically, geographically, and behaviorally, companies can target which markets to target with specific promotions or products offered.

Knowing how customers behave helps you understand how to sell them stuff—and that's where analyzing consumer behavior comes into play. Consumer choice's psychological and sociological aspects are intricate yet valuable to firms wanting an upper hand as they make products or devise strategies for particular markets.

Finding success in the market doesn't happen in a vacuum—it happens by being better than others. That's where competitive analysis comes into play. This section will help you assess your competitors, emphasizing benchmarking, SWOT analysis, and strategic positioning.

Markets are dynamic, meaning they're constantly changing. By seeing the big picture through industry and market trend analysis, companies can detect trends before they become issues. Companies can base their long-term operational plans on changes such as consumer preferences, technological advances, and economic forces, among many other factors.

You can be as innovative as possible, but if there's no demand for it, it won't sell. Product demand and market size can inform ways to determine whether products will fly off the shelves or flop hard. Your marketing strategies will be vital if you understand what customers want or need.

Data interpretation and reporting is the final chapter in our journey of market research & analysis; that does not mean it is less critical than other chapters. At this stage, we have analyzed the data and drawn conclusions; now we must present these findings so that others can easily understand what happened during the collection process. Data interpretation helps us make strategic decisions within our institutions so that everyone knows what it is all about when they look at them.

The market is constantly changing and can be challenging to keep up with—especially when trying to stay ahead. That is why we are here. Numerous opportunities exist for businesses who want to thrive in this field but identifying them necessitates a profound comprehension of market dynamics. The sooner you grasp these nuances, the faster you will shoot ahead.

4.1 Introduction to Market Research

Understanding market dynamics is a critical part of any successful business plan. Market research and analysis work as a compass in the ever-changing world of commerce. They help businesses navigate consumer preferences, industry trends, and competitive landscapes. This section deeply examines market research and comprehensively examines critical decision-making.

Market research is more than just a process—it's at the heart of strategic planning. It helps in understanding the market's intricacies, seizing opportunities, and avoiding risks. We must realize that this isn't just another item on our checklist, but a strategic imperative.

Designing a market research plan highlights the next cornerstone—acknowledging that a well-thought-out plan sets us up for success. In this segment, we'll learn about systematically identifying research objectives, determining appropriate methodologies, and allocating resources effectively. As markets change swiftly and the landscape shifts continuously, adaptability becomes our greatest ally—so let's ensure we stay agile throughout our journey.

Data collection techniques are the foundation for effective market research. They take theory and turn it into actionable insights. Here, we explore methods such as traditional surveys and interviews and cutting-edge data analytics techniques powered by artificial intelligence applications. By weighing the pros and cons of each technique, businesses can fine-tune their approaches based on the unique demands of their research objectives.

As markets grow increasingly diverse, businesses must understand the art of market segmentation, partitioning diverse markets into uniform segments, for targeted marketing strategies; thus, products will align with specific consumer needs that they've sought in other areas or brands. By exploring various segmentation criteria, such as demographic, psychographic, geographic, and behavioral factors, we can shed light on the relevance of these variables in shaping market dynamics.

Analyzing consumer behavior follows suit, highlighting how consumer preferences and decision-making processes shape markets. We deeply delve into the psychological and sociological factors affecting consumer choices. As businesses gain a more robust comprehension of what drives purchasing decisions, they can begin to craft products and strategies tailored to genuine market demands.

Knowing your enemy is important—competitive analysis acknowledges this as essential to success in any market. This involves dissecting competitors using benchmarking, SWOT analysis, and strategic positioning. By understanding rivals' strengths and weaknesses, businesses can fortify their position in the market while identifying untapped opportunities.

Our journey into market research will uncover a critical piece of strategic business knowledge. Understanding the market is at the core of every successful enterprise, so it would be good for us to get started here.

We will explore how market research connects with strategic decision-making. I'll show you why insights are so important by giving examples of how these strategies have been used successfully in other companies. Going through each step together will make it easier for your business to make informed decisions when we start mapping out which directions are most advantageous.

There are two types of market research: qualitative and quantitative. Each has its own characteristics and benefits. Qualitative research examines opinions, while quantitative research is all about numbers. Here we discuss those specifics to help you understand which method will be most helpful, depending on your goal.

Definition and Purpose of Market Research

At its core, market research is a multidimensional process that helps us better understand the market. It involves collecting, analyzing, and interpreting data to prepare us to deal with complex consumer trends and competitive dynamics. In layman's terms, it's our compass in the jungle of commerce; it helps us find practical information—not just numbers or surveys but qualitative insights, perceptual nuances, and strategic implications. Any company needs to know what its target audience wants so it can align its position accordingly.

Market research is designed to enable decision-makers to see into the future—identifying opportunities before they pop up, assessing risks early enough to mitigate them, and positioning their products or services in prime locations before anyone else.

Market research helps us understand what makes the market tick and how each gear fits together. It constructs a roadmap for how your business should operate strategically in the coming years. Its importance cannot be stressed enough; when utilized correctly, it is the foundation for any successful business strategy.

The Role of Research in Business Strategy

Market research aids businesses with customer insight into needs, preferences, and behaviors, leading companies to develop products and services that resonate with customers. This work drives demand and helps form long-term relationships, which are vital for any company. A company must have a solid understanding of its customers or other market trends to avoid investing in ventures that don't meet expectations.

By researching prospective competitors, businesses gain strategic advantages. New players can emerge swiftly and disrupt established markets in today's globalized economy. To stay ahead, companies must understand their competition thoroughly by finding their strengths or weaknesses; this way, they can strategize and capitalize on opportunities while minimizing potential threats moving forward. If a company isn't familiar with its competitors, it won't go far when trying to grow.

Research also heavily influences internal dynamics. By looking at internal processes such as employee engagement or organizational culture, companies can identify the areas where innovation is needed most. These two things help optimize operations within the company so everyone can get more done in less time while enjoying an overall better working experience. Understanding who has what skills within the workforce helps allocate resources effectively, so there isn't unnecessary downtime.

When businesses commit to research and development, they put themselves ahead of others by staying ready for technological breakthroughs. A proactive approach allows them to anticipate industry shifts, develop cutting-edge products or services, and maintain a leadership position over competitors.

Risk management is another area that businesses benefit significantly from when they commit to research. Contingency plans can be implemented to minimize any harm from regulatory changes, economic downturns, or even unforeseen market disruptions. These are all examples of well-known business killers that companies can avoid with knowledge and a plan.

Research isn't an optional element for businesses; it is something they need to survive, regardless of industry. Those who embrace this type of decision-making become adaptable and agile, ultimately allowing them to succeed in the long run. With so much information available today, it's hard to know what is essential and what isn't, but strategic insight always has value, so those who act on it will thrive no matter what uncertainty comes their way.

Types of Market Research: Qualitative and Quantitative

Market research is vital for figuring out who to sell to. Qualitative and quantitative research can each give you different perspectives on your target audience.

Qualitative research goes deep into consumer behavior and preferences. This method focuses on understanding why people do things rather than just what they do. This approach is all about open-ended questions. Interviews, observations, or focus groups help researchers understand the market landscape. This methodology is instrumental during product development. Qualitative data can uncover potential issues that surveys might not pick up on.

Quantitative research uses massive amounts of numerical data to find trends and patterns in consumer purchases. By collecting statistical information, businesses can predict the market and validate their hypotheses. It's much more rigid than qualitative methods but making informed strategy decisions is necessary.

There are times when these two approaches overlap. Qualitative studies often precede quantitative studies because they help guide survey-building processes and establish research hypotheses. When it is time for surveys or experiments, quantitative methods draw broad conclusions from the deep work done by qualitative ones.

Choosing between the two is straightforward once you know what each one does best. Use qualitative research to explore motivations or form new ideas based on deep knowledge of the consumer base; use quantitative research to confirm previous findings or see how well they generalize across your target population. Combining them will always be best; they perfectly play off each other's strengths to form a complete market landscape analysis.

4.2 Designing a Market Research Plan

Businesses seeking to navigate market complexities and make informed strategic decisions must design a robust market research plan. This requires thorough planning, specific research goals, and a reasonable selection of appropriate research methods.

Creating precise aims for studies is the first step in designing market research plans. These objectives guide the entire study so that it lies within rational boundaries. Articulating specific and clear-cut aims for investigation helps link it with general business policies. Whether you are trying to understand what customers prefer, assess market trends, or evaluate how well new products perform in terms of quality or value, clearly spelled-out goals will influence subsequent decisions about methods used, selecting a sample population, and the data analysis techniques to be employed.

Different questions asked during investigations require different approaches to studying them to generate meaningful conclusions from the results obtained. Qualitative methods, including focus groups, interviews, and observation, have depth and context since they delve into details of consumer behavior and perception, respectively. Conversely, quantitative means like surveys, experiments, and statistical analysis provide the coverage needed for more generalizations and solid statistics. The art lies in combining these methods to understand markets comprehensively.

Planning for a survey involves considering many logistical aspects involved in this process. These include, but are not limited to, defining who our target audience will be, determining what sample size we will need, establishing when exactly we will collect our data, and determining when we will analyze it. Besides this, good preparation also requires contingency planning on how any challenges encountered will be handled, ensuring that everything runs smoothly throughout the project. This includes defining research objectives, selecting proper research methods, and planning the steps for conducting a survey to help businesses win in a changing world.

Setting Research Objectives

Setting research objectives is a holistic undertaking that incorporates diverse dimensions, all of which contribute to the richness and effectiveness of an overarching plan for conducting research. Because this process encompasses studying an actual problem, researchers delve deeply into understanding intricate details about such issues by examining their complexity and implications. Another form of this exploration can involve in-depth literature reviews, checking industry trends, or examining the historical context around the study area. This helps develop objectives that are based on a more profound understanding of the subject matter.

A collaborative approach to setting research objectives brings together different viewpoints and expertise. Involving industry stakeholders who know industry forces, market trends, or company goals is among several ways this teamwork occurs. Researchers add value by making objective-setting processes participatory and through contributions from decision-making personnel, subject-matter experts, and other interested parties. As such, collaboration ensures that research objectives align with global organizational targets, thus creating realistic studies.

In a dynamic business environment, research objectives are not static entities. Therefore, when developing strategic-oriented research objectives for a business organization's projects, there should always be awareness of potentially changing future circumstances. Consequently, researchers must be responsive to fluctuations in market conditions or new technologies that emerge as well as shifts in consumer behavior during the data collection period, leading to the adaptability of the set targets and, accordingly, basing them on prevailing market situations and the needs of consumers. These must remain flexible enough to capture any new developments, so that they will never lose touch with what is happening at any given time.

The strategic orientation of research objectives involves carefully considering the potential impact of the research outcomes. This means ultimately not just gathering facts but exploring answers that can provide solutions for the organization. The research objectives aim to develop new products, improve marketing techniques, or even streamline organizational operations. This practical application reinforces why research objectives must be set strategically to inform and improve different aspects of business strategy.

Selecting Appropriate Research Methods

The selection of research methods is a critical element that will shape the quality and pertinence of findings, an essential aspect of developing an extensive research design. The decision on research approaches depends on how research questions are framed, how much insight is being sought, and the purpose of the study.

We have looked at the way that researchers combine qualitative and quantitative methods

As well as choosing between them, researchers must also consider specific methodologies within each category. The choice depends on the objectives of the study and its practical limitations. For example, if someone would like to know cultural perceptions, an ethnographic method, involving immersive fieldwork and participant observation, could be appropriate. On the other hand, if the aim is to establish the impact created by a marketing campaign, a closed-ended questionnaire might be more applicable.

Research methods are acceptable only when they comply with ethics, and they must be realistic based on available resources, time limitations, and expertise. There must be a balance between the gains and losses brought by each technique and the research objectives; the choice must be relevant to the study purpose and contribute significantly to a general research program.

Choosing suitable methods of scientific inquiry is an intricate decision involving reflection on what questions are being asked, how much insight is being sought, and what the aim of the investigation is. The choice between qualitative or quantitative methodologies or mixing them depends on how much one wants to know about something and the limitations of a specific line of investigation. Accordingly, researchers can ensure that their chosen approach is methodologically sound and capable of delivering meaningful and relevant insights when they carefully align it with the unique aspects of their problem.

Planning the Research Process

A central element of planning a research program entail identifying the target audience. It's vital to identify those individuals or groups of interested people that one is focusing on in research. Consumers, employees, or industry experts have specific characteristics, preferences, and behaviors. They are instrumental in selecting appropriate research methods and designing the right tools to use during fieldwork.

Sample size determination is another critical concern at this stage. The size of the sample has a direct impact on the reliability and generalizability of the research findings. A small sample may yield results that are not statistically significant, while a substantial sample could incur additional expenses and logistical complications. Striking a balance between these two requires careful consideration regarding research objectives, diversification within the target population, and the desired confidence level in outcomes.

Any good plan should consider key milestones like a literature review, research design, data compilation, analysis, and reporting. A well-arranged timeline keeps researchers on track, enabling them to make proactive adjustments by responding to unanticipated opportunities or challenges. Proper timing becomes especially crucial where rapidly changing markets call for up-to-the-minute insights.

Designing a research process involves characterizing the target audience, valuing sample size, setting realistic time frames, confronting anticipated difficulties, and maintaining ethical principles. This period of strategy formation establishes a basis for practical research work by guiding through the intricate terrain of research to obtain significant findings that will add to an overall pool of knowledge in the area concerned.

4.3 Data Collection Techniques

Proceeding to data collection marks a crucial stage in research, as the methods employed during this phase significantly influence the depth and validity of the findings. Researchers have a range of data collection techniques that span a continuum of methodologies suitable for different aspects of their study question. Examining data collection techniques involves investigating how researchers gather, analyze, and interpret data.

Survey instruments and questionnaires are part of the arsenal for collecting information. These approaches are based on structured queries to achieve numerical figures for a broader sample of a population. Survey instruments allow researchers to gather facts, measure attitudes, and quantify responses systematically through face-to-face interviews or online interactions. The structured format employed by surveys enables uniformity, allowing for statistical analysis while representing views held by individuals belonging to targeted communities at particular times.

Additional qualitative dimensions, in the form of interviews and focus groups, supplement the survey methodology. Through individualized interactions or team discussions, researchers get opportunities to detect subtleties in viewpoints informed by participants' motivations and the often-complex human experiences behind them. Interviews bring insights into people's lives, while focus groups generate diverse opinions, leading to rich results.

Researchers can observe actions for useful information using non-participant observation studies, among other methods available through research designs. This puts them into natural environments, so they gain a first-hand understanding of habits like daily routines, relationships, and contextual factors affecting them. Such immersive methods extend to long-term involvement intended to capture cultural nuances alongside the social dynamics influencing lives. The age we live in today has introduced an abundance of information, allowing for data collection methods based on secondary sources. Thus, researchers who need valuable components may rely on literature review archives rather than carrying out such studies independently. This approach enables the examination of general trends, industry comparisons, and other previously ignored areas. Secondary data helps refine research, economize resources, and provide a historical perspective.

By now, it should be clear that there is no one-size-fits-all solution when choosing a method. Researchers should consider various aspects of the research question concerning the goals they want to achieve, the target population's characteristics, and the nature of the research problem while evaluating the pros and cons of each technique. This exploration into various methodologies will help researchers navigate the data collection terrain, which is very complex, and enlighten them more on the essential tools behind any meaningful and comprehensive outcomes from this process.

Surveys and Questionnaires

Surveys and questionnaires are invaluable instruments in any researcher's toolbox. They provide a structured way to gather information from various people. The main idea behind surveys is to systematically ask a representative sample predetermined questions and get quantitative data that can be analyzed statistically.

One of the things that makes surveys so great is how versatile they are. You can administer them through various mediums, such as in-person interviews or over the phone. This flexibility allows researchers to adapt their methods according to the characteristics of their target population.

The structure of surveys ensures consistency when collecting data, which is critical for subsequent statistical analysis. Researchers can quantify attitudes, behaviors, preferences, and opinions within the study population by asking closed-ended questions with predetermined response options. This quantifiable data can then be analyzed using different statistical techniques to identify trends and patterns that contribute to a comprehensive understanding of the research question.

The success of a survey depends heavily on how well it is set up and its appropriateness for the task at hand. When formulating questions, researchers must consider clarity and relevance. Also, length and wording could deter potential participants from finishing the survey, so those need consideration, too. Pilot testing will play a vital role in ensuring reliability and validity.

Sample selection is another crucial aspect that affects the results' generalizability. Rigorous sampling techniques must be used so that whatever sample you end up with accurately represents your larger target audience. The more representative the sample is, the more robust the generalizations will be.

Surveys and questionnaires offer researchers a systematic and quantifiable way to collect data. Their adaptability, versatility, and potential for statistical analysis make them suitable for many research contexts. When set up correctly, these tools will give you all the quantitative information you need to understand what you're looking into.

Interviews and Focus Groups

Interviews and focus groups are both qualitative methods. They provide a dynamic way for researchers to collect data from human experiences, thoughts, and perceptions. Unlike surveys, these two methods aren't structured by questions that limit people's answers. Instead, they are meant to give participants a space for deep thinking and reflecting on their lives.

Individual interviews allow the researcher to adapt to the participant's response by asking more profound questions on the spot. The growing conversation will get more and more personal as time goes on. Giving the participants an open platform can bring out unspoken motivations and make it easier for them to express themselves freely.

Focus groups are interactive sessions between a small group of participants facilitated by a researcher. They bring together different perspectives in real time so people can react to each other's viewpoints, which can lead to diverse insights on the research topic.

Though they share some similarities, interviews and focus groups are also different when collecting qualitative data. Interviews focus specifically on personal experiences, but focus groups were designed to explore the shared belief systems created by societal norms.

For these two methods to work effectively, you need a skilled researcher who can ask follow-up questions without deviating too much from the main topic. They must also be able to listen actively while encouraging the participant when necessary. Creating a comfortable atmosphere is also essential because interviewees often share deeply intimate memories or thoughts.

The qualitative data gathered through either method forms an interpretative approach used during analysis. Researchers use this method because it shows patterns among specific topics.

Overall, interviews and focus groups play essential roles in thoroughly understanding human experiences and perceptions, as they use an open-ended approach during questioning.

Observational Studies and Ethnographic Research

Observational studies and ethnographic research make the most of the data collection process. These two methods are designed to capture behaviors, interactions, and cultural nuances in their natural settings.

Observational studies involve watching people or groups in real-life situations. This method documents naturally occurring behaviors, providing an unfiltered view of the subject matter. Researchers may participate with them or keep their distance using a non-participant approach. The idea behind these hidden tactics is that participants will act more like they typically do if they don't know researchers are watching them.

Ethnographic research takes this immersion even further, as it relies on researchers becoming deeply embedded in the community or setting under investigation. They spend ample time in daily activities, rituals, and social structures to understand how things work there. Ethnography depends on this 'insider's perspective' because it can help one truly understand why people do what they do—and see how cultural dynamics and societal norms influence it.

Both observational studies and ethnographic research are meant to capture real-world phenomena at their core—which isn't something structured methods like surveys or experiments can offer right away. When you can witness someone's behavior through an observational lens, you'll be able to understand a lot about them better. This ecological validity also enhances the findings' external applicability because it represents the authenticity of everyday situations.

Despite their advantages, such immersive approaches also have some drawbacks: Their unstructured nature requires high skill in observation, interpretation, and reflexive engagement from the researchers. Ensuring your presence doesn't disrupt the natural flow of behaviors or violate people's privacy is no easy task. As researchers venture into the field, they must be careful not to overstep any boundaries with the people they're studying.

Both observational studies and ethnographic research offer a unique lens into human behavior within society's many layers—so long as researchers execute them correctly. Their immersive nature and emphasis on context provide a depth of understanding that complements other data collection approaches.

Utilizing Secondary Data Sources

Using secondary data sources is a strategic approach to research that involves exploring existing datasets, literature reviews, and archived records. This way, you can find out more without collecting primary data. It's cost-effective and efficient because it relies on information already available.

The first advantage of secondary data is the time and resources saved. Researchers can use collections from other studies or historical records to quickly get the necessary information. You can also examine trends in patterns or phenomena over a long period of time, providing historical context to enrich your analysis.

Some examples of secondary data sources are publicly available datasets, scholarly articles, government reports, and organizational records. As a researcher, you need to thoroughly check the reliability and relevance of these sources to validate your findings. The credibility of the original data collection methods, the sample's representativeness, and the consistency of the measurements are crucial details for evaluating the quality of the secondary data.

This method allows researchers to examine different dimensions and perspectives within their topic. By synthesizing information from multiple sources, they can draw better conclusions than just one source. This integrative approach contributes to a more comprehensive understanding of the subject matter.

Working with secondary data is challenging. The researcher might face problems like some information being unavailable, or a need to align different datasets. There could be inconsistencies between original studies and variances in methodologies used during research that'll influence the output. Documenting everything will help keep things organized so there's no confusion when reporting on limitations later.

Ethical standards are essential when utilizing secondary data, since we're still discussing someone else's work here, even though we're just using it for our own benefit. Researchers must ensure that what they access is used responsibly while respecting the original intent. This means respecting participant confidentiality, getting permission if needed, and acknowledging contributions made by the original creators of the data.

Using secondary data sources is an excellent way for researchers to explore their topic effectively and efficiently. Information from existing datasets, literature reviews, or archived records has always been there, just waiting to be used, so why not take advantage of it?

4.4 Understanding Market Segmentation

Navigating the complex market effectively is like solving a Rubik's Cube, but it's not one cube; it's more like trying to get every color in the world on each side of the square. One building block that can be used in any marketing plan is 'Market Segmentation.' This process organizes markets into many different segments based on specific criteria.

Segmenting can be used to target and understand consumers' needs, preferences, and behaviors. Just imagine if all your customers were cats and you made a product just for them, but when you started selling it, you found out that another segment of your market was comprised of birds. That's why we tailor our approach to each segment, so we don't just keep throwing darts at the wall and hoping they stick.

Each segmenting criterion has many types, from demographic and psychological elements to geographic and behavioral dimensions. These are then used to identify homogeneous groups within the overall market to understand their characteristics, which are used in creating strategies explicitly aimed at them.

The benefits here are much more significant than just knowing your customers better; it can lead businesses toward success by allowing them to target their audience with products, messaging, and promotional efforts. This efficient use of resources ultimately creates stronger brand loyalty, because people see how well we know them and feel connected to us, because we share similar attributes.

Selecting targets from these segments is where strategy comes into play again. We look for markets with good growth potential or ones where the company's core competencies align best with what they want and need. It's essential to find balance because, while there might be great potential for growth in some areas, you must also consider if your organization has what it takes to compete effectively in those areas.

Understanding market segmentation is crucial to the success of any marketing strategy. It's like a map leading us to the pot of gold at the rainbow's end.

Criteria for Segmenting Markets

Market segmentation involves categorizing the market into diverse groups that are similar enough to consider meaningful segments. The criteria picked are the building blocks for creating a granular strategy focusing on consumers and their characteristics.

One of these many criteria is demographics, which organizes consumers based on age, sex, income, education, occupation, and family size. These attributes can quickly identify people at the same stage in life as others or with similar backgrounds. Lifestyle criteria look deeper into the individuals that make up your consumer base. This examines values, attitudes, interests, hobbies, and personality traits. You can create emotional marketing messages by discovering what makes your customers tick.

Geographic segmentation involves grouping people based on where they live, such as country, region, city size, climate, or population density.

Behavioral segmentation does precisely what it sounds like it does—it looks at behavior. This approach considers purchasing patterns, brand loyalty, and responses to marketing stimuli to form groups of people who similarly interact with products or services.

Benefit segmentation acknowledges that everyone likes things for different reasons and groups them according to what they see as the beneficial value from a product or service. Usage rate categorizes heavy users versus light ones. Marketing campaigns can be enhanced if you know which group uses your product more frequently. Brand loyalty classifies those who stick with brands versus those who switch around often. The list goes on.

When all is said and done, these strategies aim to help marketers better understand their target audience so they can more effectively target products or services to them.

Benefits of Market Segmentation

The benefits of market segmentation are vast, benefiting marketing departments' strategies. Businesses that segment their target audience can target particular groups, leading to tailored marketing campaigns. This approach allows these organizations to develop a more relevant message that can lead to higher conversion and engagement rates.

Companies need to dig deeper than surface-level information about potential customers. By looking at each customer individually and studying their psychological factors, lifestyle choices, and behavioral patterns, they will gain more insights into what makes those individuals tick. Product development and services can be created from there, with that specific audience in mind.

Market segmentation is also useful when it comes to a resource allocation strategy. When this method is used correctly, businesses can focus their energy where it will benefit them most. This also applies to marketing, product development, and distribution channel budgets.

One assumption a company should always make is that all customers are different. If one product works for everyone it is lazy and incorrect. Instead, companies should create products designed to meet specific consumer segments' needs and preferences, increasing their perceived value tenfold.

Business owners should always look for what sets them apart from competitors so they can use it in their own favor. By understanding the attributes of each segment's values, businesses can differentiate themselves from the competition, ultimately increasing brand appeal and strengthening their competitive advantage.

All forms of communication depend on being understood correctly by the receiver. Language barriers between cultures limit how far your brand will go if you don't consider how different audiences respond to messages differently.

Market segmentation provides businesses with flexibility regarding crunch time. When markets change frequently, companies must adapt alongside them; otherwise, their competitors might catch them off guard.

Approaches to Target Market Selection

It is necessary to evaluate the market's needs to understand where the most significant potential for business growth lies. As organizations move through complex consumer landscapes, tapping into target markets becomes critical for focusing resources and matching company products with the specific needs of those chosen segments.

Market potential assessment allows businesses to comprehend what market segments are more likely than not to grow. By analyzing population trends, economic indicators, and the wants of emerging consumers, companies can position themselves appropriately within expanding markets so they can succeed long into the future.

Aligning with a company's strengths and core competencies is a pragmatic approach to selecting a target market. Businesses must analyze the services they can provide better than their competition to identify which segments would most benefit from their expertise. This ensures that the markets picked will fall nicely into line with a business's strengths, creating an advantage over other competition.

Organizations need to look at how many competing businesses there are and any barriers that may prevent new competitors. By doing this, we can avoid situations where our services or products become overcrowded by others when entering specific markets.

Resource allocation is significant when choosing a target market. If your business needs more resources, some segments may need to be avoided until you obtain those resources. When looking at distribution channels, marketing budgets, and production capabilities, it's clear that each segment will require its own portion of these resources. Thus, companies must align themselves with those requirements so that efficiency is achievable and returns on investment are maximized.

Understanding consumer behavior and preferences is just as important as anything else in this whole process. To ensure we hit all areas correctly, businesses should analyze each segment's buying habits, motivations, and choices. What we learn from this will allow us to pick markets that strongly resonate with our values and thus drive customer engagement and loyalty.

No matter what the marketing objective is, it must be met by choosing the right target market. We can use these objectives to see which segments they'll work best in. If the end goal was more market share, we'd have to choose different segments than if we wanted to launch a new product entirely. Strategic coherence ensures all efforts are directed towards outcomes that align with broader goals.

When picking a target market, practical considerations such as access and regulatory factors must also be considered. By looking at how easy entering those markets would be through regulatory compliance, distribution networks, and legal considerations, companies can make more informed decisions on where their products would serve customers best.

Analyzing the consumer lifecycle within segments is essential for spotting long-term opportunities. It helps us understand how much customers want what we have and whether they'll return for more later. Putting effort into those areas will lead us toward long-term profitability.

4.5 Analyzing Consumer Behavior

Knowing how consumers behave is vital to marketing strategies. It lets companies understand what shapes purchasing decisions and the process through which people buy things. This section delves into consumer behavior, touching on elements that influence choices, what goes on when people make decisions, and some insights from behavioral economics that help with marketing.

The different factors in consumer behavior are like threads in a tapestry. These threads represent how complex purchasing decisions are. Understanding the factors influencing consumer purchasing decisions shows marketers just how many considerations there are between psychological elements and situational influences, from personal reasons to social ones. The more these factors are studied, the more marketers can create strategies that drive their customers' choices and preferences.

The consumer decision-making process provides a roadmap for businesses trying to make products people will want to buy. From recognizing a need for post-purchase evaluations, this intricate journey is broken down into stages like information search and evaluating alternatives. Knowing how people go about this process helps businesses position their offerings so that people will perceive them positively.

There are also behavioral economic insights that take economic principles and add psychological twists. This approach recognizes that individuals sometimes act irrationally because emotions or social contexts interfere with logic. Once these insights are explored and understood, marketers will know what value consumers see in their products and why they choose certain things over others.

A deep dive into this topic reveals that consumer behavior isn't as simple as saying, 'People buy things.' There's so much going on underneath the surface involving various factors and processes that affect choices differently depending on who you're targeting or what kind of business you run. No matter who or what you're trying to market to, these layers must be unfolded if you want your endeavors to resonate with anyone.

Factors Influencing Consumer Purchasing Decisions

Purchasing something is one of the most complex things humans do. Tons of influences shape how we decide to give our money away. They're like puzzle pieces. When put together, they form a picture we call consumer choices. When marketing professionals start picking apart these factors, it's easier for them to see what makes us tick and why, what we want, and, more importantly, what triggers us to open our wallets. This section explores the complex world of consumer purchasing decisions.

Psychology plays a major role here. Thoughts, feelings, and motivations play pivotal roles in shaping purchasing decisions. Personal experiences, lifestyle, and individual tastes influence consumer preferences, impacting product perception. Marketers use this information to get into your head, but also, they try to figure out the emotional and cognitive triggers that get you to open your wallet.

Social factors mess with our heads, too, because, as humans, we're sociable beings at our core. Friends, family, and peers influence norms and values in us from an early age (and throughout life). Social influence comes in many forms, such as 'societal expectations,' 'word-of-mouth recommendations,' and even 'social media interactions.' Marketers dig deep into these societal cues to tailor their goods or services.

Cultural factors? They've got their way of messing with you too. Believe it or not, cultural backgrounds, subcultures, and societal norms are deeply ingrained in a society's values, beliefs, and customs play a huge role in making up who you are as a consumer. These are so integral that marketers have realized that, if they can align their products with those same values, it's game over.

Personal & individual characteristics have some weight regarding your purchasing decision, even if it doesn't appear like it. Demographics such as age, sex, income, and occupation may seem irrelevant, but they're essential to marketers. Lifestyle choices, personality traits, and self-concept also contribute to your consumer identity. Understanding these details helps them create targeted campaigns that appeal to specific segments.

This next one is obvious. Situational factors like time constraints and urgency will always impact consumers' willingness to purchase. Marketers try to optimize situations depending on how much people need their product or service, hoping it'll bring home the bacon.

The last factor is perception, which is impacted by sensory experiences and cognitive processes. So many things influence how we interpret information and make choices, like branding. The way something looks can be the push or pull needed to make a sale for marketers.

Understanding all these automatically loaded influences is essential for businesses seeking meaningful connections with consumers. Once you get it down pat, you can tailor your strategies specifically for those motivations and preferences; ultimately driving successful consumer engagements.

The Consumer Decision-Making Process

The consumer decision-making process is just that—a process. But it's not straightforward. It's dynamic and intricate, full of twists and turns as people consider whether to purchase. And even though it's so chaotic, the stages within this process show us how consumers navigate choices, evaluate alternatives, and ultimately decide what they want or need.

The first stage is problem recognition. This happens when customers realize the difference between where they are now and where they want to be. Many triggers for problem recognition exist, such as unmet needs, desires for improvement, and advertising ploys—all can set someone off spending money to fix something.

The information search is next in line. After realizing that an issue needs addressing or a desire needs fulfilling, consumers search for information to help them better understand what's happening and ideally find solutions. The ways people can go about searching for information are endless—personal experiences and word-of-mouth recommendations are familiar sources, but online reviews or expert opinions work, too. How much time someone spends looking for information about their problem depends on how much they care about solving it, how complex the issue is, and personal preferences.

Evaluation of alternatives comes up after an information search has been completed, either super thoroughly or barely at all. At this point in the journey to purchase something new, consumers weigh the pros and cons of different brands or products by comparing them side-by-side. Quality vs. price and features vs. reputation influence how someone might make their final decision.

Finally, we're into purchase decision territory. This is where customers choose which option to buy after evaluating all the alternatives. What do you think influences their choice the most? Are these the attributes of the selected product? Promotional offers? Sales incentives? Peer recommendations? I genuinely don't know. But whatever it is, it signals the end of the evaluation journey.

The post-purchase evaluation wraps everything up. After a consumer has paid for something and used it, they take a step back to evaluate whether their expectations—as well as any other standards or needs—were met. How satisfied they are with their purchase can depend on perceived performance, quality, fulfillment of needs, and more. These evaluations shape future decision-making by influencing attitudes toward a brand and impacting brand loyalty.

Throughout this process, psychological, social, and situational factors work together, or against each other, to influence each stage. Emotional considerations and brand loyalty also add more layers to a disordered landscape. And here's one final twist: sometimes consumers jump back into earlier stages after progressing through them once. That is not always the case, though—that depends on the level of involvement required by the decision.

All these complicated variables might leave you scratching your head, wondering how anyone expects marketers to connect with their target audience. But honestly, if you look at these five stages individually and what happens within them, you'll find all the information you need to tailor your strategies appropriately. Provide relevant information when people are searching for knowledge about what they want and need; address concerns when customers start comparing brands; and create positive post-purchase experiences, because we know people will evaluate how satisfied they are with your product or service afterward.

This process is undoubtedly challenging, but understanding it helps businesses build trust with their customers—something that becomes increasingly difficult as our world evolves.

Behavioral Economics: Insights in Marketing

The mix of behavioral economics and marketing dives deep into our brains. The brain is a mysterious thing. With every twist and turn, we reveal how we think when making choices. Behavioral economics can bring to light all the biases, cognitive shortcuts, and emotional influences that go into choosing what we want as consumers. It's a way to understand how individuals make decisions when shopping.

At its core, behavioral economics recognizes that people don't always pick things based on rational thought alone. We're influenced by emotions, cognitive biases, and even social contexts. Marketers can use these insights to their advantage by understanding how consumers perceive value and respond to different stimuli.

One important insight is the concept of loss aversion. It says that we'd rather not lose what we already own than gain something new of equal value. Marketers can use this insight to create a sense of urgency, or to make the risk of missing out seem more significant than it actually is.

Another great insight is the concept of anchoring. Our first thoughts can stick with us forever after seeing something for the first time. This is handy when marketers need to get information across or strategically price items.

When you tell me I can't have something, my desire for it doubles. The endowment effect suggests people place higher values on items just because they own them. With knowledge like this, marketers could use free trials or offer samples of products or services that will increase the likelihood of subsequent purchases.

Defaults are safe bets because they're familiar to us. People are inclined to stick with default options because they're afraid anything else won't perform as well as the one thing they know works. Marketers should position preferred options as defaults if they want those choices to align with organizational goals.

The actions and choices of others tell us what's safe and what's not. We like to feel secure, so marketers can use testimonials, user reviews, and social media endorsements to create a sense of community and trust in people who might try a new product.

The more choices there are, the worse it is for the consumer and marketer. The paradox of choice suggests that too many options make us anxious and unhappy with our final decision. Marketers should keep this in mind when trying to sell something big. The more choices, the harder it will be for customers to narrow down what they want. We've always said emotional branding is critical; now we have proof. Once we understand what triggers emotions in our target audience, we can appeal to them through ads, narratives, and experiences.

Behavioral Economics Insights in marketing get you thinking about everything that goes into choosing any store. Understanding these insights allows you to build better strategies tailored to cognitive biases, emotional responses, and social influences. This intersection between economics and psychology gives you a framework for creating more effective campaigns that connect brands with consumers on another level.

4.6 Competitive Analysis

To survive in a constantly changing market, you need to know your competition. This section is all about understanding competitive analysis, a crucial part of business management that will help you make strategic decisions in the current economic climate. In it, we'll discuss the methods and insights needed for businesses to succeed by gaining an edge over their rivals.

Figuring out who you're up against is half of the battle. Identifying your competitors involves thinking more deeply than just considering who offers similar products or services. It's about recognizing the various elements of competition, such as substitutes and potential entrants. You'll also need to understand how these players fit into your positioning strategy so that you can anticipate market dynamics.

We'll discuss tools and frameworks for competitor analysis, which are necessary for companies looking to break things down systematically.

Learning from competitor strategies and positioning might be one of the most essential parts of competitive analysis because it provides insights into consumer preferences and potential areas of differentiation between rival companies. Examining where others have left gaps in their positioning strategies allows enterprises to identify better potential niches and strategic opportunities that align with their strengths.

Identifying Your Competitors

Finding your way through the competitive landscape is a core part of strategic management when building a lasting business. Knowing your competitors goes deeper than just recognizing companies with the same products or services as you. It requires a more extensive look at the competition, from businesses in your sector to those indirectly influencing you. This knowledge is crucial for all companies that want to position themselves correctly and anticipate market dynamics.

Most people first think of their direct competitors when they hear the word 'competition.' These entities are all fighting for the same set of customers. They offer very similar products or services and often share target audiences. Understanding these competitors' strategies, strengths, and weaknesses can grant you foundational knowledge of your immediate competitive landscape. With this knowledge, businesses can figure out how best to position themselves by capitalizing on their unique strengths and identifying areas where they could stand out more. Other factors businesses must consider include substitutes and alternatives that meet similar consumer needs. While these may be different from what you sell, they do fulfill comparable purposes, so it's still essential for businesses to be aware of them. By knowing about these alternatives, companies can anticipate shifts in customer preferences and identify threats to market share before it's too late.

Potential entrants are another aspect of competition worth considering. These companies may currently be operating outside your specific market, but they're capable and determined enough to appear one day soon. Assessing potential entrants means understanding their strengths, resources, and any barriers you might face when entering your market.

In addition, some complementary products or services enhance or supplement what you offer. You probably would think of something other than these as traditional competition, but they can influence customer choices and the market. Having relationships with complementary providers can create opportunities for mutually beneficial partnerships.

It's worth noting that identifying competitors shouldn't be done once and then forgotten about. Keeping up with them, as they change constantly, is vital to staying ahead of the competition in your market. Assessing the landscape regularly will grant businesses the knowledge they need to make informed strategic decisions, adapt quickly when trends start shifting, and build a solid defense against ever-evolving competition.

Tools and Frameworks for Competitor Analysis (SWOT, Porter's Five Forces)

In the world of business, understanding your competition is vital. But that's easier said than done. The competitive landscape can be confusing and chaotic. There are many factors to consider and paths to take; it can feel like navigating through a maze. Let's consider two valuable methodologies: SWOT analysis and the Porter's Five Forces framework.

SWOT is an acronym for strengths, weaknesses, opportunities, and threats. By creating this internal-external matrix, you gain insight into the organization's current state and strategic environment. Strengths and weaknesses look inward; they assess resources, capabilities, and internal processes. Recognizing these factors allows businesses to leverage their strengths and address weaknesses—optimizing internal operations.

Opportunities and threats pertain to the external world in which organizations operate. Companies can get ahead of the game regarding growth by analyzing external conditions such as emerging trends or untapped markets. Conversely, threats encompass all company challenges due to market trends, competitor actions, or economic factors. Being aware of these dangers allows companies to navigate around them before they even arise.

Michael E. Porter developed Porter's Five Forces to help companies understand profitability within their industry on a deeper level. Five forces shape competitive dynamics: the influence of buyers in negotiations, the role of suppliers in talks, the potential threat posed by new entrants, the possibility of substitute products or services, and, finally, the level of the competitive rivalry itself.

The bargaining power of buyers is a measure of how much influence customers have over price negotiations and terms agreed upon in contracts. In other words, how much sway do consumers hold? High bargaining power means customers can dictate most things, leaving businesses with little control, while low bargaining power gives companies more say in decision-making, which could be good for them. Similarly, for suppliers, a strong bargaining power could negatively affect the actual cost of a good or service.

Regarding new entrants, easy entry and cheap costs can be disastrous for existing companies. If fresh competitors can easily penetrate the market, it's time to start worrying. The more substitutes there are in an industry, the harder it is for businesses to retain customers. Finally, the intensity of competitive rivalry examines the competition between existing industry players. This takes things like market concentration and product differentiation into account.

SWOT analysis and Porter's Five Forces framework are two tools that provide insight into competitor analysis. SWOT focuses primarily on internal and external factors specific to your organization, while Porter's broadens the scope by assessing the broader industry landscape. By combining these approaches, you'll gain a strategic advantage over your competition by better understanding internal capabilities and external market dynamics, allowing for resilience and adaptability as competition evolves.

Learning from Competitor Strategies and Positioning

In the fast-moving business game, you can always continue learning from your competitors' strategies and plotting. It's not just about observing their actions on the field; it's also about carefully analyzing them, interpreting them, and turning them into fuel for your winning strategy.

Understand that a competitor's overarching scheme often holds the keys to success or failure. You can dissect these things by looking at their products, services, pricing system—everything. By doing so, you may find patterns in what they do that may contribute to their success or perhaps even their potential for failure

Another thing you'll want to understand is how your brand is perceived by other people compared to competitors. Perception means everything in this world. That means you'll need to analyze every aspect of your brand's presence: branding itself, messaging, and the customer experience. But there's more to learn from competitors than clever marketing tactics.

For example, if there is one thing all businesses could learn from their competitors, it's how vital adaptability is. In an ever-changing market—whether it be consumer preferences or technological advances—those who don't change with the times are most certainly doomed to failure.

Studying your rivals could also reveal the practical ways they engage with customers. This includes trying to figure out how they communicate with customers and manage relationships using any number of strategies. Not only will this give you a deeper understanding of your rival businesses, but it will also allow you to build better relationships with customers.

Successful competitors are generally ahead of trends, paying attention to and being attuned to shifts in consumer behavior or industry trends. And if they aren't, they are constantly adapting and innovating new product offerings based on unmet needs within consumers themselves.

Just remember that studying competitors doesn't mean emulating them straight out of the gate—because, let's face it, why would you want to be a carbon copy of someone else? That would be boring. It's always good to differentiate and discover what competitors aren't doing.

4.7 Industry and Market Trend Analysis

Understanding industry and market trends is essential for navigating the complexities of business. This section delves into methodologies to spot market trends, and to identify how social, economic, and technological trends impact businesses, and forecast future changes.

Forecasting future market changes requires businesses to examine current trends, analyze historical data, and apply predictive modeling techniques to predict what may happen next in the market landscape. This process allows companies to build informed strategies to navigate uncertainties, capitalize on emerging opportunities, and ultimately mitigate risks associated with future market fluctuations. Industry and market trend analysis should be helpful for any company trying to adapt its strategies, innovate its offerings, and position itself for success in this increasingly competitive world.

Methods for Identifying Market Trends

In the business world, keeping up with market trends is essential. It helps companies adapt to changes to take advantage of opportunities and stay competitive. There are many methods for identifying market trends, each designed to help businesses get ahead of their competition by revealing patterns and emerging developments in specific industries or markets. These methods allow companies to make informed decisions, anticipate changes, tailor strategies, and take advantage of evolving consumer preferences.

Market research is a method that uses systematic data collection to understand market dynamics. It analyzes surveys, interviews, focus groups, and observational studies to provide insights into consumer behavior and expectations. Businesses can learn about the factors shaping trends by studying this qualitative information.

Data analysis and analytics are quantitative methods that allow businesses to scrutinize large datasets efficiently and extrapolate trends from them. This approach lets companies know what correlations exist between different data points. They can also forecast future developments based on past ones, which gives them a data-driven perspective on emerging trends.

Trend tracking is a method whereby companies monitor various indicators, such as social media mentions or online discussions, to identify emerging patterns in consumer behavior. Real-time data allows for quick responses and agile decision-making in an ever-changing environment.

Competitor analysis tells businesses how their competitors are doing relative to themselves. Companies gain valuable insights into evolving customer demands by investigating what products they're launching, marketing initiatives they're taking part in, or how they're engaging with consumers.

Expert interviews provide industry professionals with unique perspectives on potential trends because they have extensive experience within specific sectors. In addition to other methods, expert interviews add qualitative depth to trend analysis.

Consumer feedback is essential because it comes directly from your target audience; you know exactly what your customers want or need when you hear from them personally rather than through a survey or social media post.

Scenario planning allows companies to brainstorm various scenarios that could play out in the future. This method lets businesses assess what changes must be made to their strategies based on different plausible outcomes.

These methods create a comprehensive understanding of market trends. They let companies respond to changes quickly, take advantage of emerging opportunities, and navigate the complexities of a rapidly evolving marketplace.

Impact of Social, Economic, and Technological Trends on Businesses

In a constantly changing business landscape, several factors shape its dynamics. Social, economic, and technological trends all have an enormous influence on how businesses operate and strategize. This section will examine these trends' multidimensional impact on the business world.

We'll start with social trends reflecting changing preferences, values, and behaviors. Recently, there has been a shift towards sustainability and social responsibility. Consumers now prefer businesses that align with ethical values; they want to know precisely what they're getting into before purchasing. Businesses are also being called upon to practice environmentally conscious activities to stay aligned with their consumers' expectations and remain competitive in this new eco-conscious marketplace.

Simultaneously, the rise of social media has revolutionized communication and brand interaction. Today, businesses must manage their online reputation while responding to customer feedback via social media platforms. Now, customers hold all the power; they can amplify their voices through platforms like Twitter and Facebook, causing significant damage to the brand image of any company that isn't careful or responsive.

Economic trends dictate a business's financial health and ability to handle disaster situations resiliently. During periods of economic growth, firms can invest in R&D, expand their market presence, and attract top-skilled talent. When economic downturns come around, focusing more on cutting costs and diversifying your investments becomes necessary. Hence, you only have some of your eggs in one basket.

Globalization is another economic trend that businesses need to be aware of if they hope to continue succeeding in the long term. Borders are becoming less restricted daily, meaning companies need flexible strategies to survive global competition while abiding by international regulatory frameworks.

Technological innovations have been shaking up industries left, right, and center, causing some companies that reject digital transformation to fall behind those who embrace it. AI automation and the Internet have brought unexpected disruptions. Businesses must learn to leverage technology to improve efficiency, streamline processes, and deliver innovative products and services.

Decisions no longer need be based on instinct. Big data analytics has enabled businesses to extract insights from big datasets, which allows for better strategic decisions, personalized customer experiences, and optimized operational efficiency. This new focus on data might come at the expense of privacy and security.

The dance between these trends creates an intricate business environment, demanding a strategic planning approach that is both holistic and adaptable. Successful businesses can navigate these forces, picking up opportunities while mitigating risks.

Forecasting Future Market Changes

Forecasting the future is a smart move for any business trying to survive in this fast-paced, competitive world. In this section, we will talk about predicting market trends and understanding factors that come into play when they do so. This includes things like consumer behavior, technological advances, and economic fluctuations.

It's important to know what consumers do before they do it if you want your business to last. As society changes rapidly, so do consumer preferences. This is influenced by cultural shifts, demographic changes, and emerging trends.

If you stay ahead of technology, you won't have as much to worry about while trying to ride the wave of change. It can give businesses a fresh perspective on consumer preferences and shifts in market dynamics—both precious things in this age, where everything eventually gets replaced by something even better. But staying technologically relevant isn't easy, given how fast innovation moves today; artificial intelligence, automation, and other disruptive technologies require constant attention if you don't want your business processes to end up outdated.

It's also important to know how technological change affects whatever goods or services your company provides. Understanding macroeconomic trends gives more than just bragging rights at parties—inflation rates, interest rates, and overall economic growth can all give businesses an idea of where market conditions are headed and whether the journey will be smooth sailing. We're not saying anything will be perfectly predictable, but at least you'll be more informed about pricing strategies, investment opportunities, and resource allocation.

These days, you have no choice but to consider events happening on the other side of the planet; too, since they could significantly affect your business, depending on what it is. The interconnectedness of economies runs deep, and any change to trade agreements, geopolitical tensions, or international regulations could turn everything upside down in no time. Forecasting for these influences can help your business prepare for potential disruptions and capitalize on new opportunities as they come.

Sustainability and corporate social responsibility have become integral components of business strategies. While this is a good thing, it does make things a little more complicated. Market changes are now heavily influenced by environmental and social considerations. Knowing the impact of environmental regulations, changing consumer attitudes towards sustainability, and potentially new market niches will allow you to be prepared for whatever comes next.

Thinking ahead never hurts anybody, either. With scenario planning, you can imagine various scenarios and their impacts before they even happen. This will allow your company to develop flexible strategies with which you can adapt swiftly to unforeseen circumstances. Forecasting future market changes is challenging, but doing so allows businesses like yours to navigate the complexities of the market while positioning themselves for success in an ever-changing world, which also means sustained success.

4.8 Analyzing Product Demand and Market Size

At the center of practical market analysis is knowing what your customers want. This means understanding everything that goes into building preferences: age trends, cultural influences, and evolving behaviors. The old-fashioned way of doing this is through surveys and focus groups, but you can also use data analytics and AI applications.

Knowing what customers want is just as important as knowing how much they'll pay. Companies need to look at how current customers behave while studying emerging trends in technology or regulatory changes that could bring in new ones. That way, they're ready with their strategy when those future customers arrive.

The balance between supply and demand drives everything from pricing to availability to overall market healthiness. Knowing where you stand here involves looking at production capacity, distribution channels, and the regulatory environment—everything that makes up a company's systems for getting products out there. Learning more about product demands and market sizes will help businesses become better decision makers, with a long-term perspective on success.

Techniques for Estimating Market Demand

Knowing the volume of demand for your goods and services is crucial to planning a business strategy. Countless techniques for estimating demand give you different insights into what customers prefer and how they behave.

One basic approach involves surveys. Surveys let businesses ask their target audience questions directly to collect valuable information about customer preferences, needs, and buying habits. By carefully creating survey questions and ensuring that your sample is representative enough, you can gather meaningful data to gauge the market size.

Another way to understand market demand is through focus groups. Get a bunch of people as varied as possible in one room to discuss and share their thoughts about a product or service, and you'll receive qualitative insights. By letting people talk among themselves with only some light guidance from moderators, businesses can learn how much weight certain factors hold in consumers' decision-making processes. You can also observe customer behavior in real-life settings, giving you precious insight into what they want. Instead of wondering why customers make confident choices when they buy products or interact with them in person, you'll be able to see their genuine reactions by doing so.

Data analytics has become one of the most powerful tools available for accurately estimating market demand. Because it involves analyzing vast amounts of information, it allows businesses to identify trends and patterns they wouldn't have seen otherwise—facts that uncover more about consumer behavior than any other technique.

With social media monitoring's popularity on a steady rise, it's no surprise that many companies are using it to estimate demand for their products or services today... and tomorrow. Social media conversations let them tap into what kind of sentiment their target audience holds at any given moment. That real-time feedback gives businesses helpful insights into what customers will likely want next.

Artificial intelligence apps are another modern-day approach businesses have begun taking advantage of. Using machine learning algorithms to analyze gigantic amounts of historical data is another way to predict future product demand. The more accurate the prediction, the more informed the decision-making process is, ultimately leading to better actions. Collaborative filtering is a technique that's commonly used on e-commerce and online platforms. Businesses can make personalized recommendations by studying what similar customers like and dislike about specific products or services. They know that their recommendations directly influence buying decisions—which then helps them estimate how many people will want whatever specific thing they're selling.

Assessing Market Potential and Growth Projections

Finding the market's potential is essential to planning a business's future. Mathematically, market potential is the maximum point of sales in a market. Businesses can measure it by looking at some factors affecting demand. Demographic shifts, cultural influences, economic indicators, and technological advances play their part in a market's size. Businesses can use these insights to create strategies to align with new opportunities.

Knowing trends is also crucial when estimating the amount of growth that will occur. Whether driven by technology or society, these new developments give businesses good information about what might happen next in the market and how they should plan for it. Economic factors also heavily affect the numbers you see after scanning this data. Businesses need to consider GDP growth, employment rates, and inflation to see if there's enough room for them in an economic environment.

Finally, we have the technology. As always, advances today open doors and are suitable for innovation and more money-making opportunities. We've seen big companies do amazing things by keeping up with it all just like they were supposed to, taking advantage of everything new thrown at them.

When projecting future growth, businesses must consider population growth, too. It's about more than just the company itself here; industry trends and regulatory changes are playing such a significant role in whatever comes next that you'd be silly not to pay attention now.

You'll want to know who your competition is, no matter where you work or whether you've already started your business. Looking at the competition provides insight into who's in the market and how significant their share is. Once you've got that, the world is yours.

Demand-Supply Dynamics in Market Analysis

Understanding how demand and supply interact is vital for market analysis. These forces shape pricing, availability, and the equilibrium in the market, which determines how businesses adjust to changes in consumer demand. As a base concept, demand is all about the number of products or services consumers can buy at a given price. Determinants businesses should explore include consumer preferences, purchasing power, and external factors like cultural shifts or economic conditions. By knowing these elements, companies can make informed pricing strategies, marketing efforts, and product positioning decisions.

Supply refers to how much producers can offer the market at prices. Factors determining supply are production capabilities, resource availability, technological advances, and regulatory constraints. Businesses' ability to meet demand depends on how well they manage their supply chains and optimize their production processes. Pricing is where demand-supply dynamics get interesting. The point where demand and supply intersect is called the equilibrium point; it's the point where pricing stabilizes in a balanced market because demand = supply. If either of those factors fluctuates, everything will be off balance, and the market will move toward a new equilibrium.

Price stability can be disrupted by changes in either supply or demand, which eventually get reflected in price. Businesses need to navigate through those fluctuations with precision if they want to maximize revenue while remaining competitive. Keeping this balance intact is hard work for businesses because things like changing customer preferences or unexpected events could disrupt everything.

To measure how customers react to changes in price, the elasticity of demand comes into play. Elasticity measures the responsiveness of the quantity demanded or supplied when price fluctuations occur. Elasticity helps companies anticipate customer behavior when there's a change in pricing, which in turn impacts production decisions.

External factors also strongly influence these two forces, so businesses must stay vigilant when navigating them. Regulatory changes, economic downturns, or global trends can all significantly impact how these forces behave, so companies must adapt their strategies to keep up with the times. Understanding demand and supply is the key to market analysis, which will help shape pricing, availability, and overall equilibrium. This allows businesses to respond faster to consumer changes and optimize their functioning in this ever-evolving business landscape.

4.9 Data Interpretation and Reporting

With the world relying more on data-driven decisions than ever, organizations seek thorough analysis and insightful reporting to guide their choices and gain a competitive edge on the market.

Gathering insights from different research methods is a great start, but more is needed. Researchers must dive deeper into the raw numbers to fully uncover everything hidden within them.

Turning raw numbers into actual information is challenging. Researchers must use appropriate statistical methods, such as regression or multivariate analysis. The goal is to ensure that any conclusions drawn from the data are accurate, so they can be used as reliable benchmarks for future projects or decisions.

Researchers should also present their findings in a way that anyone can understand. Complex tables filled with numbers might make sense for someone who knows how to read them, but they're guaranteed to confuse anyone else who looks at them. Pie charts and graphs are much easier on the eyes and show patterns or outliers more intuitively. No matter how thorough your research is, if you convey your findings well, they will be more useful to everyone trying to act on them, like stakeholders. That's why reports must contain actionable insights to help users take steps toward their goals, whether optimizing market strategies or addressing customer needs.

Having complete control over how you interpret data will provide a solid foundation for creating reports that drive business success. Once you learn how to properly analyze market research data, use statistical methods and visualization techniques, and create actionable reports and presentations, you can turn raw numbers into insights that will foster innovation and growth in any company.

Analyzing Market Research Data

When deciphering the nuances of market research data, you need to be sure you are extracting the most valuable insights possible. This means analyzing it comprehensively using various methodologies and techniques. This all starts with data cleaning and preprocessing. During this step, researchers identify any inconsistencies, errors, or missing values in the dataset before doing anything else. By manipulating this data correctly, they can ensure it is accurate and trustworthy for analysis moving forward. They also eliminate biases that could hinder the final results during this stage.

Once the data is clean, exploratory tools give researchers a preliminary understanding of what they're working with. Histograms, scatter plots, summary stats, and other graphical representations help identify patterns, trends, and outliers in the data that couldn't be found otherwise. With a basic knowledge of what they're looking at from their exploratory data analysis (EDA) findings, researchers can finally move on to analyzing more specific parts using statistical methods. Several different ones are used, depending on what information is explicitly needed. Descriptive statistics summarize an overview of the entire dataset, while inferential statistics help draw conclusions based on sample data. More advanced techniques, like cluster or factor analysis, may be used to dissect consumer behavior.

Although statistical methods are useful for breaking down numbers quickly and easily, qualitative techniques should still be implemented for a better overall understanding. Methods like thematic or content analysis give insight into consumer attitudes beyond just numbers, which paint a clearer picture when combined with quantitative findings.

Finally, contextual factors need to be considered throughout the whole process. Researchers have to understand who their sample demographic is comprised of, so they know how accurately these results represent a target market later. Sensitivity analysis also checks for any bias present during the data collection.

Analyzing market research data is challenging because it involves so many steps. Doing it correctly is paramount for an organization's success. By employing the proper techniques and being aware of context, researchers can unlock valuable insights that will be used to make strategic decisions in the long run.

Utilizing Statistical Methods and Data Visualization

For market research, more than primary data is needed. Don't worry; I'll break this down into more easily digestible sections.

Statistical methods provide a way to find patterns or trends in your data. These stats can also help you find the core values of your data, which is incredibly useful when comparing variables.

Inferential statistics allow you to predict an unknown population based on sample data. Hypothesis testing helps researchers validate their hypotheses and make better decisions with the information at hand. Advanced statistical techniques allow researchers to examine complex datasets more deeply. They are usually used by more experienced researchers who know what to do with this information.

Now, let's move on to visualizing all that pesky number crunching. Charts and graphs make spreadsheets much easier to understand and provide a quick overview without wasting too much time. Bar charts and pie charts are great for showing distribution, while line charts and scatter plots are best for relationships between variables over time.

Once you have this under control, start playing around with interactive visuals like heat maps and bubble charts; each reveals new information about your dataset that you may have missed. There are also geographic mapping visuals, which offer spatial context, facilitating regional analysis and market mapping. Infographic storytelling techniques combine visuals with narrative storytelling to communicate critical insights to different audiences.

So good luck. You've got everything you need to dig deep into your market research.

Chapter 5

Developing Your Business Model

Business models are at the heart of any venture. They provide structure and define how businesses create, deliver, and capture value. Entrepreneurs must understand the key elements that make up these models to articulate their value proposition, identify target markets, and establish sustainable revenue streams. By analyzing successful strategies from various business model archetypes, individuals can adapt them to their unique circumstances and objectives.

The chapter also explores practical tools like the Business Model Canvas, a visual framework that breaks your business's blueprint down into bite-sized chunks. Iterations of this canvas help entrepreneurs understand their value proposition, customer segments, distribution channels, and revenue streams while setting the stage for strategic decision-making and execution. Value creation and delivery emerge as central themes here. It highlights the importance of addressing customers' needs while leveraging resources to deliver superior offerings. Strategy is scrutinized through competitive advantages, emphasizing differentiation, cost leadership, and market positioning to achieve sustainable growth.

Any company's financial aspects are focused on revenue generation, cost management, and economic sustainability—profitability, good cash flow, and capital allocation ensure long-term viability and resilience. In an era where environmental consciousness has become paramount, sustainability serves as one of two primary focuses through endeavors such as incorporating sustainability principles into operations—thus helping pursue growth opportunities conducive to scalability expansion.

5.1 Introduction to Business Models

Exploring the concept of a business model will show us how companies operate in the economy. At its core, a business model encompasses the most basic framework for how companies create value, deliver value to consumers through supply chains, and capture value through profits.

A robust business model acts as a roadmap for strategic decision-making. It will help guide resource allocation and market positioning decisions so companies can adjust to shifting market dynamics, seize emerging opportunities, and manage risks effectively.

As technology advances rapidly, businesses must keep up with their competitors by innovating new models that cater to today's consumer preferences.

By understanding what goes into making up a business model, why they're essential, and how they've grown digitally over time -- individuals can better prepare themselves for whatever comes next when it comes to forming strategies or developing new ideas within organizations anywhere.

Exploring the Concept of a Business Model

A business model is a plan that shows how a company creates, delivers, and holds on to value. It's the starting point for an organization when it starts building out its strategies, operations, and revenue streams. This blueprint is essential for managers and investors, since it defines what a company does and how it can succeed.

A business model represents a company's essential parts—its target market, value proposition, cost structure, and critical activities. These elements work together to form one cohesive strategy that leads the team to long-term success.

The first part of any business model involves identifying your target market. Defining the audience you want to serve is crucial when customizing products or services to fit their needs.

Once you know who your customers will be, you want to offer something that will keep them around—this is where your value proposition comes in handy. A strong one will draw customers in while keeping competitors at bay.

Revenue sources are crucial if you want your business model to succeed. It's all about finding different ways your company can make money. This could be through selling products directly or using ad revenue from other sources.

You need money before worrying about making more—this is where understanding your cost structure comes into play. Knowing how much money you're spending on things like production costs versus marketing expenses gives an insight into what's eating away at potential profits.

Key activities drive progress toward turning the business model into reality. Identifying these tasks helps companies use their resources effectively while delivering on what they've set out to do.

Other aspects of business models, like partnerships or distribution channels, may also be necessary for success.

Customers want change often, so staying ahead of the curve is crucial to longevity in an ever-changing market.

By analyzing and refining your model, you can identify where to optimize operations, which will ultimately help you thrive.

The Importance of a Strong Business Model

First and foremost, a strong business model provides clarity and direction. Determining things like target market, value proposition, and revenue streams gets everyone on board with one vision. All decisions made after will be based on what's best for the company's goals.

A well-designed model also facilitates resource allocation. By understanding how much is spent on generating costs and creating value, businesses can optimize their operations for maximum efficiency and profitability.

Also important is differentiation and competitive advantage. Companies need every leg up to stand out in today's ever-changing world, where the competition and people's preferences constantly change. A unique value proposition supported by a robust business model can be all it takes to set a company apart from the rest.

Resilience, as well as adaptability, are also vital factors a solid business model brings. Markets are constantly in flux, so being able to navigate trends, emerging technology or unforeseen disruptions will ensure longevity when others start to falter.

You need to consider investor confidence. When presenting your ideas to potential investors or other entrepreneurs, nothing speaks louder than a clear plan of action for how you'll make money. Trust me when I say there is no way of overstating how critical a robust business model is.

Evolution of Business Models in the Digital Age

The digital age has changed the way we run businesses. = Concepts that were once frowned upon have now become vital =. It's a sink-or-swim mentality; if you don't keep up with the times, your business will likely end up in trouble.

One of these concepts is 'disruptive innovation.' This is a relatively new idea that has come about thanks to digital technologies. Newbies on the block can challenge established companies because they can provide innovative products and services that blow their competition out of the water. For example, transportation was revolutionized when ride-sharing platforms became popular. Another prime example would be streaming services reshaping the entertainment industry as we know it today.

Data monetization has also been a big part of this evolution in technology. Since data is so easily accessible now, organizations have started using it as a strategic asset, and it's proven successful. Companies can use data analytics to optimize operations and create personalized consumer offerings. By doing this, businesses have unlocked new revenue streams and created tailored customer experiences, which helps improve decision-making capabilities.

Platform-based business models are another concept that has emerged in recent years, thanks to technological advances. Platforms act as intermediaries by connecting users, producers, and consumers under one roof and allowing them to interact with each other through transactions or value exchanges. E-commerce marketplaces like Amazon connect buyers and sellers, and social media platforms like Instagram connect users and advertisers.

Finally, one of the best things about living in this era is how easy it is for anyone to establish their own personal brand or start a small gig. All they need is access to social media sites to advertise themselves or sell products on online marketplaces such as Amazon or Etsy.

Thanks to the digital age, there is no limit to how far entrepreneurship can go. Digital platforms and online marketplaces provide individuals with the opportunity to monetize their skills, assets, and time on a flexible basis. It also allows people with unconventional work schedules or those who want to avoid being tied down by a full-time job to make money. This can apply to freelancers offering services on digital platforms or even drivers participating in ride-sharing services.

If you think about it, this shift towards 'gig-based' models has implications for labor markets, regulatory frameworks, and the future of work itself. With more industries going in this direction, time will tell how permanent these changes are.

As we continue to move forward in this digital era, one thing is for sure: business models have never been so dynamic. And if you aren't ready to adapt your model based on new technological advances, your company will not survive for long.

5.2 Core Elements of a Business Model

The success of any business relies on its business model, which acts as the framework for how the company creates, delivers, and captures value. The core elements of each model drive its viability and sustainability in the market. With that being said, these elements come in many forms, including the value proposition given to customers, strategies used to generate revenue and monetize offerings, cost structure and profit margins involved with operations, and the distribution channels utilized for reaching customers and engaging with them efficiently.

The customer value proposition is found at the heart of every business model. It's where a company articulates the unique benefits or values that their products or services offer their target customers. A compelling value proposition is essential for attracting and retaining customers in a competitive marketplace. By understanding who your customers are, what they need most, and what problems they want solved, you can design your offerings, accordingly, setting yourself apart from competitors.

Revenue stream identification and monetization strategy development are crucial for a successful business model. Revenue streams include all sources of income a business generates, like product sales or advertising revenue. In contrast, monetization strategies involve determining pricing structures, such as recurring revenue models that extract value from your offering.

Alongside solidifying a flow of income, understanding the cost structure and profit margins associated with the business will help ensure financial sustainability and profitability. It's important to manage expenses wisely across functions like production or administrative work while optimizing cost structures to maximize profit margins.

Effective distribution channels and strong customer relationships go hand-in-hand with operating a successful company. Distribution channels are the ways products or services are delivered through direct sales or partnerships with other retailers. Meanwhile, building strong customer relationships is something businesses should pay attention to, as loyal customers drive repeat business and word-of-mouth referrals, which can attract new customers more efficiently than traditional marketing methods.

Customer Value Proposition

Every successful business has a customer value proposition. It's the one thing that separates it from its competitors. There are thousands of options out there, so it would be nice to know why we should choose your product.

A customer value proposition expresses the unique benefits and value that a company promises to deliver to its target customers. It is the heart and soul of any business strategy and helps guide product development, marketing efforts, and customer engagement initiatives.

Businesses must understand what their target audiences need, want, or even hate about the similar products they sell. Companies can tailor their offerings to meet specific customer demands by walking a mile in their shoes.

These tailored offerings should identify functional benefits and consider emotional and social ones. This will help build deeper connections with customers.

Customers don't care how big or small you think your features are. They care about how it'll improve their lives or solve a problem they have in front of them. The customer value proposition needs to speak directly to them by offering convenience, saving time, or fostering a sense of belonging—things that customers can resonate with personally.

Happy customers tend to become brand ambassadors, meaning they will advocate for your brand and recommend it to others without even being asked.

Sure, today's business landscape is competitive. By staying current on customer needs, embracing innovation, and delivering exceptional service, any company can establish an advantage over everyone else on the market.

Revenue Streams and Monetization Strategies

In the business world, figuring out how to make money and keep things going is crucial. You also want to be able to grow. This can happen if you understand how to monetize your product or service effectively. Revenue streams are the different forms of revenue a company generates through its customer offerings. One way to achieve this is by selling products directly to subscription-based services. Having multiple sources of income helps businesses stay on their feet even when things go wrong.

A monetization strategy involves finding ways to extract value from your customers without making them feel like they're spending too much money. Finding the right price for your product is essential for staying competitive and maximizing revenue. The last thing you want is for customers to think there's a cheaper alternative elsewhere.

One popular model companies use is the freemium model. This gives people access to basic features for free, but more features come at a cost. While it may look like you're trying to get people hooked so they pay more later on—which is true—this gives users who don't yet have enough incentive to buy into premium offers the chance to try everything before committing.

Subscription-based models are ubiquitous in today's streaming media platforms, such as Netflix and Spotify, and rightfully so—they work. Charging a recurring fee for an ongoing offer allows companies to keep their books balanced by knowing how much money they will make monthly from subscriptions alone. Outside those two main methods of generating cash flow, businesses can also explore indirect monetization strategies such as advertising, sponsorship, or affiliate marketing. These involve leveraging customers' attention and engagement with third-party advertisers or partners.

Companies could consider implementing tactics that help them gather data from customer interactions and analyze it later to find opportunities to optimize what they already have or introduce new campaigns. Doing this helps build a more personal customer experience, which can increase the value proposition overall.

Cost Structure and Profit Margins

Cost structure and profit margins are essential for a business model. They affect an organization's financial health, sustainability, and competitiveness. Understanding and managing costs is crucial for optimizing profits, maximizing efficiency, and succeeding in the market over the long term.

Cost structure refers to the expenses a business incurs while producing its products or services. These can be divided into various categories: fixed costs, variable costs, and semi-variable costs. Fixed costs, such as rent, salaries, and utilities, do not change, no matter how little or how much you sell. Variable costs, like raw materials, labor, and distribution expenses, change along with production. Semi-variable costs share elements of other cost structures: fixed and variable components that adjust based on activity levels.

Optimizing cost structure involves reducing expenses without sacrificing quality or customer experience. If applicable, streamlining operations may involve renegotiating supplier contracts or even using technology. Profit margins show the difference between revenue from sales and the cost of making your product or service available to customers, expressed as a percentage of revenue.

The three main kinds of profit margins are <u>gross margin</u>, the difference between revenue and direct expenses; <u>operating margin</u>, which reflects profitability after accounting for indirect expenses; and <u>net margin</u>, which is ultimate profitability after all expenditures have been subtracted. Maximizing these margins involves strategically increasing prices or decreasing direct expenses, respectively, so that you are getting more out than you put in.

Distribution Channels and Customer Relationships

A business model needs solid distribution channels and customer relationships. These two things can shape how products or services are delivered to customers and how relationships are nurtured to drive loyalty.

Distribution channels can include direct sales, retail partnerships, e-commerce platforms, wholesalers, distributors, and third-party marketplaces. Your decision on a distribution channel depends on target market demographics, product features, geographical scope, and organizational goals.

Multiple distribution channels can allow companies to expand their reach and penetrate new markets faster. This also allows them to cater to diverse customer preferences and buying behaviors. Optimizing efficiency and accessibility are a few things that should be noted when it comes to effective distribution channel management. You want your products or services readily available when and where customers need them.

On the other hand, customer relationships can involve any interaction between businesses and their customers. This includes pre-sale inquiries, post-sale support, and feedback mechanisms. Building trust with a customer base is crucial. When a company has a satisfied customer, they tend to buy more from them repeatedly. They do this because they like what they've got so far, so why not get that again? They'll also recommend the company's product or service to others and provide constructive criticism.

With the rise of technology, businesses have been able to tailor interactions specifically for each customer, making them much more accessible than ever. Using mobile apps and social media, companies now have access to data analytics tools to observe who's buying what and offer tailored experiences that resonate with each customer.

Now, businesses can utilize digital marketing channels like email marketing, social media advertising, and content marketing at all stages of the purchase journey, which is fantastic. In doing so, businesses can build brand affinity, drive customer loyalty, and differentiate themselves in a crowded marketplace.

Distribution channels and customer relationships are core elements of a business model. They influence the way products or services are delivered to customers and how relationships are nurtured to drive loyalty and satisfaction. Through optimizing distribution channels, harnessing technological advances, and prioritizing investments in customer relationship management initiatives, businesses can elevate customer experiences, cultivate brand loyalty, and attain sustainable growth within the market.

5.3 Analyzing Business Model Archetypes

Analyzing business model archetypes can give us a deep insight into how businesses across different industries operate.

I know there's no one-size-fits-all solution to running a business. That's why I've compiled an extensive collection of overviews and examples that give you an idea of where your next venture might take you.

Overview of Common Business Model Patterns

Understanding the landscape of business model archetypes requires a thorough examination of the common patterns contributing to successful ventures across different sectors. Dissecting these patterns can give entrepreneurs a deeper understanding of businesses' strategies to create value, gain market share, and encourage growth.

The subscription model is popular these days. As we've seen, subscriptions allow companies to offer products or services regularly in exchange for payment. Businesses that employ this model often provide ongoing value through access to exclusive content, software updates, or premium services. Companies in the media and entertainment, software, and consumer goods industries have adopted the subscription model as an effective way to foster customer loyalty, predictability and drive long-term revenue.

As mentioned, the freemium model is another modern archetype. This involves offering basic versions of products or services for free while charging for premium features or additional functionality.

Marketplace models such as e-commerce and platforms are essential in many businesses. They connect buyers with sellers and help facilitate transactions between them. Examples include online retail platforms, freelance marketplaces, and service-based platforms where they make money through transaction fees, commissions, or advertising. By building scalable economies, marketplace models create value for buyers and sellers.

The on-demand service model has become increasingly ubiquitous thanks to technological advances that have disrupted traditional industries like food delivery and ride-hailing services. Because this model offers instant access, people's lives have become increasingly convenient and flexible, and businesses operating within the on-demand service model have tapped into new market opportunities.

Analyzing standard business models gives entrepreneurs insights that they can use to drive their ventures to success. Whether it's subscription models, freemium approaches, or marketplace platforms, companies can leverage them to innovate and create value for their customers.

Adapting Standard Models for Unique Business Ideas

When entrepreneurs work with business model archetypes, they change the models a bit to adapt to their unique business ideas. These existing models give you an excellent way to succeed, but sometimes they don't fit with what you're doing. When you realize this, you need to develop ways to shape them into your value proposition and cater to your target market.

People like to modify existing frameworks for niches or specialized customer segments. People love things tailored for them, so if you could find a niche within an industry, customers would be more likely to choose you over another company. For example, if someone made a subscription meal kit service but it was based on dietary preferences or cultural cuisines, then that could set them apart from the rest of the food delivery market.

Another thing people will try is integrating new technology or processes to enhance their customers' experiences. If people see a new way they could do something they're used to, especially emerging trends such as artificial intelligence, they will want to use that instead of old methods. For example, in P2P lending, someone might incorporate blockchain technology, improving transparency and trust within the process and making it more appealing.

Creating a solid brand identity and focusing entirely on giving customers a fantastic experience is critical in today's marketplace, where competition is higher than ever. Even though everything mentioned helps get eyes on your brand, once customers click on your site, they will expect nothing less than fantastic branding if you want them to return.

Sometimes, when taking risks, some adaptations don't go as planned—which is normal. The most important thing about making changes is being fast enough to keep up with changing markets, so once something doesn't work, you can move on to the next change. People who embrace a culture of innovation and agility can quickly bounce back from failures.

Although it's always great to come up with something completely new, sometimes you can use what already exists and make a few changes to unlock your full potential. By doing this, you could open doors no one else noticed, set yourself apart from every competitor out there, and stand out even in the most ever-evolving business landscapes.

5.4 Designing Your Business Model Canvas

The Business Model Canvas is an incredible tool for entrepreneurs. It helps them visualize, analyze, and refine their ideas. Created by Alexander Osterwalder and Yves Pigneur, it provides a structure for breaking down all aspects of a business into separate but interrelated parts. With the nine building blocks, you'll be able to understand your vision better than ever before.

Here, I'll explain what each segment does so that you can see why it's so important. Once you've understood its purpose, you can make better decisions when populating each block with relevant information and insights.

The main work begins with filling out each segment of the canvas. This is where you gather data and conduct market research to fill it effectively. You must identify your target customer segments, articulate unique value propositions, and map out how you'll reach them using channels. Resources, activities, and partnerships can help deliver value propositions efficiently and sustainably.

This is an ongoing process because real-world insights often lead to adjustments on the canvas. As new opportunities arise or challenges manifest through customers' or investors' feedback, revisions must be made.

Step-by-Step Guide to Using the Business Model Canvas

The first step in using the business model canvas is knowing its nine fundamental building blocks. Each block represents an integral part of a business model: customer segments, value propositions, channels, customer relationships, revenue streams, key resources, key activities, key partnerships, and cost structure.

After becoming familiar with these blocks, entrepreneurs can start filling in the canvas however they want. This means identifying which customer groups the business should target and defining them as precisely as possible.

Understanding customer needs will help entrepreneurs craft value propositions that address pain points and deliver perfect solutions.

Filling Out Each Segment of the Canvas

Completing each field of the Business Model Canvas is essential to establishing your company comprehensively and effectively. Every piece represents an aspect of business that, when aligned correctly, forms a cohesive structure to support strategy and objectives.

Customer Segments: The first segment determines which target customer segments you're looking to serve. This means understanding their needs, preferences, and behaviors before categorizing them based on their shared characteristics or attributes. By doing this, entrepreneurs can personalize value propositions and marketing efforts so that they pull at the right strings for each specific group.

Value Propositions: Value propositions articulate what makes your product unique. It could be something as simple as solving unmet needs, providing better experiences, or offering what no one else does. To craft a compelling statement, you must understand customer pain points, market trends, and competitive dynamics.

Channels: The channels section identifies all the touchpoints and distribution routes along which your company will reach its customers. These include online platforms, physical retail locations, and any partnerships you might have with distributors or resellers. Entrepreneurs have almost unlimited channel options, like direct sales teams or partnerships, but selecting the most effective ones will help you maximize your marketing efforts.

Customer Relationships: This step addresses how you plan to communicate with customers post-launch. Will there be personalized interactions? One-on-one consultations? Or some self-service option? The goal is to establish positive relationships that foster loyalty, satisfaction, and repeat business.

Revenue Streams: This segment details where the money will come from. One-time sales? Subscription fees? Licensing agreements? Advertising revenue? Diversifying revenue streams helps keep cash flow moving smoothly while ensuring financial stability.

Essential Resources: The key resources segment identifies the resources necessary for delivering value propositions and executing strategies effectively. These encompass a wide range of physical assets (equipment/facilities), intellectual property (patents/trademarks), and human capital (employees/partners). Each plays an essential role in the success of your business.

Key Activities: The key activities segment outlines the core processes your business needs to operate to deliver value to customers. This could be anything from customer service or sales to manufacturing or supply chain management. Focusing on different activities that drive value creation and differentiation will help you find a balance between effort and efficiency.

Key Partnerships: The crux of key partnerships spotlights external collaborators who play a role in supporting the business model and achieving its objectives. These could include supplies, suppliers, distribution partners, or strategic alliances with other businesses. By leveraging these relationships, entrepreneurs can give their resources an edge, ultimately enhancing the company's competitiveness and scalability.

Cost Structure: The cost structure segment outlines business expenses. Fixed costs like rent and salaries remain constant regardless of production levels, while variable costs fluctuate based on the amount of product produced. Understanding both types of costs is critical to ensuring a business's financial sustainability and profitability.

Filling out each segment of the business model canvas is vital for designing a comprehensive and effective business model. Taking your time to consider each element ensures that you develop a plan that's well-aligned from top to bottom—value for customers creates revenue, which drives long-term success.

Iterating and Refining Your Business Model Canvas

The development stage of the business model allows creators to adapt and improve as they work through feedback and, in turn, respond to customer needs and market dynamics. This consistent work-in-progress way of working will optimize resource allocation and make the creators better at what they do over time. It's all about fine-tuning their strategies, optimizing resource allocation, and making things more effective for everyone involved.

Once you collect feedback from customers, investors, and partners, you can start reworking your canvases based on it. Evaluate each segment of your current canvas individually. Then, consider how aligned it is with your business's overall strategy and objectives. Use this information to prioritize changes that will have the most impact on the industry.

Entrepreneurs must prioritize conducting market research and analysis throughout the iteration process to recognize emerging trends, competitive threats, and fresh opportunities. This proactive approach enables entrepreneurs to adjust their business models effectively, capitalizing on evolving market conditions to sustain a competitive advantage.

While working through this process of trial and error with your current ideas, you should constantly be testing them. Experimentation is key here, so don't take it lightly. If one idea goes differently than planned, move on to another until it's perfect.

Throughout the iteration process, entrepreneurs should maintain a flexible and adaptive mindset, embracing failure as an opportunity for learning and growth. Some iterations will yield the desired results.

5.5 Value Creation and Delivery

Creating and delivering value is essential to success in the modern business world. It's the key to maintaining a competitive edge. The essence is understanding how value works as your business grows, is delivered to your customers, and is sustained over time. This section takes a deep dive into value creation and delivery, offering tips and strategies for entrepreneurs to build sustainable companies that will thrive in the long run.

The first step in any business model is identifying how value is created. What unique products or experiences does your business offer? Value creation should be the building block of everything you do in your company, from production to employee training to customer engagement.

Once you've figured out what added benefits your product or service will provide, it's time to think about how it will reach the customer once they buy it from you. From start to finish, an optimized system needs to be in place that eliminates waste while delivering quality and convenience. By integrating technology into things like distribution channels and supply chains, businesses can discover ways around road bumps that competitors might run into during growth.

Quality control and customer satisfaction are closely related factors that should always be remembered. Happy customers will return when they know they can trust every product from your assembly line. In today's online shopping-dominated world, satisfied shoppers are one good review away from bringing new people through your doors, a free form of advertising no company should ever downplay.

Value creation and delivery are at the core of all successful business models in today's fast-paced world, driven by social media marketing campaigns. By prioritizing these values in every aspect of their company structure—whether through lean manufacturing or excellent customer service—entrepreneurs can build a brand that will have no issue growing and thriving.

Outlining How Your Business Creates Value

At the heart of any business model is the question: how do you create value? Understanding and articulating how your business generates customer value is necessary for a robust and sustainable business model.

Value creation starts with knowing what customers need, want, and hate. By doing market research, getting customer feedback, and analyzing trends, entrepreneurs can discover ways to address unmet needs and provide meaningful solutions that resonate with their target audience. This customer-first approach forms the basis for creating valuable customer relationships.

Product innovation is one-way companies add value. By developing innovative products or services that offer features or benefits not provided by competitors, businesses can set themselves apart and attract customers searching for fresh solutions. Doing so may involve investing in R&D, using brand-new technology, or partnering with outside teams to spread new ideas.

Another strategy is creating excellent service experiences. Your reputation improves when you provide support quickly and kindly; people consider your offerings more valuable than those without a personalized service. To execute this approach, train employees well so they know how to help every kind of customer; implement systems that tell you what customers think; without them having to say anything to you; and optimize processes so each service experience feels reliable enough for people to recommend it to friends.

If you achieve it, operational excellence can also create value for customers. People like paying less for something they could find elsewhere. By ensuring operations are smooth and cheap enough, businesses can produce high-quality goods at low prices for consumers who want both reliability and affordability. Some steps here include adopting lean principles, automating specific processes, or negotiating good deals to keep costs as low as possible while staying efficient.

A brand's reputation is valuable to a lot of people. By building up your reputation and focusing on the intangible aspects of your company identity, credibility, and good vibes, customers will see more in what you offer than in the product or service itself. If you're wondering how to build up this kind of vibe, spend money on marketing and branding, nurture loyalty between yourself and customers, and make sure that you always give back to your stakeholders, so they'll trust you for years to come.

Creating a compelling value proposition for your business is a multifaceted process. It requires complete knowledge of customer needs, competition dynamics, and market trends. But with a customer-first mindset, innovation as a top priority, excellent service at the forefront, optimal operations running in the background, and an unbeatable brand reputation, entrepreneurs can create something valuable that'll become their company's backbone.

Efficient and Effective Delivery Systems

Creating fast, innovative ways to get your product into customers' hands is critical to building a successful business. Building an efficient delivery system starts with streamlining the internal workflow. You want to ensure you're producing as much as possible without wasting time or money, allowing you to deliver your goods or services at peak efficiency. By using lean principles, automated technologies, and continuous improvement initiatives, businesses can run more efficiently while responding faster to customer demand and changing markets.

External processes are crucial when designing an adequate infrastructure for getting products out. That's why systems must be well designed with distribution in mind from the start. Whatever channels you use—direct sales, online marketplaces, or retail partners—they must be able to reach customers effectively so that they will go through you rather than anyone else.

Logistics management can make or break delivery speed. This includes all the necessary steps, like ensuring inventory is available and optimizing transportation routes. If you get this right, things get where they need to be faster, and orders are coordinated so there aren't any delays or mistakes along the way. Ordering accuracy can significantly boost satisfaction levels because people want to avoid dealing with shipping errors.

Technology is at the heart of this process because it makes everything more visible when implemented correctly. It lets you see everything as it happens in real time, so companies don't miss opportunities.

Quality control measures should be standard across the board for any business. Monitoring and gathering customer feedback will help improve service levels and product quality, building trust and a reputation that customers can consistently rely on. To that end, businesses should focus on creating a satisfying customer experience instead of giving them the bare minimum.

Creating an efficient delivery system is the way to build a successful business model. By optimizing internal processes, strategically designing distribution models, effectively managing logistics and fulfillment operations, implementing technology improvements, and committing to quality control and customer satisfaction, businesses will have built something reliable enough to last into the foreseeable future.

Ensuring Quality and Customer Satisfaction

Quality and customer satisfaction are two vital pillars of any business model. Building a loyal customer base, creating a good brand reputation, and driving sustainable growth come from developing a business model focused on these aspects.

It all starts with the commitment that everything should be done to the highest standard—whether it is the product design or manufacturing process. Companies must set rigorous quality standards and stick to them consistently so their products or services will meet customers' expectations, if not exceed them. This may involve implementing quality management systems, regular inspections and audits, and investing in employee training to ensure they comply with the set standards.

Customer satisfaction is equally important for businesses, as it helps them understand what customers need or want. Feedback can be gathered through surveys, reviews, and direct communication channels to identify improvement areas and promptly address concerns. Listening to their customers actively and swiftly and addressing their feedback will show how committed a company is to delivering perfect customer service, thus creating stronger connections with their target audience.

Of course, effective communication also plays a significant role. Businesses must be transparent when dealing with customers—clear product information and pricing. Responding promptly to customers' concerns shows a high level of reliability, leaving no room for negative feedback.

Besides quality and communication, consistency is equally important. Customers should have consistent experience when interacting with your business entity—from initial interaction to post-purchase support. Consistency creates trust between the company and its customers, making them feel like you're reliable and encouraging them to purchase from you again.

Businesses can differentiate themselves by offering services or features that enhance the overall shopping experience for customers, such as personalized recommendations, convenient payment options, or extended warranties, which give peace of mind to those who choose to buy them alongside their products or services. By surpassing customer expectations, businesses can create the potential of customers willing to endorse their products or services to others.

By sticking with quality in everything they do, actively listening to customer feedback, communicating efficiently, ensuring consistency, and providing value-added services, businesses can create strong relationships with their customers, thus positioning themselves for long-term success.

5.6 Competitive Advantage and Strategy

In today's rapid-fire business world, success means staying ahead and finding an edge over your rivals. We dive into the nitty-gritty of competitive advantage and strategy. It examines how companies can pinpoint, cultivate, and leverage their unique strengths to outperform competitors and flourish in our increasingly crowded marketplace.

Identifying and developing competitive advantages requires a deep understanding of a company's strengths, weaknesses, opportunities, and threats. By running through an exhaustive analysis of internal capabilities and external market dynamics, businesses can find areas where they're second to none while also finding areas for improvement. This could mean funneling funds into research and development or leveraging proprietary technology or intellectual property to further develop products or services.

Aligning a business model with a competitive strategy is vital for fully leveraging a competitive advantage. A business model explicitly created with this strategy in mind allows smooth execution while maximizing impact simultaneously. For example, tailoring value propositions, distribution channels, and revenue streams enables businesses to make sure all angles are covered with their unique strengths under consideration before stepping into the ring.

Anticipating and responding to competitive forces involves being aware of what change is coming and adapting strategies to maintain one's place within the competition. By keeping a close eye on competitors' movements as well as industry trends and customer preferences, businesses can get ahead of any issues that may arise before others do so—and thus respond faster than anyone else can. This might involve adjusting prices or enhancing products preemptively against incoming threats from other firms trying to steal from your customers. Regardless of the specific tactic, it all comes back to being adaptable and quick on your feet.

Identifying and Developing Competitive Advantages

When developing a business model, identifying and cultivating competitive advantages will make or break a company's longevity in a cutthroat market. This section examines the various strategic considerations and methodologies for identifying and creating these competitive advantages.

This can be done using a comprehensive analysis of the business's internal strengths and external market dynamics. By understanding their unique capabilities, proprietary technologies, and intellectual properties, companies can create something they know no competitor has.

Once identified, it's essential to nurture these newfound advantages so they can continue to be effective in the long term. This can be done by putting more money into R&D so they can innovate new products or services within their framework. A popular method of avoiding competition is building up barriers of entry like patents or trademarks, which would legally protect your work from being copied elsewhere.

Continuous improvements must always be made to keep up with customer changes in taste and preference, as well as in the marketplace itself. To stay ahead of competitors, businesses can implement feedback loops that gather insights from customers and employees. Routine performance evaluations will help highlight where improvements need to be made internally, and further training initiatives will allow employees to learn from those mistakes. By following these steps, entrepreneurs give themselves the best possible shot at sustained success in today's brutal business landscape.

Aligning the Business Model with Competitive Strategy

Ideally, aligning the business model and competitive strategy is critical to achieving lasting success in today's market. Let's examine how to accomplish this alignment and optimize resource utilization to maximize your competitive advantage. Defining strategic goals and priorities is the first step to aligning the business model with the competitive strategy. This means understanding who your target market is, what they want, and where you fit into the industry.

Next, you need a comprehensive understanding of your competition—their strengths, weaknesses, and anything else that can be mined for an upper hand in the marketplace. With this information, you'll be able to develop a business model that leverages your company's strengths while minimizing risk along the way. From there, businesses must ensure that their business model aligns with their value proposition and positioning strategy. In simpler terms, does what you sell resonate with customers? If not, it may be time for a pivot.

Operational elements must also align with both models. Distribution channels must reach target customers efficiently, revenue streams should be diversified enough so that no one threat wipes out everything, and costs must also stay manageable. Adapting quickly allows companies to keep up with changes in competition or technology, which will always benefit those willing to evolve as needed.

Aligning these two plans can be challenging, but if done right, it can unlock untapped potential within any organization, allowing them to soar past competitors.

Anticipating and Reacting to Competitive Forces

In the world of business, anticipating and reacting to competition is crucial for any successful business.

A solid anticipation plan begins with understanding your competitors' strengths and weaknesses, market trends, and new competition. Regular competitor analysis allows you to see who could threaten you or what would boost you, allowing companies to anticipate competitive forces and formulate strategic responses accordingly.

Staying attuned to changes in customer preferences is easier than it sounds. Gathering insights through research or getting feedback about how people feel about your services can help you adjust your plans to better meet their needs than the competition.

The business must also be aware of its internal challenges. This involves assessing the business's strengths and weaknesses by constantly checking up on SWOT (Strengths, Weaknesses, Opportunities, Threats) analyses. Regular meetings allow companies to anticipate internal challenges and devise strategies effectively. You must ensure that your company reacts swiftly when a challenge arises. This requires agility and flexibility in responding to changing market conditions, competitive threats, and customer feedback.

Finally, we reach the point where we see if everything worked out well. We do this by tracking key performance indicators, gathering customer feedback, and adjusting strategies based on real-time data.

5.7 Financial Aspects of Business Models

In the corporate world, you need to understand finance to succeed. This section looks at all things finance-related within business models, from revenue and costs to financial metrics and ratios and even break-even analysis and planning.

Projecting revenue and costs allows you to estimate how much your company will make or lose over time. You'll have to figure out how much you can charge for your product, how many sales you can make in that time, and how much it costs to produce one unit or service of whatever you're selling. The more accurate this estimate is, the better off your company will be when it is time to allocate resources and invest.

Key financial metrics and ratios for assessing business model viability are numbers that tell you whether or not your plan is going to work out in the long run. They're profitability, liquidity, and efficiency indicators. Having good scores on these measures means that your business is probably financially stable enough that you'll be able to grow later down the line.

Break-even analysis and financial planning ensure your business plan stays in good standing. Break-even analysis tells you exactly what price point needs to be hit for total revenue generated by sales to match the total cost of providing those sales. Financial planning aims to achieve long-term goals by managing cash flow properly, since we all know that nothing's going anywhere anytime soon without any money coming in.

Projecting Revenue and Costs

Estimating revenue and expenses is essential to any business plan. It gives you an idea of your company's finances and helps determine if your business model is viable.

Revenue projection can be done in several ways. It could involve predicting the sources and amounts of income that the business may generate, including sales, service fees, or licensing agreements. To project revenue accurately, companies must consider market demand, pricing strategies, sales volume, and potential growth opportunities. By analyzing historical data and customer feedback, companies can better understand what's realistic regarding projections.

Cost projection involves estimating all the expenses your company will accumulate over time. This includes production costs, labor costs, overheads, and marketing expenses, to name a few. For accurate cost projections, companies must consider factors such as material prices, labor rates, rent, and utilities. Businesses must also conduct thorough research to make sense of their estimated cost projections.

Financial models like income statements and cash flow statements are commonly used in this process. They help businesses analyze economic data to forecast future performance more quickly and evaluate different scenarios for their financial health before making any decisions on pricing strategies or resource allocation. Remember that this requires continuous monitoring and adjustment as market conditions change so that the plan remains relevant.

Predicting revenue streams allows businesses to see how much money they'll bring in during a given period. Taking these steps ensures that businesses use resources wisely without being wasteful by spending money they don't need to spend

Key Financial Metrics and Ratios for Assessing Business Model Viability

Understanding and applying key financial metrics and ratios is paramount to creating a business model. These metrics give businesses valuable insights into their economic well-being, operational performance, and efficiency. With this information, decision-makers can make informed choices about where to improve their businesses and mitigate risks.

One fundamental metric you're probably thinking of is revenue. It holds significant weight as it measures how much money your company brings in by doing what it does best: selling things or services. Analyzing revenue trends over time can reveal patterns and indicate the effectiveness of sales and marketing strategies.

Profitability ratios are essential for determining if a company is making any profit. Specifically, gross, operating, and net profit margins tell you how effectively your business operations generate profits.

Cash flow metrics are vital for assessing liquidity (how easily cash can be converted to pay bills) and overall solvency (think paying off debt). Quantifying these two dimensions will help you understand how stable your finances are.

Efficiency ratios evaluate different aspects of leveraging resources to generate more money. I'll be looking at asset turnover (revenue generated per dollar invested), inventory turnover (how many times inventory was sold within a period), and accounts receivable turnover (how efficiently debts were paid off)

Leverage ratios help measure debt management, which has enormous implications for risk levels associated with borrowing too much or not enough from lenders.

While crunching numbers is essential, you must also consider what other businesses are doing and how they perform. Comparing yourself to others can give you a better sense of where you're succeeding or falling behind. From there, you can build strategies to push your performance while keeping the competition at bay.

There are plenty of metrics and ratios to analyze regarding financials. By getting into the nitty-gritty of them, entrepreneurs and leaders alike can make informed decisions that put their company on track for sustained growth.

Break-even Analysis and Financial Planning

Break-even analysis is paramount in financial planning. It serves as a crucial tool for entrepreneurs and business owners to evaluate the feasibility and capability of their ventures. Analyzing the point at which total revenue matches total costs gives them insights into the minimum sales required to cover expenses and generate profits.

The first step in break-even analysis is counting fixed and variable costs. As we've seen, fixed costs stay consistent regardless of production or sales levels, meaning you'll pay them every month. Variable costs go up when production increases. They include expenditures on raw materials, labor, and utilities.

By understanding how much their business costs to run, entrepreneurs can calculate the break-even point, which represents the level of sales needed to maintain a neutral financial position, otherwise known as covering all expenses.

This part of your planning will give you critical insights into pricing strategies, production plans, and overall strategy.

Besides finding that sweet spot where profits begin to show up on your ledger, financial planning looks at various aspects like budgeting resources effectively and forecasting results in the long term to set solid goals for your venture.

Looking ahead, it also involves using scenarios like sensitivity testing; which assesses how changes in the volume of sales, pricing, or operating costs will impact financial performance; so that entrepreneurs are ready for anything.

It's also crucial because even though nobody wants to think about it, sometimes things don't work out. With detailed financial projections, investors can decide whether to fund a company based on its potential return on investment.

To ensure this happens, these projections must demonstrate an understanding of your market, industry dynamics, and competitive landscape.

In conclusion, developing a robust business plan that includes break-even analysis, understanding cost structures, and thorough planning is critical to creating a solid foundation for long-term success. If you get this right, your future self will thank you.

Chapter 6

Writing a Comprehensive Business Plan

Writing a comprehensive business plan is one of the most vital steps for an entrepreneur or established business looking to scale up. It's essentially the roadmap that guides your organization through operational processes, strategic moves, and financial milestones.

Your business plan is a collection of goals, vision, and strategies that work together to form your venture. It describes your mission statement, target market, competing landscape, and anything else you'll need to make it big. Through research analysis and good old-fashioned planning, entrepreneurs can construct a practical concept for their ideas, all while identifying potential challenges with actual solutions.

The Executive Summary acts as a punchy overview that captures the most critical aspects of your venture. A well-crafted summary can stir up enough interest in stakeholders to get them thirsty for more on how you will accomplish everything you want. The main sections include a unique value proposition and financial projections.

After finishing the executive summary, you'll describe your business in full detail by following up with a description section. This part gets into the nitty-gritty details about where the concept came from; its history, why it exists; competitive advantages; mission/vision; and what makes it unique.

To succeed in today's markets, you'll also need extensive market research, so you know exactly which buttons to push when trying to attract customers. By understanding trends and consumer habits, businesses can tailor their strategies accordingly, which means better chances of capitalizing on emerging opportunities effectively.

If things start taking off as they should, then, sooner or later, someone will have to step up as the leader who carries this whole thing forward. Organization management explains how everyone needs to be positioned so the company doesn't stumble along its path to greatness. It also helps to hand out some roles and responsibilities to the management team, so they know what they're doing.

Your venture will offer products or services. This part should explain precisely what you're selling or providing to customers and why they should care. By articulating these unique selling points, businesses can resonate with their audience and carve a niche in the market.

Marketing and sales do what it says on the tin; they cover how you will get people through the door or online. This section will outline all the branding initiatives, promotional campaigns, and sales tactics that will be used to drive revenue growth. Customers are demanding creatures, but a comprehensive approach can keep them around for a while.

You've got your plans, product, and marketing all figured out, so now we need some funding. The Funding Request portion of your business plan will break down how much money you need from potential investors. To get them even more interested, explain how this cash boost will be repaid plus interest.

Refining your business plan is all about continuous improvement. That means you should constantly seek feedback, analyze metrics, and apply those lessons to make your plan more effective. The goal is to have a plan that's agile, resilient, and competitive, so it can withstand the challenges of the market.

Presenting your business plan is a whole different ball game. It takes planning and preparation to tell an engaging, visual story to convince people to risk their money or reputation on your idea. Use every tool when presenting, including stories, visuals, and compelling narratives.

Ultimately, crafting a business plan isn't about checking off some boxes—it's about creating a strategic blueprint for entrepreneurial success. If you can articulate your vision in a way that resonates with stakeholders, you'll have something powerful to propel your venture forward. But remember that getting there takes vision, diligence, and creativity. However, the payoff will be worth it.

6.1 Introduction to Business Planning

Starting a business can be a scary prospect. You're flying blind and need a roadmap to ensure you stay on the right path. That's where a business plan comes in. It's like the blueprint for your company—it outlines how you'll get from point A to point B, but it goes much deeper than that.

Here, we'll explore why business plans are such an integral part of success and look at two approaches for putting one together: traditional planning, which involves building highly detailed strategies, and lean startup planning, which prioritizes being flexible and willing to experiment. By learning about both methods, you can feel more prepared as they enter this new phase of their professional journey.

Purpose and Significance of a Business Plan

Understanding the intricacies of the business world can be confusing and complicated, but it's not impossible. A strategic roadmap makes all the difference. The business plan lays out everything you need to know about starting your own successful venture. In this section, we'll delve into what exactly a business plan is, why it's essential, and how it guides entrepreneurs like yourself toward success.

A business plan isn't any old document; it's a living, breathing organism that embodies your vision for your company, its goals, and its strategy. Things like market research, competition analysis, and financial projections can seem daunting at first glance—but when you have these things in place, you're armed with something powerful: direction.

One of the most important uses of a business plan is as a blueprint for decision-making and resource allocation. Having such an organized framework set up from day one will empower you to make informed choices about what actions will help or hinder your daily progress. This framework also helps keep everything aligned with your overarching goals, so that even when opportunities come knocking on your door, they don't send you spiraling off course.

The prospect of external funding is the moment every entrepreneur dreams about. But none of those dreams will come true without a solid business plan. Investors look for viability, scalability (the ability to grow), and projected returns—all of these are clearly laid out in any comprehensive business plan worth its salt. On top of instilling confidence in potential investors, even having one completed shows lenders or stakeholders how serious and excited you are about bringing this thing to life.

People won't follow someone who doesn't know where they're going. A business plan serves as a way for entrepreneurs to articulate why they're so passionate about what they're doing and helps them say it in a way that gets people excited. Whether it's pitching potential investors, attracting strategic partners, or recruiting top talent, having a compelling narrative that shows the unique value proposition of your company will always make a more significant impact than just saying, 'I'm doing this because I think I can make some money.'

Developing a business plan also requires entrepreneurs to exercise their critical thinking skills in ways other processes don't. They have to conduct thorough research into the market and their respective industry space, analyze current and future trends, and anticipate challenges ahead of time. The result is an entrepreneur who understands their business environment better than anyone else, putting them miles ahead of anyone trying to compete with them.

It's much easier to pivot when something isn't working if you can confidently look back at your plan and see where things went wrong. Moreover, regularly updating your plan keeps you current on market conditions and lets you take advantage of new opportunities.

Types of Business Plans: Traditional vs. Lean Startup

If you were to make a comprehensive plan that outlines every vision, goal, and strategy for your venture, it would look something like a traditional business plan. These documents typically cover every part of the business, such as market analysis and financial projections. They provide an in-depth overview of all aspects, including target markets and operational structures. They'll also touch on marketing strategies and economic forecasts.

The main advantage of traditional business plans is their level of detail. By examining customer preferences and competitive dynamics, entrepreneurs can make informed decisions and solidify growth strategies. On top of this, they also act as a communication tool by allowing entrepreneurs to share their visions with investors or lenders.

The downside of traditional business plans is that they're time-consuming and resource-intensive to develop. Also, these types of plans become rigid when they are finished—they don't allow for quick pivots based on feedback or new opportunities.

There is a much more flexible approach to business planning called lean startups. These highly iterative methods allow for rapid experimentation before reaching conclusions regarding business hypotheses. The primary goal here isn't to create a comprehensive plan but rather to get products or services out onto shelves or into circulation as quickly as possible, while still testing assumptions.

Lean startups are quick to pivot, based on feedback gathered within short periods after being released—hence why documents will be changed frequently to adapt to those iterations made by entrepreneurs.

Advantages to this approach include the fact that they can help identify potential pitfalls early on and allow for a quick fix before they become too detrimental to the business. Lean startup business plans are known to foster creativity and adaptability within team members by nurturing innovation and a desire for continuous improvement.

The lean startup approach isn't suitable for every venture or industry. Those who work in industries that require extensive research or upfront investments may find it difficult to adopt this method. Those looking to secure traditional financing may have trouble because these types of documents lack the depth and detail required to secure large amounts of money from investors or banks.

The decision between a traditional and lean startup business plan depends on the venture's unique character, the entrepreneur's goals, and the market's workings. Traditional business plans offer a breadth that's good for businesses that need comprehensive strategies and extensive market analysis. Meanwhile, lean startups prioritize agility and experimentation to stay adaptable in fast-paced, uncertain fields. Understanding their strengths and weaknesses can help you choose which approach will best guide your ventures to success.

6.2 Executive Summary

Creating a clear and compelling executive summary is critical to building a business plan. It acts as the door to the business plan, letting those involved in the project know what it's about. A good executive summary will give stakeholders a brief picture of your venture's vision, goals, and strategies. In this section, we'll delve into the art and science of crafting an executive summary that effectively communicates the essence of your business plan, while highlighting key points that capture interest.

An executive summary, a strategic tool, sets up the way people will read through your business plan. Its purpose is to distill all the most critical information into something quick to read but impactful enough to leave a mark on readers' minds.

Crafting this kind of statement requires you to consider who precisely you're targeting. You need your ideas to be distilled into simple language. This way, anyone can understand them. And not only do they need to understand it, but they also need to resonate with it. The aspects of your work that are most relevant and compelling should shine through for them.

Striking this balance between brevity and completeness can be tricky, though. No one wants their hard work skimmed over because it's written like stereo instructions. Yet, simultaneously, you don't want to toss everything at someone and bore them out of their mind.

Your statement should highlight what sets you apart from competitors and puts you in a position for success in general. Focus on being unique and specific about who you're targeting and showing off what makes you better than everyone else.

Let some emotion flow. People usually have short attention spans when reading anything related to work or school. Someone reading through this for investment purposes or insight is going to need something that captures them. Show confidence, show excitement, and give your statement a pulse so whoever is reading it can feel what you're trying to do. This way, people can come away remembering not just the information you gave them, but also how they felt while learning it.

Crafting a Clear and Compelling Executive Summary

Short and sweet is the name of the game for an executive summary. It must say precisely what you need to captivate, persuade, and inspire action.

Start by boiling down your core message to create something more potent; dropping any unnecessary details or complexities along the way. Each word should matter here, and your reader should have no problem following through on your journey.

When you write your summary, keep things simple, because simplicity is critical. Avoid jargon or complicated phrases; instead, think about explaining concepts to children—simple enough for them while still getting your point across.

Remember urgency. Writing these summaries is supposed to lead to action in real life. You've got to make sure what you're providing clicks with heart and brain alike, so people know why they should care.

Speaking of making people care, bear in mind exactly who'll be consuming this content throughout each step of production—what are these people looking for? What do they need to know? Do you know what their aspirations or challenges are? You should. This way, your summaries will cater to what your readers want.

It's time to go over this with a fine-toothed comb. When you think you're done editing your summary, give it an extra once-over to ensure everything reads smoothly.

All in all, crafting executive summaries that work is a mixture of art and science. It depends on how creative yet concise you can get while still making sure your reader understands everything they need to understand. If done right, these summaries have the power to draw people in and make them act—leading both you and them towards success.

Highlighting Key Points of Your Business Plan

The key to a successful business is clearly explaining the Business Concept. Without it, nothing else matters. You need to clearly define your product or service, so people know what it does. This should include a unique selling proposition and how this thing will fill a void in today's market. Paint a vivid picture of what sets your idea apart from competitors and why customers flock to it.

Next comes Market Analysis, where you'll gather data on the competition and identify target demographics. It's fantastic that you have an idea for something great, but if there isn't demand for it, or if there are too many others already doing exactly what you want, then you're heading towards failure. Highlight all findings that validate your product or service idea and show that you understand where everything sits around you.

Strategies are next in line, building from marketing to sales all the way to financials—they're all important. Detailing these is key when proving that you can hit every goal and objective created by management. It's also an excellent opportunity to showcase how well you know your company through strategy suggestions that build on strengths while mitigating weaknesses.

A crystal ball would be nice, but since we can't use that, we have financial projections instead. They give us insight into our money situation before we even get started on anything else, with revenue forecasts, expense projections, cash flow statements, and break-even analysis.

Investors see the business world a bit differently to do—everyone knows this. It's not the idea that brings them aboard but also the management team. They want to know that there's experience behind this and that it won't run by a complete novice who pieces things together as they go. Point out your team's roles and responsibilities while highlighting advisors or mentors at any level.

No matter how foolproof you think your plan is, it can just take one push for everything to fall apart. Risk Management is often overlooked, though it shouldn't be. Bring up key risks and uncertainties with strategies on mitigation, so investors see you're self-aware enough—and act proactively towards anything that could threaten their investment.

Speak with passion and purpose throughout each section of your business plan, market analysis, strategies, financial projections, and anywhere else it's applicable. This way, the people who matter will know how much blood, sweat, and tears went into this whole thing from day one, and see the passion you have for your project.

6.3 Business Description

Regardless of your business type, every part needs a descriptive mission statement. These statements help people understand why your company exists in the first place. Think about it as a guiding light for decision-making processes that align with your values and principles.

The vision statement takes that one step further by vividly depicting how you'd like things to turn out. A well-made one will inspire everyone connected to the project and give them purpose. These two statements seem empty on their own. That's why objectives exist; they provide concrete milestones and benchmarks so you can measure progress towards those goals you set up earlier.

Now, we get into tangible aspects—structure and history. The structure includes all things legal, including governance and taxes. It explains all legal entities behind it, how operations run, and where governance should come from. Each type has advantages and disadvantages depending on ownership and management structure. Knowing how your organization operates internally helps create reasonable expectations and accountability for everyone involved. Meanwhile, history establishes credibility through listing triumphs, challenges, setbacks, and failures. By documenting everything along the way, you honor those who came before you, and future employees can also learn from this information.

The business description is the entrance into the business plan, a summary that positions the venture. By outlining the mission, vision, and objectives, entrepreneurs show what they want to accomplish. Describing structure and history offers insights into how things were set up and where they went. As you write your plans, craft this section with clarity and foresight. Doing so will set you up for success in the entrepreneurial landscape.

Detailing Your Business's Mission, Vision, and Objectives

Arranging a business's mission, vision, and objectives is central to every business plan. These three elements shape an organization's direction, strategies, and decision-making processes. By thoughtfully considering these three elements, entrepreneurs can clarify their purpose and inspire stakeholders.

The first element, the mission statement, is said to be the North Star of any business, which encapsulates its core purpose and reason for existence. This statement alone should always guide its operational initiatives and strategic decisions, in alignment with its values and aspirations. A well-crafted mission statement involves distilling the company's essence into a concise declaration that communicates its unique value proposition and its societal impact. It should answer questions like why it exists as a business and how it seeks to make a difference.

Similarly, the second element, the vision statement, paints ways to inspire people by rallying them around shared views for success rather than guiding long-term plans. In this statement, employees must also see themselves succeeding as they strive for greatness or pursue excellence with customers or partners working alongside them.

Objectives provide roadmaps for translating visions into actions by providing milestones, thus tracking progress as you work towards your strategic goals. This element needs to be specific, measurable, achievable, relevant, and time-bound (SMART) since it's often structured around concrete benchmarks and milestones that will be used when analyzing progress over time. Whatever goal it is, whether increasing market share, expanding into new markets, or enhancing operational efficiency, all these require efforts to be focused, with resources allocated effectively so that progress can easily be monitored and analyzed periodically.

The business plan is incomplete without the mission, vision, and objectives. These provide a framework for strategic alignment and organizational coherence, which guides decision-making at all levels of an organization. By articulating a clear and compelling mission, vision, and objectives, entrepreneurs can inspire stakeholders and attract talent, which is crucial for their growth and success. Though it is complex, it's always possible to distill these ideas into concise statements that resonate with authenticity and clarity.

We should mention how essential detailing this part of your business plan can be; it helps you articulate your purpose, inspire stakeholders, and guide strategic decision-making. By crafting compelling statements that communicate core values, aspirations, and strategic priorities, you will have aligned efforts toward common goals, charting a course for sustainable growth and success.

6.4 Market Analysis

When drafting a business plan, market analysis is the most essential section. This critical business plan component helps guide entrepreneurs through the complexities of the marketplace, providing invaluable insights into how their venture operates. It's not a superficial examination but a deep dive that requires industry analysis and target market demographics. By understanding these complex elements, you can lay out the groundwork for growth down the line.

Understanding your market well is fundamental to success in any business venture, whether it's about industry trends or regulatory frameworks. Immersing yourself in these intricacies helps you anticipate challenges and identify opportunities early on. You must gather data from multiple sources, such as industry reports and expert opinions, and conduct primary research like surveys, focus groups, and interviews to gain firsthand insights into customer needs, preferences, and behaviors.

Analyzing your competition is also essential to researching your market. By understanding where competitors may fall short, you can capitalize on those weaknesses, effectively differentiating yourself from them. Industry Analysis also involves evaluating their strategic positioning, product offerings, pricing strategies, distribution channels, and marketing tactics.

Target Market Demographics provide insights into ideal customer characteristics, needs, and preferences. Knowing this information will allow entrepreneurs to identify target customer segments and tailor their marketing strategies accordingly. In addition to variables such as age, gender, income, education, occupation, and geographic location, psychographic factors also play a crucial role in understanding one's target market.

Knowing what you're up against is crucial in business. It can help you see where the gaps are and how to take advantage of them. Even knowing the market inside out will do wonders for your sales, marketing, and distribution strategies. This is an excellent mindset for developing your strategy to beat your competitors. If you're starting or have been in the game for a while, analyzing yourself in terms of your industry standards is vital. From there on, assessing who has got what will help you grow more effectively than ever before.

Demonstrating a Deep Understanding of Your Market

No section of a business plan is as important as demonstrating an understanding of the market. This becomes the basis for strategic decisions and allocating resources for a company. Entrepreneurs must know everything about that specific market and how their customers behave, so they can navigate competition and find their own spot in the market.

Knowing industry trends and dynamics is critical to understanding your market. You can do this by considering macroeconomic factors like regulatory frameworks, technological advances, and consumer preferences. Knowing what's happening helps you see potential threats coming long before they arrive.

Consumer behavior is also fundamental to understanding. By knowing what makes customers tick, you will have insights into why they buy things in the first place. Depending on your niche, this could look like brand preferences or product expectations.

Competitor analysis gives insights into competitors' strengths and weaknesses so that you can efficiently strategize around them while gaining an edge in comparison. By evaluating competitor positioning strategies, businesses can identify gaps in services they don't offer, giving them room for differentiation. Market research is also vital because it provides actual data-driven insights, lowering the chance of failure.

Industry Analysis and Target Market Demographics

Understanding the ins and outs of the industry landscape is as important as knowing who your target market is. A deep understanding, based on both industry analysis and demographic information, can drive a business to success.

Analyzing an industry involves looking at all aspects in which you would compete. This includes competitors, opportunities, regulations, and trends. Doing this lets you know what you're getting into before you do it. You'll be able to understand who your competition is and where they're weak. You'll see areas of growth or disruption that may be worth exploring yourself. And most importantly, you'll be aware of things such as changing consumer preferences and regulatory rule shifts that could impact your venture one day.

Once you have looked at everything your industry offers, it's time to examine every competitor. Through competitive analysis, you can evaluate their strengths, weaknesses, and strategies. Once we know how our competitors operate, we can find gaps in the market where we stand out better than them. The data acquired from this will allow us to develop strategies to gain an advantage over them.

6.5 Organization and Management

The section dealing with organization and management is crucial. It details how a company is structured and profiles everyone in charge of its direction. By outlining hierarchies and introducing the people who run things, entrepreneurs give stakeholders a clear idea of how their investment moves.

At the center of every organization lies its structure, which is a fancy way to describe how it works. Roles are key, responsibilities are essential, and reporting relationships keep everything on track. Whether traditional or flat, the structures are chosen to show what kind of business this team is running. Are roles clearly defined, or is there more room for collaboration and autonomy? How roles are meted out and information flows may seem like small details, but they offer insight into any given operation.

Then there's the management team. This group sets the tone, especially as far as leadership goes. They're in charge of day-to-day operations and keeping an eye on long-term goals. These leaders bring together different skill sets and knowledge bases—all contributing to success. How it looks can vary, but these teams usually include visionary types, who think big, and operational whizzes who make things happen. By profiling these folks, an entrepreneur gives stakeholders insight into what makes them tick.

Organizational structures come in many shapes and sizes. You probably know startups often have something loose going on initially, to allow room for change and growth later on. Different industries may need different things from teams, so flexibility is key here.

We mentioned that management teams can look different, depending on needs. It depends on industry expertise, functional skills, leadership qualities, cultural fit, and so much more. You could end up with seasoned pros or a group of kids straight out of college, who are all extraordinarily determined and willing to learn from each other. The team sets the tone for the whole operation.

The part of the business plan that discusses organization and management is the blueprint for running a business. It lets everyone know who's in charge and what their job is. That way, everyone can be accountable for what they're responsible for. A strong organizational structure makes it easy to make decisions and drive growth. When businesses are organized well, it's easier for them to use their resources and stay ahead in the market.

Outlining Your Business's Organizational Structure

The organizational structure of a business refers to its formulated arrangement of positions, responsibilities, and reporting relationships; this defines authority and hierarchy, establishes communication lines, and outlines decision-making processes. Depending on a business's size, industry type, or strategic goals, various common organizational structures may exist, each with advantages and disadvantages.

One common type is hierarchical (or pyramid) structures; these traditional models reflect a top-down authority flow. Each subsequent level of management oversees the activities of those below them while power progressively gathers at the top. Though this system provides clarity in terms of reporting relationships and accountability, it can cause bureaucracy, slow decision-making procedures, and limit employee autonomy.

By contrast, flat organizations promote an egalitarian approach by reducing layers of management in favor of more collaborative opportunities for employees and higher empowerment rates. Decision-making authority becomes decentralized as employees gain more freedom to make choices within their areas of expertise, promoting innovative cultures that accommodate flexibility and adaptability—this makes them excellent options for small businesses or startups operating in ever-changing landscapes.

Matrix structures are another alternative model combining elements from hierarchical and flat systems. Here, employees report back to functional managers (e.g., marketing, finance) and project managers, depending on the specific task they're working on at any given time. This dual relationship allows greater flexibility in cross-functional collaborations. Nonetheless, it can also lead to conflicts if not managed effectively, since it opens multiple doors for misunderstandings regarding which manager has the final say over an issue or project.

Choosing an organizational structure relies heavily on a wide range of factors, including business size, industry dynamics, stage of growth, and strategic priorities. Small businesses or startups may benefit more from adopting a flat or matrix structure since they offer flexibility, agility, and innovation. As businesses become more mature, it may be best to transition to a hierarchical model to ensure scalability, operational efficiency, and centralized decision-making protocols.

Apart from the overall structure companies decide upon, the business plan must also specify the exact roles and responsibilities of each key person within the company. This includes department heads, leaders of all levels, and any other position critical to driving the business's success. Defining roles clearly allows entrepreneurs to ensure their teams are aligned in completing tasks and conducting decision-making.

Profiles of Your Management Team

Within a business plan, when entrepreneurs create profiles for their team, they give stakeholders an idea about who will lead the ship and shape the company's future. These profiles build up trust and confidence among those involved in the project by proving that these members have enough leadership, vision, and experience to make it happen.

Each successful company has at its center a dynamic leader with exceptional visionary qualities who sets direction and inspires others to follow suit. Whether this person is an entrepreneur with out-of-the-box ideas or an executive with years of experience under their belt isn't what matters most; it's that they do everything they can to lead the team towards reaching their goals. The leadership style, values, and goals set the tone for any organization—large or small—and help shape its culture, allowing innovation, collaboration, and growth.

Every management team consists of individuals whose skills, experiences, and perspectives collectively benefit the venture. They might be executives specialized in finance, operations, marketing/ sales, or technology; alternatively, there may be specialists responsible for product development or human resources. Nonetheless, they all have qualities that complement one another's strengths so that together, they can tackle challenges head-on while being 100% prepared if things don't go as planned.

Profiles of each member within this group will provide stakeholders with deep insight into their professional background and accomplishments while shedding light on how much each individual has contributed thus far. This information includes details such as past employment history—where did this person start? Educational qualifications—have you studied in your industry? Industry experience—how knowledgeable are you? Achievements: can you name anything significant you've done? By highlighting how well-rounded the team is, entrepreneurs show that they've thought about each individual's talents and what they bring to the table.

It isn't professional achievements that make for a great profile; it's also leadership skills, interpersonal abilities, and strategic thinking; these people will guide the business forward. There may be examples that illustrate members' leadership styles; how they make decisions and inspire those around them will prove their worth even further.

In addition to highlighting individual achievements and qualifications, profiles of the management team may also touch upon their roles and responsibilities within the organization. This includes outlining the specific oversight and decision-making authority areas for each member and their contributions to critical strategic initiatives and projects. By clarifying the roles and responsibilities of the management team, entrepreneurs foster accountability, alignment, and collaboration within the organization, ensuring everyone knows what they have to do.

6.6 Products or Services

Descriptions of your products or services are the foundation upon which your entire business plan is built. These offerings embody what sets your business apart from others in your industry. You may be offering innovative solutions to common problems, or perhaps you boast some unique value and convenience for customers. Either way, a very clear understanding of what you sell will help stakeholders better understand how this venture plans to launch successfully.

In addition to describing these offerings in detail— another thing worth considering is how long they'll be relevant for, as well as how they'll be delivered to market (the service delivery method).

Understanding the delivery process will streamline operations for any service-based company out there.

These two components highlight the operational execution and strategic planning of any given business idea. By detailing features and how an item solves customer's pain points, entrepreneurs demonstrate their ability to meet market demand.

Outlining service delivery proves your foresight and strategic thinking—showing potential partners you've put some thought into adaptation when faced with adjusting to changing market conditions or customer expectations.

Descriptions of Your Products or Services

At the core of every business plan is a detailed description of the products or services that form the center of the venture. This section is vital for communicating the value proposition, unique features, and benefits that set the business apart in the market.

Descriptions of products or services begin by articulating their core value proposition—the primary benefit or solution they provide to their customers. Whether we're talking about solving a problem, filling a need, or enhancing life quality, this proposition communicates the unique value they offer to their clients. By defining it clearly, entrepreneurs create the groundwork for subsequent descriptions by establishing an overarching benefit that all users can expect from their offerings.

Beyond listing these values, some unique features and functionalities may help to distinguish them from any competition. These may include product specifications, technical capabilities, and design elements. The idea here is simple: highlighting distinctive features showcases innovation, creativity, and attention to detail, reinforcing the value proposition in this fierce marketplace.

These descriptions also provide insights into the advantages and benefits customers can expect from these products. These might be tangible things like cost savings, or intangible things such as peace of mind, status, or emotional satisfaction. Through this list, entrepreneurs try to demonstrate their understanding of customer needs, showing off their ability to deliver and resonate with target audiences.

You will also need information on pricing and delivery options, which helps put into context how much quality is being offered and at what cost. The transparency around these facts builds trust with consumers while facilitating well-informed decision-making, eventually making a sale more likely.

Information on Product Life Cycle or Service Delivery Method

The life cycle of a product starts with an idea and then goes through several other iterations before reaching its final form. Each stage has its own set of hurdles and opportunities. The first phase is pure development, which includes researching, testing, and designing the perfect product. After that comes the introduction, where you market, sell, and distribute this new creation to catch some buzz. You've been envisioning the growth stage since you came up with the idea. This is when sales are booming, and production has never been faster. After growth comes maturity, when sales become stable. Then there's nothing left but to either move on or find something new that'll catch people's attention.

Another aspect of a product's life cycle is how it gets delivered to customers' front doors (or whatever delivery method you use). These channels can take many different forms, whether physical or digital. This also includes customer service if anything goes wrong during customers' experience with your business.

The fun begins once you integrate these insights into your business plan, because plans can be explicitly made around specific stages of a product life cycle or service delivery method. This includes enhancing current strategies such as pricing and marketing. They must fall within the boundaries set forth by these insights while keeping customer satisfaction at the forefront. With these things in mind, you'll be able to keep your product relevant and prosperous for years to come.

Any business plan worth its salt must include information about the product life cycle or service delivery method. Entrepreneurs need to understand how products and services will be managed, primarily through their lifecycle and the delivery method. Doing so helps develop strategies that adapt and evolve with an ever-changing marketplace and customer base. With a combination of planning and strategic execution, entrepreneurs can put themselves in the best position to find long-term success and sustainable growth in today's dynamic marketplace,

6.7 Marketing and Sales Strategy

The marketing and sales strategy section serves as the compass guiding you through the ever-evolving market, outlining the strategies and tactics that will drive customer acquisition, revenue generation, and sustainable growth. At its core, this section lays the groundwork for success by defining how a business will attract customers, engage them with their product or service, convert them into clients, generate revenue to fund operations, and ultimately scale out.

This is where you find the in-depth plans for what strategies and tactics your business will employ to reach its target audience, build brand awareness, and drive sales. Whether it be traditional advertising methods or breaking down barriers with direct sales efforts through social media engagement or digital marketing, these plans provide a roadmap for reaching customers and achieving revenue goals when followed correctly. Clear objectives, target audiences, and messaging strategies all need to be defined to ensure every aspect of your marketing strategy is aligned with your overarching goals. The marketing mix concept is an integral part of marketing in general, so naturally, it would be included here too.

The four Ps: product, price, place, and promotion all point towards decisions around product development, such as pricing strategies while using distribution channels and promotional tactics to draw customer interest. By carefully crafting these elements into your next big thing, you can create something that resonates with customers while driving sales by analyzing market trends and competitive dynamics before developing strategies to differentiate yourself.

On top of all of this, we have the sales forecast, which provides us with projections about what future sales numbers might look like based on an analysis of both market demand for our current products or services along with our own sales strategies for products or services. This critical tool for financial planning can then be used to make decisions around production, inventory management, and marketing investments. Entrepreneurs can use this tool to anticipate revenue streams, identify potential bottlenecks or challenges, and develop strategies to mitigate risks and capitalize on opportunities. By analyzing historical sales data, market trends, and customer behavior, you can create a realistic forecast that will allow you to stick with your business's objectives.

We're talking about specific tactics and activities that will be employed to make our goals a reality. These could include details on advertising campaigns, promotional events, sales promotions, lead generation activities, and customer relationship management strategies. By outlining these specific activities, entrepreneurs ensure that their marketing and sales efforts are targeted to measurable goals, which should then be aligned with the overall objective of the business

A business blueprint's marketing and sales strategy section helps bring customers in, increase sales, and make money. Entrepreneurs will do this by clearly defining their marketing and sales plans, saying how they will market their products, and guessing how much money they think they'll make. Through careful planning, precise execution, and constant refinement, entrepreneurs can set their businesses up for a bright future where they grow consistently and make cash. With all that said, the marketplace is constantly changing, so it's essential to be flexible and ready to adapt at any moment.

Defining Your Marketing and Sales Plans

Regarding business planning, the importance of defining comprehensive marketing and sales plans must be considered. These plans become strategic roadmaps that help guide entrepreneurs through the complexities of customer acquisition, brand positioning, and revenue generation. When objectives, strategies, and tactics are clear for entrepreneurs, they ensure their marketing and sales efforts are focused on what they should be.

A deep understanding of the target market is at the core of every marketing plan—those individuals or organizations a business aims to attract and serve. This includes conducting extensive market research to find the demographics of critical customers, along with surveying their preferences, behaviors, and pain points. Can businesses effectively tailor their strategies by segmenting markets into groups based on shared characteristics or needs? It's not about understanding your customers, though; if you want to stay ahead, you also have to keep an eye out for trends in your market.

Once you've defined your target market from your previous work, entrepreneurs have something real to build on. Figuring out how to use this information is where it starts to get fun. What kind of strategies do these people like? What products have performed well for them before? The list goes on.

Sales channels also need some attention when discussing your sales plan. Setting targets as well as training sales teams will take some effort. Once all this is planned, customers should have one cohesive experience after another—smooth sailing until they decide whether they want what we have.

KPIs (Key Performance Indicators) are ways we measure progress on these things, so they need some thought. Some ideas to consider include metrics such as CAC (Customer Acquisition Cost), CLV (Customer Lifetime Value), conversion rates, sales pipeline velocity, and return on investment (ROI). By setting specific goals, entrepreneurs can get a feel for the effect of their marketing on sales, allowing them to adjust.

Marketing Mix and Sales Forecast

A business's marketing mix and sales forecast are crucial for the venture's success. These two key components help guide strategic decision-making, allocate resources efficiently, and drive revenue growth.

The marketing mix, also known as the four Ps—product, price, place, and promotion—is a fundamental framework for creating and implementing marketing strategies. Each element serves a unique purpose in shaping customer experience and influencing purchasing decisions.

Product: Refers to the tangible or intangible benefits that businesses offer customers. This includes more than services; it also involves features, packaging, branding, and additional value-added features. Companies must understand their target market's needs and preferences to develop products that meet or exceed their expectations.

Price: This reflects how much customers are willing to pay for products or services. Pricing strategies can differ depending on competition levels, perceived value (how much value customers think they're getting), cost structure, and demand in certain markets. By closely analyzing customer behavior in specific markets, businesses can find prices that maximize revenue while staying competitive enough to remain profitable.

Place: refers to where products or services are made available to customers. Distribution channels can range from physical stores such as wholesalers and distributors, to digital platforms like websites or mobile apps. The main goal here is finding which distribution channels will work best for your target market so you know that they will see your offering at the right time.

Promotion: involves various selling techniques used to communicate your value proposition with potential customers before persuading them to make a purchase. Examples include advertising campaigns, public relations efforts, and direct mailings. By creating compelling messaging, businesses are able to raise awareness about their offerings, leading to higher interest and conversions.

In addition to defining the marketing mix, businesses must also develop a sales forecast to estimate future sales volumes and revenue. These insights are valuable for planning and allocating resources efficiently. To get started on a sales forecast, you'll need to analyze historical sales data, market trends, and other factors that may impact performance. By identifying patterns, businesses can make more accurate forecasts, leading to improved decisions.

It's important to note that businesses should rely on something other than their historical data because this might lead them in the wrong direction. They should consider factors like market conditions, shifts in consumer preferences, and new competitors or products. Updating these forecasts regularly will allow business owners to adapt quickly while staying competitive against potential threats.

6.8 Funding Request

In the complex world of business planning, the funding request section is critical to achieving entrepreneurial success. This part of the plan is a roadmap for acquiring the financial resources necessary to turn vision into reality and fuel growth. Entrepreneurs provide their financial needs and requests in this section, in addition to other future financial strategies.

At its core, the funding request presents entrepreneurs' capital requirements for starting up, operating, and scaling the business. They need to go through start-up costs, operational expenses, and investment requirements across multiple areas, including product development, marketing, sales, and infrastructure. After quantifying their financial needs concisely but accurately, they can give stakeholders an honest look at how much money it will take for the venture to succeed.

While presenting their financial needs, entrepreneurs must come up with a funding request that specifies where they want their money from. This could be equity financing or crowdfunding platforms, among others. Aligning these requests with what they need from providers shows off their knowledge about strategic visions and financial acumen.

The future planning end encompasses how entrepreneurs expect to control and allocate assets moving forward, so that there is enough support for ongoing operations and company expansion. With detailed projections like budgets or cash flow forecasts, managers know when money will be coming in versus money going out over time. By doing this, they can make informed decisions on resource allocation so that profitability stays high.

In addition to day-to-day operations, money matters, such as managing revenues, are also considered here. Maintaining sustainability requires thinking long-term because market conditions can change rapidly. Not only do you have to check current performance, but you should also forecast future indicators while adapting your strategy. By clearly stating needs and funding requests, entrepreneurs set themselves up to take on investments that align with their goals.

Presenting Your Financial Needs and Funding Request

One of the most essential parts of a business plan is showing how much money you need and how you will get it. This section is the heart of your financial needs. You'll detail what capital you need at every stage of your business: starting up, operating, and growing. By working out these needs precisely, you can then articulate exactly how much money you want to request from investors or lenders.

The first step in assessing financial needs is breaking down all the places where capital will be used in your business. Entrepreneurs will evaluate start-up costs, operational expenses, and investment needs by looking at product development, technology infrastructure, and staffing.

Once entrepreneurs know how much money they need for their businesses, they begin requesting funds from various sources depending on their goals for their company/industry. They might consider equity financing, debt financing, venture capital, angel investors, or crowdfunding platforms. Investors like seeing a customized funding request because it shows that entrepreneurs have done prior research about what kind of investment opportunities are available in their specific market.

It's not enough to ask for money; entrepreneurs must also provide a compelling reason for why someone should give them funds. This includes explaining the market opportunity for their product or service compared to competitors and backing up claims with thorough market research and analysis. The infusion of capital will allow entrepreneurs' companies to reach strategic milestones faster than if they didn't receive any investments, so it's worth noting that developing an argument here could make or break an investor's decision.

Stakeholders don't want vague explanations of what funds will be used for—they want specifics about where each dollar is going, so they feel better about lending money in the first place. With a clear breakdown of initiatives, entrepreneurs can show investors they have a plan and give them peace of mind that their money won't be wasted on unnecessary expenses. This will make stakeholders more inclined to invest in their companies.

Future Financial Planning

In the context of a business plan, future financial planning is like a compass, which allows entrepreneurs to navigate the turbulent and always-shifting marketplace with poise and precision. This critical section outlines strategies for managing financial resources, optimizing revenue streams, and ensuring long-term profitability and sustainability for the venture. By predicting future financial performance, spotting potential risks and opportunities, and developing strategies that can mitigate obstacles and capitalize on chances, entrepreneurs can lay a solid foundation for their business.

At its core, future financial planning involves creating detailed projections. Entrepreneurs estimate sales volume, expenses budgeting, and cash flow projections to understand what's ahead. They don't pull these numbers out of thin air; they utilize historical data and market trends to make them as realistic and aligned with their goals as possible. With this information, forecasting performance becomes simple, allowing businesses to gain insights into potential revenue streams, cost structures, and cash flow dynamics.

Another critical aspect of future financial planning is identifying potential risks and uncertainties that may impact on the company's health or finances. These can be anything from changing regulations or economic downturns to operational issues or supply chain disruptions. Once these problems are known, entrepreneurs can develop contingency plans that will help minimize any damage caused by them.

Avoiding disaster isn't enough for most businesses—they want to strive for success, too. That's why future financial planning also encompasses strategies for optimizing revenue streams while maximizing profitability. Generally, businesses do this by expanding markets into new territories or launching new products or services. Other ways include trying to improve efficiency, so costs go down, leading to those profitability margins going up.

Beyond day-to-day operations, it also takes capital to make a business work. That's why future financial planning also involves assessing the structure and financing options of the company to ensure optimal use. They might look at what kind of loans they have or even go out and try to find other sources like venture capitalists. Once everything is in place, though, it allows businesses to minimize their costs, keep some flexibility, and position themselves for success over the long term.

Future financial planning within a business plan is essential for ensuring that a venture can survive the long haul while also being profitable. By creating projections, identifying risk, opportunities, optimizing revenue streams, and assessing financing structures, entrepreneurs can build a set of strategies that will allow them to wade through complex waters with ease.

6.9 Financial Projections

Financial projections hold more weight than most projections within a business's blueprint. This part of the plan serves as its economic backbone, giving stakeholders insight into a company's viability and sustainability. Using intricate data from projections and statements, entrepreneurs can provide a look at what a company's financial health will look like in the future. They can use break-even analysis to assess a company's position and to properly inform decision-making and strategic planning.

The heart of this section is the depiction of financial data through projections and statements. You can use historical data, market research, and industry benchmarks to forecast future revenue, expenses, and cash flows. Projections then give us a detailed view of how well a company is likely to do over time. Many people make decisions based on these projections alone, so they need to be taken very seriously.

As well as break-even analysis, entrepreneurs also analyze key ratios, such as liquidity solvency and profitability metrics, to get an idea of what value they are creating for stakeholders. Through this analysis, they will be able to evaluate things such as gross profit margin, and debt-to-equity ratio, allowing them to gauge where they stand financially at any given time.

The idea of financial planning might have you thinking about when businesses invest in something new, like expanding into new markets or investing in product development, but that's not the main point. You use these projections for initiatives that involve optimizing operational efficiency. When business owners know what they're going into before doing so, they can drive confidently forward, resulting in success down the line.

Depicting Financial Data through Projections and Statements

In a business plan, the most dynamic part is usually the financial information. It uses projections and statements to help stakeholders determine how financially healthy and viable that venture is. This section should provide an in-depth snapshot of the financial performance that is expected to happen over a certain period, offering insights into cash flow dynamics and expense management. By creating these detailed predictions, entrepreneurs can guide their businesses toward growth and success.

The process starts with previous financial data, such as income statements, balance sheets, and cash flow statements. Entrepreneurs look back on this information to find trends or patterns that they can learn from. This could be figuring out which products are selling better than others or what factors may have led to their business doing poorly in one year. If they know what has gone wrong, they will have an easier time preventing it from happening again.

Once past data has been analyzed, entrepreneurs will use forecasting techniques to understand future performance. This could involve examining market demand or pricing strategies for potential sales projections, which would help entrepreneurs estimate future expenses and revenue more accurately.

Entrepreneurs don't stop at estimating revenue, though—they also create balance sheet projections. Balance sheet projections show assets, liabilities, and equity over time, so entrepreneurs can see whether things look good or not quite right in the future. If everything has looked great on paper for around six months, but recent changes haven't been positive for the company's liquidity (cash in hand), solvency (ability to pay debts), or stability, it would be best if a new strategy wasn't implemented.

They also develop cash flow projections because it's essential to consider when money is coming in and when it is going out (and how much). This way, entrepreneurs can anticipate when cash needs may become more demanding, and whether they will be able to make their financial obligations.

Incorporating all these projections into the business plan will give it more structure and make it easier to understand. Researchers have found that tables, charts, graphs, and narrative descriptions are the most effective tools to illustrate key financial metrics in a way that is best understood by anyone who looks at them.

Break-even Analysis and Financial Position

When it comes to business plans, a break-even analysis and financial position evaluation are essential for checking profitability, managing costs, and ensuring that the business is sustainable. By conducting these critical analyses, entrepreneurs and stakeholders can determine whether their companies can cover expenses, how much profit can be made, and whether they're on a solid financial footing in the marketplace. The critical point in the break-even analysis comes from determining when total revenues equal total costs, meaning no profit or loss. This point serves as a massive milestone to let entrepreneurs know what level of sales or income is needed so that the business can cover its fixed and variable costs. When they do this analysis, they'll gain insights into what volume sales should be, pricing strategies, and cost structures that would drive success.

The whole process begins with entrepreneurs being able to identify all the different types of fixed and variable costs related to their business. Once these have been locked down, entrepreneurs can calculate more accurately where their next move should be.

For example, to get exact numbers, use this formula:

Break-even point = Fixed Costs / (Selling Price per Unit—Variable Costs per Unit).

Knowing exactly how many units need to be sold allows entrepreneurs to assess their performance up until now and see where improvements could be made.

Besides knowing about your own break-even point, it's also good to understand where you stand financially compared to other ventures in the marketplace. To do this, you'd analyze vital financial ratios such as liquidity ratios, solvency ratios (e.g., debt-to-equity ratio, interest coverage ratio), and profitability metrics (e.g., gross profit margin, net profit margin). By assessing these different metrics, entrepreneurs can identify how well they'll be able to meet short-term obligations, manage debts and generate profits.

Knowing your business's financial position also allows you to understand where you stand in the market. A current could show promising signs of liquidity but also too many idle assets that need to be used. Meanwhile, a low debt-to-equity ratio could show underutilization of leverage or an excessively conservative financing strategy. This information lets entrepreneurs make informed decisions by optimizing their financial position and maximizing shareholder value. When entrepreneurs get all these insights back, it gives them the power to inform strategic decisions about their business's future. It's time to figure out what they're doing right and wrong so that they can focus on doing more things right. If the break-even point is too high, they can look at opportunities for reducing costs or increasing sales volume to ensure long-term sustainability. At the same time, if there are liquidity constraints or solvency issues, they'll know it's time to improve cash flow, strengthening their business positions financially.

6.10 Refining Your Business Plan

Refining your business plan from an idea to something actionable is crucial. It's the step that separates the people who talk about it from those who do it. In this section, we'll go over the process of reviewing, editing, and polishing your plan so that it accurately represents the vision you have for your venture. We'll also touch on tailoring it to different audiences, because some people want to hear everything you say.

The process starts with a review of what you already have. It would help if you went through each section with a fine-tooth comb, analyzing its clarity and questioning its consistency. You'll need to consider whether what you've written will get you closer to your goals and whether there's any missing information or mistakes in general. The goal here is simple: get the bad stuff out so that we can replace it with good things.

After reviewing comes editing, and now we're getting closer to being done with this. Ensuring everything in the document is comprehensible sums up this step, but there are other things we need to consider. We don't want anyone reading our plan and thinking they're back in science class; keep jargon out of here. People also like short messages, so ensure critical concepts are communicated effectively. After all that is said and done, we can polish it all up into something shiny. Adding pictures helps illustrate thoughts faster than words ever could. You also need to check that grammar is okay, and formatting is clear.

In addition to our overall polish, we also need to ensure our different versions aren't copies. For example, we won't pitch our investor partner document during a meeting with potential investors. Everyone has interests and priorities, so try customizing your pitch to address their needs.

The process is about making the document better than what you started with. Through careful refinement and customization, you'll turn your vision into something tangible. For now, though, it's time to get to work.

Tailoring the Plan to Different Audiences

There's no such thing as a one-size-fits-all business plan. Entrepreneurs know they need to tailor their message to different audiences to get the best results. Whether you pitch investors, partners, or internal stakeholders, the goal is always to make a connection and get support.

When it comes to investors, they like to see numbers. Focusing on your business's value proposition and growth potential can help them see dollar signs. You'll also want to highlight critical financial and revenue projections. And don't forget about scalability and competitive advantage—these buzzwords attract significant investment. You'll be more likely to get funding by emphasizing what they care about most.

Potential partners require a different approach. Instead of trying to show how profitable your venture is, you need to demonstrate strategic alignment. Show them how their partnership will benefit both parties in terms of profit and growth potential. But don't forget that collaboration is a two-way street—make sure you showcase your own track record and capabilities so they can also trust you. With this approach, you'll foster credibility and find allies who can help grow your business.

Internal stakeholders like employees or board members have different concerns entirely. They want to know how your plan aligns with their goals within the organization, if at all. Make it clear what each stakeholder needs for the plan to succeed; this way, everyone knows where they fit in the puzzle right at the beginning. Show them how each role contributes to success; people are more likely to buy in if they feel valued from day one.

Beyond content aligning with objectives and culture, entrepreneurs must also adjust tone when necessary; language presentation matters when trying to appeal to an audience's interests. What might sound appealing or formal in one meeting may not sound that way in another. A persuasive and conversational tone can sell the audience on your business, while a more analytical one may seem too dry to some.

Different formats should be considered when presenting different plans. For example, you won't want to present investors with a 100-page document. Instead, provide them with an easily digestible executive summary or pitch deck highlighting your business's key features. By contrast, internal stakeholders will require more information, so don't be afraid to go into depth with their documents— it's what they'll expect. By adjusting your format for each audience accordingly, you avoid the confusion of overwhelming them or missing out on something important.

Tailoring the business plan to different audiences is a must. Doing so will ensure its impact is maximized and it stays relevant and effective as a strategic tool. You can increase buy-in by changing the content, messaging, tone, language, format, and medium with which you present your idea to resonate with investors, partners, and other stakeholders or audiences. It's all about communicating effectively to gain support for your venture. Using this strategic approach can help you communicate the value proposition of your business's vision and strategy.

6.11 Presenting Your Business Plan

Revealing your business plan for the first time can be nerve-wracking, but it's also an exciting way to showcase all the hard work you've put into creating and designing something fabulous. This section will help you understand how to give the perfect presentation to appeal to anyone interested in investing, joining your team, or offering constructive criticism. Going up and presenting information may seem like a simple task, but there's so much more that goes into it than that. Entrepreneurs have one job when delivering a business plan presentation: get everyone listening and super invested in what they're hearing. You should want investors and members of your board alike to leave with goosebumps because they are so excited about what they heard. And sometimes, that'll require you to go off-script with some high-energy storytelling—trust me, it works.

Diversifying your approach has merit. Your audience will respond better to pretty charts or real-life stories about others succeeding through similar ventures. It's all about figuring out how to make people think 'wow' at every turn. You also need to be ready for any questions or feedback. The ability to answer inquiries without hesitation helps you to come across as knowledgeable and trustworthy. No matter how great your idea is now, there's always going to be room for improvement further on down the line. It would be wise to not only accept feedback but also actively seek it out. Whether someone has a suggestion or wants clarification on something from earlier in the meeting, make sure to implement a culture of acceptance and continuous learning. Your business plan will change and evolve over time, but it will always move in the right direction if you follow these strategies.

Pitching your business plan is a big deal. It's like the moment you cross from the amateur to professional level in entrepreneurship. Because of that, it requires a lot of prep work. One must plan, prepare for every question, and practice to execute the presentation flawlessly. By doing this, entrepreneurs have a higher chance of giving a compelling pitch that resonates with people and gets them to support the venture.

Strategies for Effective Presentation

Your audience is vital. If your message doesn't resonate with what they want, it will be hard to get them on board. Research comes first; investigate their background, preferences, and expectations so that you can speak their specific language. When you do this, your engagement will increase tenfold.

Next comes storytelling—something everyone loves. It's about weaving a narrative highlighting the problem(s) you're solving with your business venture. Doing this right off the bat conveys the essence of your vision. Visuals are always a must in presentations. Incorporating slides and various other visual aids helps illustrate your business's goal in a different light and perspective.

Keep things dynamic. Maintaining eye contact, when possible, establishes a strong connection; gestures and vocal variation ensure people don't nod off. Organization matters. Nobody likes a mishmash of information thrown at them all at once. Breaking things down bit by bit into easy-to-digest chunks ensures people understand each point better before moving on to the next one.

Last but not least, engage with your audience throughout the presentation. Ask for any response, so long as they remain engaged and attentive, whether it's questions or comments about their thoughts. Fostering a dialogue creates an environment where both parties feel heard; it also helps enhance any understanding they may need before fully committing or supporting whatever you have presented. It is crucial to be ready to adapt and turn your presentation upside down, depending on how the audience reacts. Adjust and respond quickly to their engagement, interest, or understanding. Be ready to change your pace, content, or style on the fly to keep them engaged with what you have to say. Just keep the audience interested and ensure they resonate with your message effectively by responding quickly and flexibly.

Valuable presentation strategies are essential for delivering your venture's clear vision, plan, and potential into stakeholders' minds. By knowing who you are talking to, creating an inspiring narrative, utilizing visual aids well, being confident throughout delivery—even if you're freaking out—structuring your presentation logically, getting them involved actively, and being ready for feedback.

Preparing for Questions and Feedback

Presenting a business idea isn't simply giving a speech; it's about conversing, discussing concerns, and using feedback to improve the plan. The ability to anticipate questions and prepare for feedback is vital, because this will allow you to show stakeholders that you are ready, confident, and responsive.

The first step in preparing for Q&A is reviewing the business plan. Look at each section in depth to determine potential inquiries or conflicts. Pay particular attention to market analysis, financial projections, and strategic initiatives. The more you can understand and explain the content behind these sections of your plan, the better suited you will be to answering questions. When anticipating questions and feedback, bear in mind that investors may want to know about financials, while customers may ask about user interaction with your product or service. To give tailored responses, it's essential to be prepared to answer from multiple perspectives.

Each response should be concise but detailed. Be clear, without being vague or evasive; support answers with data when available. This way, they will be confident in your knowledge of the subject. To ensure things go smoothly when it comes time for a Q&A session, practice beforehand. Responding on the spot could lead to nonsensical replies that sound uneducated. Refine messaging by rehearsing what you'd say until there is no room left for improvement.

During the presentation, it's important to create an environment where questions are encouraged. This opens conversation between both parties, strengthening understanding of ideas and building trust between everyone involved. Feedback is crucial when evaluating how well your presentation was received by an audience. It can help point out obvious strengths and weaknesses within your pitch that might otherwise have gone unnoticed. Use this feedback to enhance your plan moving forward. There's always room for improvement, no matter how strong a pitch you think you gave.

Remember, this isn't just about pitching a good idea; it's also about proving that you know what you're doing and deserve stakeholder support.

Chapter 7

Navigating Legalities: Business Formation and Compliance

The legal framework for businesses is complex but ignoring it could land you in some hot water later down the line. Better safe than sorry, right? Determining your business's structure is one of the first steps toward becoming a legally compliant company. It determines things like liability protection, taxation rules, and governance rules. This chapter provides guidance on selecting the most appropriate structure based on ownership, liability protection goals, tax treatment options, and regulatory requirements.

While this guide aims to give you the tools you need to take care of many legal matters, there will be times when outside help becomes necessary. Laws change frequently, so you'll want someone keeping an eye out for new legislation that could impact your operations or industry standards, as well as someone who can help you navigate complex legal situations, should one arise throughout the life cycle of your venture. Please don't hesitate to reach out if you need guidance or assistance from legal advisors or consultants.

7.1 Introduction to Business Legalities

Entering the world of entrepreneurship is an exciting voyage filled with promise and opportunity. As the gears start turning, business owners must remember that starting a business involves complex legalities. Knowing how to handle these hurdles and obstacles is essential, from agreement signing to regulatory compliance. Complying with laws and regulations is important, as failure to do so can lead new businesses to fines or, even worse, a lawsuit. Being familiar with industry-specific laws from the get-go will help ensure there are no legal risks involved right at the beginning. By doing this, entrepreneurs guarantee their company a solid foundation and pave its path toward lasting success. Getting a general idea of what legal necessities your startup needs will help you stay on top of things throughout its lifespan. From the registration process to risk management, you'll have insights into issues you may encounter in your journey as an entrepreneur. Structuring business entities appropriately and going over contracts thoroughly are some ways you can ensure safety moving forward. Entrepreneurship is full of endless possibilities. I understand how hard it must be to focus on legality rather than creativity when building something new. But with my guidance, I hope you can put those worries aside and continue growing without hesitation. The road ahead looks long, but you know it'll be worth it. Trust me when I say that taking care of the legalities as early as possible will save you a headache later.

Importance of Understanding Legal Requirements

Understanding legal requirements is crucial when you are starting or expanding your business, but it can also take time to grasp. Legal compliance is the foundation of a safe and stable environment for any venture. It provides the structure that helps businesses operate, make decisions, and interact with stakeholders. By fully understanding legal obligations, you can reduce risks, protect your interests, and build long-term sustainability and success.

When you understand these responsibilities, you can comply with laws that govern business operations, saving yourselves from hefty fines, penalties, or even the closure of your business. Ignorance of these regulations can lead to other severe consequences, such as lawsuits or reputational damage. Because of this, you must invest time into learning about specific legal obligations in your type of business.

With knowledge of employment laws, you will know how to create fair and compliant job offers, so there will be no room for labor disputes in the first place. Similarly, knowing how intellectual property works allows you to legally protect your products, giving you a competitive advantage. On top of everything else, understanding legal requirements is essential to protect assets and interests. Businesses carry financial risks daily, but adhering to legal principles significantly reduces exposure. Businesses create contracts every day, whether it involves clients or employees. By following contract law, you can ensure your agreements are legally binding and prevent disputes. Finally, by showing customers you abide by consumer protection laws, you gain trust, ultimately reducing any damage from lawsuits.

Strong knowledge of the law will create a culture built on transparency within your organization, which will help you grow quicker than those around you who lack this strength. Employees working under leadership who prioritize integrity are more likely to follow suit with ethical conduct and responsible business practices. External stakeholders like investors will observe your commitment to transparency and be more inclined to work with you instead of your competitors.

For entrepreneurs to continue their growth in a steady legal fashion, they must understand the requirements that come with it. Knowledge in these areas will keep them on track and allow for minimal risks. By doing this, you can build yourself up as an authority within your industry.

Overview of Legal Considerations for New Businesses

Formation and Structure

Choosing the proper structure for your business is one of the earliest decisions you'll make and one of the most critical ones. How you structure your business can determine liabilities, tax obligations, and governance requirements. Most companies have one of four main structures: sole proprietorships, partnerships, corporations, and limited liability companies (LLCs). Entrepreneurs should evaluate their options based on ownership rights, liability protection, tax implications, and operational flexibility, each of which has its own pros and cons.

Registration and Licensing

Once your business is structured correctly, it's time to register it. Entrepreneurs must register with local government authorities and obtain appropriate licenses and permits relevant to their business. Registration requirements vary hugely, depending on factors like type of business, location, and industry. If owners fail to do this, they can face fines or penalties or, worse yet, more serious legal consequences further down the road. Do some thorough research early on so you're not caught in any sticky situations later on.

Intellectual Property Protection

Securing intellectual property (IP) assets creates a solid foundation for safeguarding unique ideas, innovations, and creations from being stolen or used by competitors. These assets may include trademarks, copyrights, patents, and trade secrets. Entrepreneurs need to identify these IP assets and then enact steps to legally protect them through registration mechanisms such as trademark registration. By doing this, you will be able to prevent unauthorized use from others, thus preserving competitive advantage in marketplaces.

Contracts and Agreements

Legal agreements are essential when defining business relationships' rights, obligations, and expectations. Entrepreneurs must be diligent and take all necessary steps to protect their interests and mitigate risks. Common types of contracts include customer agreements, supplier contracts, employment contracts, and partnership agreements. Withdrawing a little bit and becoming calculated is crucial at this step because you don't want to put yourself in any vulnerable positions. It's best for entrepreneurs to seek legal advice when drafting or negotiating these contracts as they can help ensure clarity, enforceability, and compliance with applicable laws.

Regulatory Compliance

Following rules, regulations, and industry standards is necessary for every business. This includes areas like taxation, employment, consumer protection, and data privacy. Entrepreneurs must stay informed about these topics if they want their company to avoid issues down the road. Implementing policies and procedures will play a massive part in ensuring everything runs smoothly, so it's essential to have this thought through early on.

Risk Management and Insurance

Identifying and managing risks will be vital in protecting yourself financially. By assessing potential risks, you can implement strategies that allow you to prevent them from happening later in your journey and mitigate the associated risks. You know what they say; 'better safe than sorry.' Obtaining appropriate insurance coverage, such as general liability insurance, will provide more protection against unforeseen events and liabilities, which could save your ass later.

Corporate Governance and Compliance:

When running a new business, there are many legal hoops to jump through. From registering the company to creating shareholder agreements, each step is essential in its own way. It's easy to overlook these things with everything else going on around you. The unfortunate truth is that doing so may lead to some pretty big problems down the line.

You should take key steps early on to avoid these issues. Building a strong corporate governance foundation can go a long way in ensuring success and sustainability. You may not have heard of this before, but it's as simple as establishing policies, procedures, and structures designed to oversee and manage your business responsibly. Having a good board of directors and shareholder agreement can also help ensure compliance with all relevant laws.

Moreover, strong internal controls can help detect unethical behavior. It all sounds complicated, and it can be, but that doesn't mean you're destined for failure if you don't get everything done correctly right away. Make sure you're aware of what needs to be done moving forward and how important it is for your future growth. By getting advice from qualified professionals now, you'll be better prepared for whatever comes next when things start growing. Remember the little things when you are working on your new business venture. Caring for those today will set you up for success tomorrow.

7.2 Choosing the Right Business Structure

When it comes to starting a business, choosing the perfect structure is vital. It might sound like a pretty easy task, but the truth is that there are tons of options and factors you need to consider. To start off with, you have tax implications, liability protection, operational flexibility, and regulatory compliance. This section will focus on helping you choose an optimal business model that suits your needs and explore comparison charts for companies.

Finding the proper business framework takes time because you must analyze various factors such as business objectives, risk tolerance levels, plans for growth, and regulatory requirements. From sole proprietorships and partnerships to corporations and limited liability companies, each entity type has its own ownership, governance, taxes, and liability rules.

Weighing the pros and cons of each entity will help guide you on what's best for your venture, i.e., do you need simplicity or operational flexibility? Do they provide liability protection? How are they taxed? While this may sound daunting, consulting legal & financial advisors will do wonders.

Once you've checked all those boxes, it's time to get started. Registering your business with authorities is a necessity if you want to be legit, so don't skip it. After that, make sure you obtain any permits or licenses needed. Once these steps are completed, it's important to keep up with governance structures and compliance procedures so that you maintain your legally formed entity properly.

Picking out the right structure can sometimes be as hard as choosing what clothes to wear in the morning. But let me tell you, once you find one that aligns perfectly with your goals, everything gets easier from there. Through strategic planning based on careful consideration, entrepreneurs can navigate complexities with confidence and lay the groundwork for sustainable growth and prosperity.

Sole Proprietorships:

A sole proprietorship is an easy way for someone to own a small business. It is straightforward to establish and manage, so it doesn't take too much effort from you. Others can join in if they want, but all decisions are ultimately up to the owner. However, the lack of separation between personal and business assets means that you, as the owner, have unlimited personal liability for your business's debts.

Partnerships:

This involves two or more people joining together to operate a single business. There are two main types of partnerships: general partnerships and limited partnerships. A general partnership means that any debt or obligation falls equally on all partners involved, regardless of their individual contributions. A limited partnership consists of general partners who manage the business and limited partners who contribute capital but have limited liability for business debts.

Corporations:

Corporations are exciting compared to other types because they're seen as separate legal entities from their owners and shareholders. This allows the shareholders access to 'limited liability protection.' This means that if things go south in your business journey, your personal assets cannot be claimed by lenders or to pay obligations for debts or lawsuits.

Limited Liability Companies (LLCs):

As mentioned previously, LLCs offer a balance between limited liability protection and operational flexibility. They are often used by startups or small businesses that may require extra care in those two areas. One big plus is that LLCs offer 'pass-through taxation,' which means that profits and losses earned by your business are passed down to you and reported on their tax returns. This can save a lot of money.

Considerations for Choosing the Right Business Entity:

When deciding on what type of entity you want to go with, you should consider ownership, liability protection, taxation, governance and operational needs. Sole proprietorships and partnerships may be appealing, because they are simple and flexible, but beware, as they do not protect your personal assets in times of debt. Corporations will always protect your personal assets from being sold off if your business falls into debt or a lawsuit, but it does come at the cost of double taxing you when it comes to taxes. LLCs offer a balance between both sides of this table.

At the end of the day, all decisions should be based on how big or small your new company will be and what goals you have set for yourself, in both the short term and long term. It is essential to take time to evaluate the risks each structure brings before making any fast moves.

How to Choose the Appropriate Business Structure for Your Needs

Selecting the proper business structure is a significant decision that affects your venture's legal, financial, and operational aspects. With different options available, each with its advantages and considerations, it's essential to analyze your specific needs and goals when deciding on the most suitable structure for your business. Here are vital factors to consider when looking for the appropriate business structure:

Ownership and Control:

Think about how many owners you want for your business or if you wish to find a partner. Sole proprietorships and partnerships give owners full control over decision-making while keeping things simple and flexible. Corporations and LLCs offer a more formal structure, with shareholders or members sharing ownership.

Liability Protection:

Evaluate what level of liability protection you need. Sole proprietorships and partnerships expose owners to unlimited personal liability for business debts. Corporations and LLCs provide limited protection, protecting owners' assets in most cases.

Tax Implications:

Make sure you understand the tax implications of your structure. Sole proprietorships and partnerships pass profits directly to personal tax returns, while corporations get taxed twice at the corporate and shareholder levels. LLCs let the owner choose between pass-through or corporate taxation.

Operational Flexibility:

Think about how much flexibility you need to run your operations smoothly. Partnerships have minimal regulatory requirements while still being simple. Corporations and LLCs have more governance demands, such as annual meetings, recordkeeping, and compliance filings.

Growth & Funding:

Consider where your funding will come from and any growth plans. Corporations are preferred by businesses seeking external funding through the sale of stock to investors. Small businesses may find LLCs attractive due to their flexible management structures.

Regulatory Compliance:

Understand all the different regulatory requirements that come with these structures, so that you can make sure everything is done correctly down the line. Corporations and LLCs have state-specific filing procedures, such as articles of incorporation or organization, whereas sole proprietorships and partnerships have fewer but still need to comply with local licensing, and tax requirements.

Long-Term Goals:

Consider your long-term goals and exit strategy. Make sure that the structure you choose aligns with everything you plan to do, such as growth, succession planning, selling, and going public.

Professional Advice:

Don't hesitate to seek professional help during this process. The different structures are complex, and it helps to get advice from somebody who knows what they're talking about. Attorneys, accountants, or business advisors can provide valuable insights and ensure compliance with legal and regulatory requirements.

Considering these factors and seeking professional help when needed gives you the best chance of making an informed decision that fits your needs. The choice will significantly affect your business's operations, taxation, liability, and growth potential. Take your time to think about these things before choosing a path.

The Process of Forming a Legal Business Entity

There are few things more complex than legal jargon. Understanding the process of forming a legal business entity can be mind-boggling. By following these steps and considering key details, your business can be compliant and on solid ground.

Selecting The Right Business Name:

Once you know what kind of business structure you want, it's time to give your baby an awesome name. Ensure it's catchy and fitting but ensure someone else isn't using it. Look up state regulations to be safe.

Register the Business Name:

Remember, the name should be memorable, reflect the brand identity, and comply with state regulations. Fill out whatever documents your state or local government asks for, so it becomes real. And don't forget—you want this name forever, so make sure it doesn't infringe on existing trademarks or copyrights. When you've chosen a name, there's still lots of work left to do before you start printing logos on hats and slapping them on customers' heads willy-nilly, but don't worry—that day will come. The next step is registering your name with government authorities that oversee that sort of thing—this typically means filing a DBA or fictitious name registration with either local or state government entities.

Prepare and File Formation Documents:

Just when you thought the worst was behind you, here comes more paperwork. Fill out all the necessary forms associated with the business structure you have chosen. Articles of incorporation for corporations or articles of organization for LLCs require all kinds of basic info about your new venture, such as its name, address, and owners.

Obtain Necessary Permits and Licenses:

Tackling permits and licenses is another necessary chore. The specific requirements depend on exactly where your business falls within these categories: industry type (is it a restaurant or a microgreens grower?), location (is it in or out of the city?), and how you plan to operate (will you need engineers on staff?). Figure all this out and start applying.

Comply with Tax Requirements:
Nobody gets away with avoiding taxes except for maybe blood-sucking billion-dollar corporations. But that's an entirely different issue. Ensure you're doing everything with the book, because no one wants to deal with Uncle Sam's wrath.

Establish Governance Structure:
It feels like we've done a million things already, but trust me, there's plenty more ahead. This is the time to establish governance structures to manage the business as efficiently as possible. Bylaws for corporations, operating agreements for LLCs, or partnership agreements for partnerships will outline everyone's rights, responsibilities, and decision-making processes.

Maintain Compliance and Good Standing:
Once your business is formed and established, it's time to think about maintenance, which sounds terrifying, but we can't stop now. To keep your legal status in good standing, follow these steps: annual filing requirements, tax payments, and permit renewals. If you fall behind, you will see your whole operation go down the drain with fines, penalties, or loss of privileges.

Setting up a legal business involves several key steps and factors you need to consider. You must follow the law and have a solid foundation for your business. With professional support and careful planning, you can get through this process and build an enterprise that's both successful and on the right side of the law.

7.3 Registration and Licenses

Regulations and licensing requirements imposed by federal, state, and local governments are applied across different industries. These licenses regarding health and safety standards or industry-specific regulations are crucial. You'll find all kinds of permits that differ from one another based on the location or type of activities that will be conducted. If you have a food-based company, health permits are needed, as well as food-handling permits. Construction companies need permit building blocks, as well as environmental ones. The process of acquiring these licenses can be confusing, so entrepreneurs must conduct their own research. Identifying which license or permit applies is essential for avoiding legal issues and penalties later. Following this research, you may find that certain documentation, such as applications or fees, may be needed for submission approval. Depending on the jurisdiction, some can be obtained online through portals, while others require an in-person visit to government offices or regulatory agencies. And yes, some prerequisites are required before approval is granted.

Registration isn't a one-time thing—it requires ongoing work that could extend throughout your entire career as an entrepreneur. Renewals and updates must be made periodically to ensure continued compliance with regulations. Depending on where your business is located, this might mean updating information or paying fees. Double-check everything, ask professionals for help when needed, and stay informed about regulatory changes to keep your business in tip-top shape.

The Basics of Business Registration

It's the first step in getting your business up and running, but it can be a doozy. Business registration seems cut and dry: formalize the entity, pick a name, and fill out some forms. But there are many moving parts to it all.

And knowing what those are is crucial for anyone looking to make their entrepreneurial dreams come true.

Choosing the Right Business Structure: There's no one-size-fits-all when it comes to choosing how your business will be structured. Sole proprietorship, partnership, corporation—these are the most common choices, and each has its own set of implications for taxation, liability, ownership, and governance. You need to look at each carefully before making any decisions.

Selecting a Business Name: Once you've landed on your structure, it's time to give that bad boy a name. This is often easier said than done — —finding the perfect balance between unique and fitting can be difficult. The name should be memorable, reflect the brand identity, and comply with state regulations. And don't forget — —you want this name forever, so make sure it doesn't infringe on existing trademarks or copyrights.

Registering the Business Name: You've got the name picked out, but there's still lots of work left to do before you start printing logos on hats and slapping them on customers' heads willy-nilly, but don't worry — —that day will come. The next step is registering your name with government authorities that oversee that sort of thing - —this typically means filing a DBA or fictitious name registration with either local or state government entities.

Completing Necessary Paperwork: Now that your new company has an official title, you must fill out all sorts of legal documents before regulators take you seriously as a business owner; and before you can open those business accounts. What exactly you'll need depends on your chosen structure and the location in which you're operating. Articles of incorporation are required for corporations, and articles of organization are needed for LLCs. These documents include details about the business, such as its name, address, and ownership structure.

Obtaining an Employer Identification Number (EIN): On top of registering your name and filling out all that paperwork, entrepreneurs may also need to obtain an Employer Identification Number (EIN) from the IRS. This number is unique to businesses and is used for tax reporting purposes. It's necessary if your company has employees or operates as a corporation or partnership.

Registering for State and Local Taxes: It doesn't matter what type of business you're in—you will eventually have to pay taxes. Depending on where your business is located and what it does precisely, different types of taxes must be registered for sales, income, and payroll. Make sure you get this all squared away early on, so you don't find yourself on the wrong side of Uncle Sam.

Necessary Licenses and Permits for Various Business Types

Regardless of what business sector you work in, or how big your company is, it's always going to be under strict regulations that require legal attention. One way to make sure you're adhering to these rules is by acquiring the right licenses and permits that will allow you to operate your business safely. In this section we'll cover a broad range of these license types that are required across various industries.

Professional Certifications: To practice professionally within their industry; lawyers, doctors, accountants, engineers, and real estate agents must all have professional certifications. These certificates are issued by state licensing boards or regulatory agencies. Requirements often include minimum educational standards along with being trained on specific topics for a decided amount of time.

Business Licenses: No matter what type of business they are, most businesses will need some sort of general business license or permit to legally operate. These licenses are issued by local governments or municipalities based on different factors such as location, industry, and activity level. They regulate how businesses conduct themselves within an area and generate revenue for local government operations along the way.

Health and Safety Certification: Some businesses, such as food services providers, hospitals, clinics, childcare services and beauty salons, and shops, need health permits. Obviously, this makes sense due to the nature of their product offerings. They also help enforce sanitation standards.

Environmental Certification: If your business produces anything toxic, you're going to need an environmental certification. Most small businesses don't fall into this category. But if you do produce waste in one way, shape or form, you'll want to get yourself familiar with the local laws around emissions so that you can properly dispose of anything harmful to the environment.

Alcohol and Tobacco Licenses: I don't think anyone would be surprised to learn that these two industries have some pretty strict licensing requirements… But did you know that they're regulated by state and federal agencies? There's no wonder it takes so long for any new alcohol-related business owners to get their business up and running…

Building and Construction Certifications: If your business involves any kind of construction, it'll need a building permit. It doesn't matter if you are working on residential or commercial projects—both require a permit.

Transportation Certification: Any company that uses vehicles for transportation services such as taxis or Ubers will need to make sure their drivers have proper certifications. The best part about this is that once your driver gets their certification it can also be used anywhere else, they go.

Specialized Industry Certifications: Some professions require certain types of training to operate legally. For example, an insurance agent who works with securities will need different certifications than a lawyer who works for the gaming commission. Make sure you know what type of license applies specifically to you. As stated, there are many regulations small businesses must abide by when setting up shop, but having the right licenses is definitely at the top of the list. If you are unsure how to obtain one, there's no harm in asking for help from someone who does—even if it costs more money than expected.

7.4 Understanding and Managing Taxes

A company can't be successful without understanding taxes. They are vital for a business's monetary situation and affect everything from profit to keeping up with strict regulations. Each different legal structure has its own obligations and considerations. Regardless of whether your company is a sole proprietorship or an LLC, knowing the structure's obligations is key for compliance and managing finances effectively. Different structures have different tax treatments, like inconsistent tax rates, deductible options, and reporting requirements. By understanding what kind of implications your chosen business structure has, you will be able to make educated choices toward optimizing your position.

Outside of income and payroll taxes, sales tax is the most common tax that companies encounter. It gets levied on products and services' sales, as the name implies, and usually gets collected for state or local governments. Knowing your sales tax obligations such as nexus requirements is critical to follow if you want to avoid penalties. Another significant consideration for companies is income tax, since it impacts cash flow and profitability. The net income that a business entity earns is subject to business income tax, which then goes through federal, state, and local laws. Knowing about deductions, credits, and reporting requirements will help minimize liability in after-tax profits. Payroll taxes include different taxes deducted from employee wages along with contributions from employers like Social Security or Medicare. Keeping track of these calculations in a timely manner while keeping complaints can save tons of potential costs if done right. Managing taxes effectively calls for using good accounting practices with financial records being always kept well organized. Accountants play a huge part in helping businesses with their planning, compliance, and reporting when it comes to taxes alone. They also aid clients by looking into financial data while preparing returns, and giving advice that will reduce liability. Accounting software and systems have a big role in making record-keeping more accurate, financial analysis more precise, and tax reporting easier to read. Using technology to its full potential can make the process go smoother for everyone involved, while keeping up with obligations.

Key Tax Obligations for Different Business Structures

Various legal structures carry distinct tax obligations and considerations for businesses. Understanding these requirements is crucial in efficiently managing a business's financial affairs and ensuring compliance.

Sole Proprietorship: In this structure, the owner and the business are treated as one entity for tax purposes. Therefore, the owner reports business income and expenses on their personal tax return using Schedule C (Form 1040). Sole proprietors must pay self-employment taxes, including Social Security and Medicare taxes, based on net earnings from self-employment. They must make estimated tax payments throughout the year to cover income and self-employment tax liabilities.

Partnership: Partnerships are pass-through entities that flow profits and losses through individual partners' tax returns. The partnership does not pay income tax; each partner reports their share of partnership income or loss on their personal tax return. A partnership must file an annual information return (Form 1065) with the IRS showing its income, deductions, and credits. Partnerships might have state and local tax obligations, depending on jurisdiction.

Limited Liability Company (LLC): LLCs offer flexibility regarding taxation—owners can choose whether to be treated as a disregarded entity, partnership, S corporation, or C corporation. By default, single-member LLCs are treated as disregarded entities; thus, the owner includes the business's income and expenses on their personal return. On the other hand, multi-member LLCs are seen as partnerships for federal tax purposes; members report their share of profit or loss on individual returns. LLCs can also be taxed under S corporation or C corporation rules if they meet specific eligibility requirements.

S Corporation: Similar to partnerships, S corporations are pass-through entities that allocate business profits and losses among shareholders' shareholder returns. An annual corporate return (Form 1120S) must be filed with the IRS to report income, deductions, and credits. Shareholders pay tax on their proportionate share of corporate income—regardless of whether or not it's distributed to them as dividends. S corporations have certain eligibility requirements, such as having no more than 100 shareholders and being owned by individuals, estates, or certain trusts.

C Corporation: C corporations are separate legal entities from their owners and are subject to corporate income tax on profits. A corporate return (Form 1120) must be filed annually to report this information, along with deductions, and credits. Shareholders also face taxation when receiving dividends from C corporations, potentially causing double taxation of corporate profits. These structures offer benefits such as lower tax rates on retained earnings and the ability to raise capital through stock sales.

Business owners need to understand tax obligations for different business structures. Knowing the ins and outs of these obligations is critical, because it helps you figure out how to navigate the tax landscape effectively. Whether you're a sole proprietorship, partnership, LLC, S corporation, or C corporation, your company must follow the law and relevant tax regulations. The goal is to ensure that your company reports its taxes accurately and mitigates its liabilities as much as possible. You can get through all this by working with qualified tax professionals who will give you the right advice while staying updated about any tax developments.

Sales Tax, Income Tax, and Payroll Tax Considerations

Sailing through the taxation landscape is crucial to keeping your finances in check, but it can be a maze. The ins and outs of tax considerations such as sales, income, and payroll fall on you to ensure your business follows the law. In this section, we'll break down these tax considerations and share tips on how to sail successfully through them.

Sales Tax Considerations: Consumption tax may sound like something your business doesn't need, but understanding taxable goods or services is essential for all businesses. Figuring out who or what you need to pay sales tax to is challenging, with multiple rules imposing different taxes at state, local, or municipal levels. Knowing the connections between these jurisdictions and what sort of transactions are exempt from taxes will keep you in line with the law.

Income Tax Considerations: Besides impacting cash flow, which is also essential, income takes a hit when it comes to another major consideration: income tax. You've got federal, state, and local laws to worry about in addition to paying yourself enough money. Treatments differ, depending on whether you're a sole proprietor, partnership, corporation, or LLC, so reporting accurately becomes essential. Paying any amount owed in time will prevent penalties creeping up.

Payroll Tax Considerations: As if there weren't enough employee costs already; payroll tax adds even more to that bill. This includes Social Security, Medicare, Fed, and State taxes withheld from their paycheck and unemployment contributions made by employers. These must be paid regularly at responsible amounts, depending on each employee's situation.

Accounting for Taxes: Tax management requires top-of-the-line accounting practices, since accurate records around income deduction credits are required by law. To keep track of all these numbers and rules, businesses should keep everything from balance sheets to cash flow statements, and anything else that can be accounted for. Again, using accounting software will mitigate the headache of taxes and speed up your auditing process.

Tax Planning Strategies: On the bright side, there are ways to legally reduce your tax. Since deductions and credits are given out sparingly, you'll want to use these as much as possible. Timing income and expenses can be a clever way to optimize your financials and structure business transactions efficiently. I could go on about this, but I'll just say one thing: constantly think about legally avoiding paying more than you need to. You can manage your obligations effectively, optimize your positions, and achieve your goals by considering sales tax, income tax, and payroll tax implications (and implementing effective planning strategies). Regular communication with tax professionals can help you to stay compliant with laws while maximizing money-saving opportunities.

The Role of Accounting in Managing Taxes

One of the main roles that accounting has in managing taxes is maintaining precise financial records. Accountants track income, expenses, assets, and liabilities using bookkeeping software and systems. These serve as a base for calculating taxable income, preparing tax returns, and ensuring compliance with tax laws and regulations. By keeping accurate records, companies can report their activities precisely. This minimizes the risk of errors or discrepancies that could lead to audits or penalties.

Accounting professionals also play an essential role in creating strategies to decrease liabilities while maximizing benefits. They analyze financial data and assess its effect on taxes. Then they look for opportunities to save on taxes. Some common strategies include deferring income, maximizing credits, deductions, restructuring transactions, or looking into exemptions; incentives. Proactive planning will help you optimize your tax breaks while minimizing your debt.

Making sure that businesses are following all the necessary tax laws is one of accounting's core responsibilities. They keep up to date with any changes to filing deadlines, and requirements. The professionals prepare files for various types of taxes; income, sales, payroll, business, depending on what your company does or needs help with. As everyone knows through personal experience, when dealing with governments, there is a high chance something will go wrong, which can lead to audits, then fines and penalties; but not if we were prepared for them. When responding to notices and bills, accountants know precisely what's expected of them because they've already been through it before, which helps them mitigate potential penalties.

The professionals also generate income statements, balance sheets, and cash flow statements, which give further insights into how the business works. By identifying trends and patterns, accountants can help you better decide what's next regarding tax optimization or improving existing strategies. Forecasting and projections are two more things they do to help businesses make informed decisions about planning taxes and strategy.

Accounting professionals always offer support and guidance in managing complex laws and regulations. Usually, these professionals represent businesses while communicating with authorities. Inquiries, negotiations, and disputes all fall under their scope. Accounting plays a significant role in managing business taxes, so pay attention to it.

7.5 Employment Laws and Regulations

When it comes to running a business, obeying employment laws is vital. Employers must follow many legal requirements that dictate how the employer-employee relationship should be handled. Adherence to these regulations, from hiring to compensation and benefits, helps businesses avoid legal risks and treat employees fairly. Hiring workers has plenty of legal gray areas. Employers must navigate non-discrimination laws, background checks, and immigration requirements when hiring new people. Failure to do so could land employees in hot water, with accusations of discrimination or unfair practices. Understanding these rules is vital for snagging top-tier employees without courting legal trouble.

Companies must also provide their workers with certain benefits, such as health insurance, retirement plans, and sick days. When designing these benefit packages, employers should have an idea of what programs such as ACA and ERISA require. Minimum wage levels and overtime payment laws must be respected.

Employee contracts and handbooks are also essential documents with substantial legal implications. These outline the rights, responsibilities, and expectations of both parties involved in employment relationships. Businesses must ensure they're drafting iron-clad contracts that can stand up in court, while protecting the company from potential disputes.

Employment laws can be complex to wrap your head around, but failing to do so can result in significant fines or lawsuits against companies, big or small. Businesses can successfully mitigate these risks by treating employees well through fair hiring practices and honest communication about compensation, benefits, requirements, and duties. In the following sections, we'll take a more detailed look at various aspects of employment law, so you see what you're up against.

Hiring Employees and Compliance with Labor Laws

Hiring new employees is crucial to building a skilled and productive team, but it can be a legal minefield. Federal, state, and local laws ensure job applicants are treated fairly during hiring, especially regarding discrimination. Employers cannot make decisions based on race, color, religion, sex, national origin, age, disability, or genetic information. Laws like Title VII of the Civil Rights Act and the Age Discrimination in Employment Act (ADEA) require employers to focus on merit when hiring. Follow these rules to avoid ending up with costly lawsuits and reputation damage.

Employers often use background checks to learn more about candidates before extending an offer. But there are strict rules around this, too. Before you start digging into someone's past, you must first get their consent and follow specific procedures to protect their rights should any negative information come to light. Immigration laws also need to be followed when hiring workers. Every person needs proper documentation that says they're authorized to work in America. Employers must verify each applicant using Form I-9 and maintain other documents for each employee. Failing to do so can lead to hefty fines and sanctions.

Wage and hour laws differ from state to state, but one thing remains consistent; you must pay your employees properly. Minimum wage rates and overtime pay requirements may change depending on the location of your business, but they will always exist. Employers must correctly classify employees as exempt or non-exempt from overtime pay and comply with child labor regulations. Privacy is another important factor when considering new hires. All sensitive information collected during the process must be stored securely and only used for legitimate purposes. Data breach notification laws vary significantly from state to state, so make sure your operation complies with all relevant legislation. Don't let any of these legal requirements discourage you from hiring a wide range of people. If you follow the rules and keep your operation fair, transparent, and inclusive, you'll be able to attract and retain top talent quickly.

Understanding Benefits, Minimum Wage, and Overtime Rules

Benefits: Benefits are a must. They help employers attract and retain talent, especially the good kind. These packages typically include things like health insurance, retirement plans, paid time off, and other extra perks meant to give employees a little extra incentive to stick around. It's a win-win.

Health Insurance: Employers might offer coverage through a health insurance plan. Specific requirements must be met, per the Affordable Care Act (ACA). It states that employers must offer coverage to eligible employees and their dependents, provide necessary benefits, and have affordable options for workers and their families, all while following the correct protocol every step of the way.

Retirement Plans: Sponsoring retirement plans is another option. 401(K) plans are common for this purpose because they help employees save up for retirement without damaging their wallets early on. But as with health insurance, there are rules that need to be followed to keep plan participants happy and protected by law.

Paid Time Off: Employees will love it if you let them take a day off here and there—with pay, of course. PTO (paid time off) is an excellent benefit that can cover sick leave or vacation days. Though there aren't many federally required laws about PTO, some states do have mandates about how much time off should be given to workers.

Minimum Wage: The minimum amount employers are legally allowed to pay an employee per hour is called the minimum wage. The rate varies depending on multiple factors, such as location and industry type, but this number cannot be ignored or rejected; otherwise, you could find yourself dealing with some serious legal consequences.

Overtime Rules: If your employee works more than what would be considered a standard working week, they're entitled to overtime pay, which is essentially additional compensation. Overtime rates also vary by state, so make sure you get well acquainted with the regulations that apply where your business is located.

Creating Employee Contracts and Handbooks

Employee Contracts: Employment agreements are binding deals between employers and employees that spell out the terms of employment. They outline both parties' rights, responsibilities, and expectations, to avoid workplace misunderstandings or disputes. When writing these, employers should consider:

Duties: Lay out the employee's roles and responsibilities in detail. This includes their tasks, projects, and performance metrics.

Compensation: Specify compensation details like salary, bonuses, wages, and benefits. Remember to include payment conditions and eligibility for benefits.

Terms: State how long the employment will last. Indicate whether it's at-will or fixed-term employment. Include any probationary periods or termination conditions.

Confidentiality: Add provisions that protect your company's sensitive information.

Non-Compete: Consider adding clauses preventing ex-employees from engaging in competitive activities after termination.

Employee Handbooks Employee Handbooks provide comprehensive guides for anything an employee might need during their time with you. They cover workplace conduct, from leave policies to disciplinary proceedings—all the essential stuff. Here are things you should think about when creating one:

Policies and Procedures: Detail clear policies on attendance, dress code, and punctuality. Ensure that these procedures are consistent and compliant with laws and regulations.

Anti-Discrimination Policies: Create guidelines prohibiting harassment or discrimination against protected characteristics such as race or gender in the workplace.

Leave Policies: State how vacation time and sick days or holidays work.

7.6 Contracts and Legal Agreements

The backbone of a business is built on contracts and legal agreements. They govern relationships, protect assets, and ensure compliance with the law. Contracts help formalize agreements between businesses, clients, partners, and suppliers. It's crucial to draft these contracts effectively by being clear in terms of scope, deliverables, payment terms, and dispute resolution mechanisms. Negotiating contracts requires strategic communication and understanding of each party's interests, so it can be mutually beneficial.

Businesses must protect their IP rights to prevent unauthorized use of innovations or brands. Different legal mechanisms such as patents, trademarks, and copyrights provide different forms of protection for different types of IP. Confidentiality agreements, also known as non-disclosure agreements (NDAs) play an instrumental role in protecting sensitive information shared during business negotiations or collaborations. These restrict access to confidential information that could compromise your business if it fell into the wrong hands.

Throughout this section we will delve into these topics providing insights and best practices for navigating the complexities of contract drafting within the context of your business. Understanding how to properly draft a contract helps mitigate risks while protecting your businesses assets and fostering successful relationships in an ever-evolving marketplace.

Drafting and Negotiating Business Contracts

Understanding the Scope and Objectives: Before starting the contract process, an important step is understanding the scope and objectives of the agreement. This entails identifying the rights, obligations, and expectations of each party involved and defining why the deal is being made in the first place, along with what both sides want out of it. By considering this ahead of time, parties can customize contracts that precisely suit their needs.

Identifying Key Terms and Conditions: The next step in creating business deals is determining which terms are set up and who will govern this agreement. The best way to do this is by defining work or services provided at both ends, specifying deliverables, outlining payment details, and then setting up timelines and milestones. They can include provisions that relate to warranties, indemnification, limitations, and termination clauses.

Tailoring Contracts to Lower Risks: When drafting business contracts, potential risks that may occur during this agreement are considered so they can be mitigated. This means reviewing all legal and business risks accompanying this transaction, such as regulatory compliance, intellectual property rights, confidentiality obligations, and financial liabilities. Once all are examined, it's time to develop strategies and provisions that can be included to protect interests and limit exposure to liabilities and disputes.

Negotiating Terms and Reaching Agreement: After initially completing a draft of this contract, both parties must negotiate its terms and conditions until they reach an agreement. This process will involve a give-and-take type of bargaining in which each party advocates for their side but tries their best to find common ground. This is where active communication, effective compromise, and flexibility come into play, to help address concerns and reach consensus on critical issues. Participating and collaborating with the other party during this step can be crucial to achieving favorable outcomes.

Finalizing And Executing the Contract: After both sides have agreed to the final terms and conditions, it's time to finalize everything by executing the contract. To do this, the parties must review the contract that has been put together and ensure all terms are stated and agreed upon by both ends. Once everything is accurate, both parties sign the document, officially binding them to the obligations outlined in their agreement. It is wise for businesses involved in this deal to keep copies of all signed contracts to ensure they comply with legal requirements.

Protecting Intellectual Property Rights

Intellectual Property (IP) rights are precious for businesses; they include the creations of inventors, artists, and designers. This includes inventions, artworks, designs, brand identification such as logos or symbols, business or product names, and commerce images. Protecting these from being stolen or copied by others is necessary, because this can infringe upon your competitive advantage in the market. Adequate protection of IP is essential for innovation and creativity to flourish. Various legal alternatives are available to entrepreneurs seeking to protect their specific kind of creation.

A patent is given to an inventor if they create a new invention that offers an original solution that would be obscure after analyzing prior work. This exclusive right stops others from profiting from your invention without permission. Usually, these types of protections last about 20 years after you have filed your application. To obtain a patent, you must file the relevant information about your invention with the appropriate patent office.

Trademarks help customers distinguish different companies' goods and services by using signs or phrases that are distinctive legally recognized marks. Once acquired, this gives you exclusive rights over that mark for the goods and services specifically listed on your application. Trademark protection ensures competitors cannot use similar marks, which might confuse customers into purchasing their knock-off goods thinking it is yours.

Copyright protects authors' original works, including literature, music, art, and more, if it's been expressed in some tangible medium like written word or video recording. Copyright owners have exclusive rights to reproduce, distribute, display, and perform publicly any way they want, within reason, for a limited time—this generally lasts until death plus 70 additional years before it enters the public domain, where anyone can use it freely.

Trade secrets don't cover creative ideas; instead, proprietary, confidential information is kept secret by a few individuals within a business who need to know it to have a competitive edge against other companies working in the same industry who do not know this information. Protecting trade secrets is as simple as keeping them secret and ensuring you have protections that stop unauthorized people from gaining this classified information.

Protecting IP is a crucial strategy for businesses to retain the value of their ideas and unique brand identity. By being aware of the options available to them and implementing strategies early on, entrepreneurs can make sure their innovations remain exclusive, which will maximize their profits in the long run.

7.7 Regulatory Compliance in Your Industry

In this section, we will explore regulatory compliance within your industry. Following these practices is essential for businesses to succeed. Industry-specific regulations can be found in various fields, including product safety and environmental protection. Once all of these are fully understood, we can establish compliance protocols that mitigate potential risks. Ongoing compliance checks are crucial. You constantly need to ensure that everything is going according to plan. Conducting regular compliance audits and establishing robust monitoring systems is essential. If a business needs to be updated with the latest legal requirements, they're already falling behind their competitors. Companies should seek assistance from legal and compliance experts when dealing with regulations and assessing any gaps in their business model. Legal penalties, fines, reputational damage, business disruptions, and financial losses are some of the consequences awaiting those who neglect regulatory compliance.

Identifying Industry-specific Regulations

In the business world, there are many moving parts. You can't keep track of them all. That's why we have regulations to dictate what standards companies must adhere to within their respective sectors. These rules are put in place by various entities, government agencies, industry associations, and international bodies. They ensure everything moves along safely, fairly, and with integrity.

Regulations for each industry vary depending on what they're about. For instance, the healthcare industry has HIPAA to govern patient privacy while the FDA oversees drug safety. In financial services, the Dodd-Frank Wall Street Reform Act keeps financial institutions in check and aims to prevent another crisis. To find these regulations, businesses need to spend time researching and analyzing every piece of legislation that directly affects them. They must examine federal laws and state and local laws. If they want to be up to date with the rest of the world, they might need to investigate international trade.

Once you find those regulations, you'll probably need to understand how they work with your business operations. By dissecting regulatory requirements, including deadlines, reporting obligations, and enforcement mechanisms, any business owner spots things when things are going south. These regulations are there so everyone immediately knows what to do after looking through them. No one could be expected to understand them off the top of their head, let alone remember which ones have been changed recently. Identifying rules is one step to using them practically, so stay informed about updates or changes as they come out.

When businesses know how to operate legally and ethically within their respective industries, everyone wins in the long run. Start by understanding where you stand from a regulatory standpoint, then build compliance strategies and trust from stakeholders over time.

Strategies for Maintaining Ongoing Compliance

Maintaining ongoing compliance with industry-specific regulations is a dynamic and multifaceted endeavor that requires proactive planning, robust systems, and continuous monitoring. Regular compliance audits are fundamental to assessing the organization's adherence to regulatory standards and identifying any areas of non-compliance. These audits involve a systematic review of internal policies, procedures, and practices against regulatory requirements, enabling businesses to promptly address deficiencies and implement corrective actions.

Implementing robust compliance monitoring systems enables businesses to track regulatory changes, monitor compliance activities, and identify emerging compliance risks. Organizations can streamline compliance monitoring processes by leveraging technology and automation tools, which provide real-time alerts on regulatory developments, and proactively address compliance gaps. Educating employees about industry-specific regulations and compliance requirements is essential for fostering a culture of compliance within the organization. Training programs and awareness initiatives should be tailored to employees' roles and responsibilities, ensuring they understand their obligations and the consequences of non-compliance. Businesses can strengthen their compliance efforts and minimize compliance-related incidents by empowering employees with the knowledge and resources to adhere to regulatory standards.

Seeking guidance from legal and compliance experts can provide invaluable insights into interpreting complex regulations, assessing compliance risks, and developing effective compliance strategies. Legal counsel can help businesses navigate regulatory requirements, mitigate risks, and ensure compliance efforts align with legal obligations and industry best practices. Establishing internal controls and procedures ensures compliance efforts are integrated into day-to-day operations. This includes documenting compliance policies, defining roles and responsibilities, and implementing checks and balances to prevent and detect non-compliance. By formalizing compliance processes and procedures, businesses can enhance transparency, accountability, and effectiveness in managing compliance risks. Staying abreast of regulatory developments and emerging compliance trends is critical for maintaining ongoing compliance. Businesses should actively monitor regulation changes, industry standards, and enforcement priorities and adapt their compliance strategies accordingly.

The Consequences of Non-compliance

Failure to follow the rules in any kind of business can be a serious issue. The problems that arise from this can range from legal matters to financial losses, damage to reputation, and operational disruptions. For companies to even understand what they need to prioritize, these consequences need to be understood. Failure to do this will make your profits disappear, taking your company's stability with it.

Non-compliance is also bad for business in other ways. Customers won't trust you if you don't try hard enough to earn their trust, investors won't want anything to do with you if they get even a whiff of bad corporate governance or dishonesty, and business partners will let go of your hand like a hot potato. Production delays due to regulatory violations can lead customers to look elsewhere for supplies, which means a loss in market opportunities for you. If people are going through investigations or proceedings against your company, your attention, time and money will be occupied with this process rather than more important business issues. There can also be indirect costs such as litigation expenses or regulatory compliance remediation efforts, and increased insurance policy premiums could be imposed on the company. It is all too easy for businesses to look at regulations with a 'that won't happen to me' attitude. But once they understand all the risks involved with not following them, there is no reason they wouldn't prioritize this.

7.8 Data Protection and Privacy Laws

In today's world, data is vital to a business's success. For many, it is the lifeblood of their operations and decision-making processes. With the rise in reliance comes inherent risk. The more we depend on data for everything from storing information to making sales, the more susceptible businesses are to breaches and attacks.

Every company collects sensitive information, so it is necessary to protect that data at all costs. This is why we have regulations for data security and privacy. These legal frameworks are designed to prevent unwanted access or disclosure of data and identity theft. Complying with these laws ensures trust between companies, clients, and stakeholders.

The most prominent regulation is the General Data Protection Regulation (GDPR) established by the European Union (EU). GDPR requires strict compliance from any business that collects or processes personal information. Consent requirements and breach notifications hold businesses accountable while protecting EU residents' personal data.

There's a different regulation specifically for healthcare providers: The Health Insurance Portability and Accountability Act (HIPAA). This act was implemented specifically to protect individuals' health information by imposing handling standards on PHI, requiring certain things from healthcare providers.

Numerous other acts may apply depending on your industry or location, such as The California Consumer Privacy Act (CCPA), which gives consumers rights over their personal information, such as opting out of its sale.

Ensuring your company meets all the guidelines outlined in these acts can take time and effort. The best way to go about this process is by developing policies that cater to your needs while fulfilling regulatory requirements. Outlining how you handle data can make it easier for employees to adhere to and help weave a culture built upon good practices. Beyond this, developing training programs will ensure everyone knows how to comply and what to do in case of a breach. Most importantly, this commitment to data protection will show stakeholders that you care.

The Importance of Data Security and Privacy Regulations

Data security and privacy regulations are critical in a world where every aspect of business happens online. The rules are the foundation for protecting sensitive information from unauthorized access or misuse. Data security and privacy regulations safeguard individuals' privacy rights and ensure their personal data remains confidential. These regulations play a huge role in building trust between customers, stakeholders, and partners. By setting clear standards for data protection, individuals can be confident that their personal information will be responsibly handled by organizations. Trust is everything when it comes to your reputation among the public. If people believe you're responsible with their information, they'll trust you're also responsible in other areas.

Transparency is also key to these regulations. Businesses must be honest about how they use personal data and get consent from individuals before using it at all. Transparency allows for accountability, which is great because it gives individuals control over their own information and further enhances privacy rights. Following all the regulations will also help protect your business from cyberattacks. These kinds of breaches can have devastating consequences not only financially and legally but also in terms of your public reputation. When this happens, your customers will no longer consider you trustworthy, which will damage brand credibility.

Complying with GDPR, HIPAA, or Other Relevant Laws

Laws like the General Data Protection Regulation (GDPR) and the Health Insurance Portability and Accountability Act (HIPAA) set precise requirements to protect individuals' privacy rights and enforce high standards of data handling security. Organizations must understand these regulations, as it will save them from possible legal consequences in the future.

The GDPR was implemented by the European Union, and it is one of the strictest regulations regarding data protection worldwide. Even if your business isn't in an EU country, you'll still have to comply if you collect or process personal data belonging to EU residents. Some principles set forth by GDPR include obtaining consent from individuals before processing their data, ensuring all data is accurate and secure, and protecting against unauthorized access or disclosure. If a company doesn't comply with these principles, massive penalties can be imposed: fines of up to €20 million, $24 million, or 4% of global annual turnover.

In parallel with GDPR, HIPAA sets its own rules for healthcare institutions, to protect patients' private health information (PHI). Businesses that provide healthcare services or insurance must follow HIPAA's Privacy, Security, and Breach Notification Rules. The regulation imposes safeguards on PHI, like implementing administrative, technical, and physical security measures, organizing regular risk assessment tests to ensure the proper functioning of security systems, and working on solidifying the transmission process, so no leaks occur. Violations will incur significant penalties, ranging from monetary fines to criminal charges.

Apart from GDPR and HIPAA, there are other laws designed for different industries, like the CCPA (California Consumer Privacy Act), which grants the rights consumers who live in California over their own personal data, giving them rights such as accessing it whenever they wish or deleting any unwanted personal information stored. Regulations like this allow consumers to opt out of sharing personal data with businesses. One more sector-specific regulation, the Payment Card Industry Data Security Standard (PCI DSS), was created to prevent fraud and data breaches; it governs how payment card data is handled in financial services.

To comply with GDPR, HIPAA, and other similar laws, businesses must start by analyzing their current way of handling data and finding any flaws or risks. This can be done by developing a solid set of data protection policies and identifying potential threats through audits and assessments. Employees must constantly be trained in how to best protect customers' personal information, and mechanisms must be put in place so that customer demands dealing with their subject requests can quickly be addressed, along with any reported breaches.

Organizations must appoint a Data Protection Officer to oversee all compliance efforts. This person will also interact with regulatory authorities whenever necessary or when individuals must better handle their private information. By keeping track of all regulatory developments, organizations will always know whether any changes will require them to alter their current system. This requires a lot of attention to detail from employees. If these steps are taken sincerely, businesses will avoid legal consequences, while still being able to handle sensitive data confidently.

Developing Data Protection Policies for Your Business

Producing a solid, robust data protection policy is crucial. It ensures you follow the data protection laws, reduce threats, and keep personal information safe. These policies create guidelines and best practices for securely handling data throughout its lifecycle within the organization. Here's how your business can effectively develop these policies: Aim to get the purpose and scope of the policies down as soon as possible. This will help you build out the rest of it later. You'll want to establish what kind of data these policies cover and identify any legal or regulatory requirements your business may need to follow. Once you have your objectives, it's time to sort through all your data. Create categories that make sense so you know how each specific type should be handled when documented online or offline.

Allowing only authorized personnel with legitimate need-to-know access to sensitive data is essential for protecting it against unauthorized access or disclosure. Define roles and responsibilities for individuals who will be accessing this information so there are eyes on anyone who might be doing any suspicious activity. You'll want security measures in place, to fend off any attempts at gaining unauthorized access and keep it safe from being destroyed by an accident. Encryption and other security measures will keep it safe both while sitting idle and when being used.

If your information system is ever breached, preparing a plan beforehand will allow for a quick response when time matters most. An ideal strategy would include steps for certain people when a breach occurs, who notifies whom, and their roles.

Regular audits and assessments help you identify any threats before they become an issue in your organization. Establishing discipline for those who don't follow the rules will help you maintain a culture where everyone knows how necessary these measures are to their business. When developing new products, services, or processes, consider privacy. Integrate privacy and data protection principles as soon as possible to limit the chance of third-party information being hacked or compromised. Regularly checking through these policies will ensure that all new laws, regulations, and technological advances are accounted for.

7.9 Risk Management and Insurance

In business, success is all about finding your footing in an unpredictable landscape. That's why understanding and managing risk is critical to staying afloat. This section will explore risk management and insurance—two crucial ways businesses can toughen up and become more resilient.

If there's one thing, we all know about risks, it is that they take many shapes and forms. Sometimes, they're economic or regulatory; other times, natural disasters threaten our survival. But no matter how they appear, we need to examine them closely so we can spot our vulnerabilities and fight back with a tailored strategy.

The beauty of insurance lies in its ability to cough up financial support exactly when you need it most—like after property damage or a liability claim has eaten away at your funds. By doing this companies can bounce back quicker than ever before. Good insurance doesn't just help your company get back on its feet more efficiently; it also makes stakeholders trust you more. Knowing they're protected from potential damage should make shareholders sleep easier at night.

Types of Business Insurance Policies

Understanding the array of business insurance policies can be confusing, but it's crucial for organizations to guard themselves from potential risks and liabilities. We explore some of the most common types of insurance coverage and their significance in protecting businesses from various threats and uncertainties.

General Liability Insurance is a foundational coverage that shields businesses from third-party claims. It covers bodily injury, or property damage. It's built as a safety net against lawsuits due, for instance, to accidents on business premises or through operations. By providing coverage for legal defense costs and damages, general liability insurance helps businesses deal with financial risks.

Property Insurance is another vital component in managing risk. It offers protection against damage or loss to physical assets like buildings, equipment, inventory, and furnishings. The coverage guards' businesses against perils like fire, theft, vandalism, and natural disasters so they can make swift recoveries when unfortunate events occur.

Professional Liability Insurance is designed for businesses that provide professional services. It protects them against negligence claims or inadequate work allegations made by clients. The coverage covers legal defense costs and damages awarded in lawsuits alleging professional errors or omissions. Professional liability insurance is indispensable for consultants, lawyers, and accountants; because it offers peace of mind and financial protection against potential litigation.

Cyber Liability Insurance has become all the more crucial for business owners. This specialized coverage provides financial support for businesses grappling with the aftermath of cyber incidents like data breaches. With the prevalence of cyberattacks and strict regulatory scrutiny surrounding data privacy laws, cyber liability insurance has become a must-have in risk management regardless of your organization's size or industry.

If your business requires vehicles operated by employees while on company time, Commercial Auto Insurance is essential. It offers protection against property damage, bodily injury, and medical expenses resulting from accidents involving company vehicles. Whether you have a fleet of delivery trucks or one company car, commercial auto insurance ensures businesses remain financially protected while on the road.

Workers' Compensation Insurance is required by law in many jurisdictions. It provides coverage for medical expenses, lost wages, and disability benefits for employees who are injured or become ill on the job. By compensating injured workers and shielding businesses from lawsuits related to workplace injuries, workers' compensation insurance promotes workplace safety and protects both employers and employees.

The diligent business owner needs to have a Commercial Umbrella Insurance policy. It's meant to provide extra liability coverage beyond the limits of primary insurance policies. This means they'll be protected from substantial catastrophic losses and lawsuits that exceed the limits of primary policies, which is always a good thing. It also adds an extra layer of protection for businesses with high-risk exposure.

Directors and Officers (D&O) Insurance is designed to protect individuals serving in leadership positions within a company from personal liability for their actions or decisions made while performing their duties; it's like having unlimited cheat codes for the game of life. It provides coverage for legal expenses and damages that come from lawsuits alleging wrongful acts or decisions by directors and officers.

At the end of the day, keeping your company safe from various risks and liabilities should always be a top priority. Please don't look at insurance coverage as money wasted; think about it as money saved. Investing in the appropriate insurance coverage tailored to your needs will ensure long-term viability and success in an ever-changing business environment.

Assessing Business Risks and Choosing the Right Insurance Coverage

Evaluating business risks and selecting insurance protection is a crucial part of risk management for any organization. It involves assessing potential threats and problems going forward and matching the risks to the right policy solutions. Here's how to assess business risks and navigate through the chaos to get the best coverage. The ball gets rolling with a comprehensive study of all potential hazards that could disrupt the enterprise's operations, damage assets, or hurt financial well-being. Threats can come from many sources, including natural disasters, accidents, lawsuits, cyberattacks, economic downturns, and changes in laws and regulations. Figuring out what's lurking in the darkness will give businesses a better idea of what they need to defend against first.

Once you've listed your threats on paper, it's time to rank them based on their likelihood of occurring and the scale that would impact your business if they did happen. Putting numbers on each one's probability and severity will allow firms to observe which ones they should be most concerned with and dedicate their energy to them. Then money can be allocated appropriately so that everything runs as smoothly as possible, even if these emergencies ever happen.

The next step is for organizations to explore policies that shield against these dangers. This means understanding what types of coverage are available worldwide and seeing how those offerings match your company's specific vulnerabilities. You'll want to keep track of things like limits within policies, which dictate how much you'll get back if something goes wrong, deductibles, exclusions, and how much you must pay each time before they start picking up costs.

While considering different options, businesses should ensure the scope covered by insurance aligns with their risk exposures so that there are no gaps left where significant losses might still occur. Sometimes, this means getting multiple insurance policies to cover different situations. In other cases, it might mean getting a complicated policy custom-tailored to your company's unique needs. There's no one-size-fits-all solution here, so each organization must take the time to figure out its specific requirements.

Some businesses may need more than standard insurance coverage. In these cases, you'll want to explore alternative ways to handle risk financing, such as self-insurance or captive groups. These methods can give companies more freedom and control over risk management, but they still require careful evaluation to ensure the new system will work.

Ultimately, assessing business risks and finding suitable insurance coverage is a never-ending process that must be managed with deliberate caution. Through proactive management and picking the right policies, though, businesses can ensure they are properly defended against potential losses, allowing them to secure long-term success in whatever they are trying to do.

The Role of Insurance in Business Continuity Planning

The insurance industry plays quite a significant role in business continuity planning, acting as a safety net for businesses. They are always trying to ensure their resilience in the face of unexpected events. Insurance takes on many roles in business continuity planning, including financial protection, risk transfer, and strategic support to help businesses recover and thrive following a disaster or crisis.

When it comes down to it, the main priority of insurance is obviously the financial side of things. One of the primary functions of insurance in business continuity planning is to provide financial protection against losses incurred due to unforeseen events. Business interruption insurance, for example, reimburses businesses for lost income and operating expenses during downtime caused by covered risks such as natural disasters, fires, or other disruptive events. During those periods when your business has stopped temporarily due to something entirely out of your control, these guys have got you covered. This coverage helps companies maintain their financial stability and cover essential expenses while working hard to restore normal operations.

By transferring the risk of certain events to an insurer, companies can protect themselves from being hit with potentially catastrophic financial consequences due to those events. With this weight lifted off their shoulders, they can focus on what matters: running a successful company.

When it comes to a business's reputation, they've got that covered, also. Gaining trust from stakeholders such as customers or investors can be tough, but having insurance coverage in place makes things a lot easier. It can instill confidence in stakeholders and reassure them that the business has taken proactive steps to protect its assets, operations, and continuity.

Ultimately, no matter what industry you're in, taking some time to plan accordingly goes a long way. The role of insurance isn't just financial protection, either; it extends beyond mere financial protection to encompass strategic risk management and resilience building. Sorry for the bad news, but disruption is inevitable, but if you keep your assets safe, you will be ready when they come around again.

7.10 Corporate Governance and Ethics

Corporate governance and ethics are the two most important aspects of business. They guide behavior and decision-making, ensuring transparency, accountability, and ethical conduct in all business matters. At its core, corporate governance is about how companies are directed and controlled. It focuses on defining the roles of key stakeholders such as shareholders, board members, executives, and management and finding ways to oversee their activities so that everyone remains accountable. With this structure in place, your organization will be guided with integrity while safeguarding shareholder interests.

Best practices play an equally important role in shaping organizational behavior. Following principles like transparency, accountability, and ethical conduct can be the catalyst that propels you one step ahead of other businesses that don't prioritize these things. Establishing independent board oversight or implementing internal controls are great places to start when choosing which principles should be integrated into your operations.

Ethics help guide individuals' moral compasses during their time at your company. Upholding principles of fairness, honesty, and integrity is crucial for maintaining long-term relationships with stakeholders. Acting in the best interest of employees alone could spark change within society, thanks to collective effort.

Developing a code of conduct has become increasingly important due to how interconnected businesses have become through social media. It helps outline ethical standards and expectations and provides guidance on issues such as conflicts of interest, bribery, and corruption problems. As for CSR policies, they are a way to ensure you're putting forth effort where needed most, social responsibility, and community engagement without losing sight of value creation for shareholders.

These principles ultimately promote trust with major players like employees and customers while safeguarding shareholder interests. Embrace them and watch as your organization flourishes right before your eyes.

Best Practices for Corporate Governance

Best practices for corporate governance are cornerstone principles that guide companies in maintaining transparency, accountability, and ethical conduct in their operations. They serve as essential guidelines for effective oversight, which ensures that companies operate in the best interests of stakeholders while upholding integrity and ethical standards. An independent board of directors is the first essential aspect of good corporate governance. Made up of directors not affiliated with the company or its management, an independent board provides impartial oversight and helps mitigate conflicts of interest. These directors bring diverse perspectives and expertise to the table, leading to better decision-making and adequately addressing shareholders' interests.

Another crucial element is defined roles and responsibilities, a feature that cannot be overemphasized. By limiting the roles of board members, senior management, board committees, and other key participants, organizations can reduce confusion, promote transparency, and facilitate effective decision-making processes. This understanding ensures that everyone knows what is required of them, thus nurturing a culture of accountability within the organization. Ethical values and a robust code of conduct form another fundamental component in corporate governance. A comprehensive code outlines the expected behavior of employees, directors, and executives toward colleagues, clients, suppliers, and other stakeholders. By promoting ethical conduct and integrity in these interactions, organizations protect trustworthiness, improve reputation, and lower risk factors for ethical breaches.

Any business should have adequate risk management structures to anticipate risks before they manifest themselves. Proactive risk management safeguards shareholder value and assets and improves decision-making processes. Transparency and disclosure are core elements when it comes to corporate governance. Stakeholders need timely, accurate information regarding their financial position, non-financial performance, strategy, and risk, to decide whether to invest more into the business or pull out. Transparent communication nurtures trust among all parties involved, enhances accountability, and enables stakeholders to make good decisions. Shareholder engagement is essential in corporate governance, because it promotes shareholder democracy and alignment of interests. Organizations can only know their areas of weakness and room for improvement if they engage their shareholders in regular dialogue. By engaging with them, organizations can understand their concerns, address questions, and solicit feedback on governance matters. Diversity is another element that should be addressed when creating a solid board. Boards with a balanced mix of skills, experiences, and backgrounds are better able to identify new risks and opportunities with emerging trends. These practices enhance transparency, accountability, and trust, thereby driving long-term value creation while maintaining the confidence of shareholders, employees, and customers, among other stakeholders.

Ethical Considerations in Business Decision-Making

Ethical considerations abound in business. They're the principles we follow to make sound decisions that keep organizations responsible and morally upright. Let's examine what ethical thinking means for businesses. Honesty, integrity, and equity are at the root of ethical decision-making. It's about making choices while considering how they could affect everyone involved in the business. Employees, customers, suppliers, shareholders—even the whole community—need to be considered.

Transparency is an essential aspect of running an ethical business. It means communicating with stakeholders in a way that reveals accurate information about how your company works and makes critical decisions. Transparent communication can build trust and accountability with partners by demonstrating your commitment to honesty and ethics. Fairness is crucial in decision-making. When you are dealing with employees, suppliers, or other parties involved with your business, bias should never have a role in your actions. Equal opportunities for everyone must be upheld if you want to create a trusting work environment and a solid reputation.

Integrity also plays a big part in making good ethical decisions. Even when tough choices arise, or tempting opportunities present themselves, being grounded in moral values is indispensable. With integrity at their core, companies can honor obligations signed under contract and treat clients honestly at every interaction. One more thing to remember—social responsibility. A business should always try to have a positive impact on the communities where it operates while minimizing harm to the environment. Ethical sourcing, environmental sustainability practices, and philanthropy are all prime examples of being socially responsible while still aiming for success.

And then there are governance and compliance matters. Legal statutes only serve as guidelines for avoiding penalties for breaking laws, and ethical standards help you make sure you're doing things right behind closed doors, no matter what those guidelines suggest you do. But these aren't feel-good topics either—today's consumers demand ethical conduct from businesses and won't accept less. If a company doesn't make moral decisions, when necessary, its reputation could be trashed, and customer trust might never be rebuilt. Ethical thinking is a clever way to build strong consumer relationships and boost brand loyalty in the long run.

Ethical considerations are the blueprint for making sound business choices. When you do better with your customers, suppliers, staff, and community by upholding integrity, transparency, fairness, social responsibility, and compliance, you're doing well with your own organization. And that earns you more than moral points. Those choices solidify resilience and reputation so you can stay on top of your game in today's business world.

Developing a Code of Conduct and Corporate Social Responsibility Policies

Developing a solid code of conduct and corporate social responsibility (CSR) policies is one of the most important things a business can do to ensure its employees are well-behaved and respect society and the environment. A code of conduct lays out expectations for what everyone involved in an organization should do. It sets the core values and principles that should be followed. By doing this, it establishes a culture of integrity, respect, and accountability.

In a similar but different way to a code of conduct, CSR policies outline more about the business. They show their dedication to sustainable practices that go beyond profits. They help society and the environment by pinpointing areas where help is needed most. The specifics can range anywhere from social equity initiatives to ethical sourcing strategies. Ultimately, though, this isn't just some piece of paper—by formalizing these policies, businesses take responsibility for their actions while pledging to make a positive difference.

It's crucial that these frameworks are developed with collaboration at the forefront. To include as many perspectives as possible in decision-making processes, it would be best practice to involve various stakeholders such as employees, management, customers, suppliers, and communities themselves. Engaging with these groups brings about more ownership of any resulting policies or documents made afterward. To be effective in driving ethical behavior across an organization's entire chain of command, these frameworks must align properly with each other and with an organization's mission statement. The philosophy here is that, if ethical practice is integrated into every aspect of daily operations, growth will come naturally while you are also benefiting society at large.

Transparency helps build trust between organizations and everyone else involved with them, including stakeholders. Therefore, it is essential to communicate ethical and social responsibility initiatives openly and honestly. This means disclosing information about CSR efforts, so stakeholders can hold organizations accountable and contribute to their enhanced reputation. Regular updates are also needed to ensure these frameworks stay relevant. As we all know, business practices change on a day-to-day basis these days. To remain relevant in modern times, regularly reviewing the code of conduct and CSR policies can help identify areas for improvement, leading to innovation—all underpinned by the commitment to ethical conduct and social responsibility that these policies entail.

For any organization hoping to navigate the complexities of today's world while upholding ethics, making a meaningful social impact, and making money in a sustainable way, there isn't a better way than developing a comprehensive code of conduct and CSR policies.

7.11 Staying Informed and Seeking Legal Assistance

Seeking legal help and staying current are crucial parts of managing a business. Especially now, with the ever-changing regulatory landscape, companies need to be able to adapt. This section delves into how important that is and emphasizes why people should seek expert advice to protect their business. In a world that's changing fast, being informed about regulations and industry standards is vital for businesses. It helps them navigate potential problems while also taking advantage of opportunities. This means staying current on changes in legislation, court rulings, and any new rules that may impact their industry. Ultimately, it allows people to identify risks early on and adjust accordingly. Being informed also means being one step ahead of everyone else. Businesses can stay compliant with laws and make more ethical decisions by staying aware of legal developments.

Knowing all those things can only get you so far without understanding the intricacies of legal matters. At some point, it's necessary to turn to an expert for guidance. They'll be able to assess risks better than anyone and help guide your decision-making process in a way that allows you to stay true to your goals. Legal experts are there to draft contracts, resolve disputes, or ensure regulatory compliance. The most beneficial aspect of this is risk mitigation. Lawyers are explicitly trained to spot holes within operations or policies before they cause significant issues. This saves money and, even more importantly, time—which will always be your most important asset as a business owner.

Another critical role lawyers play is in ensuring compliance with laws and regulations. With so many different requirements across industries, this is challenging, especially with the proper expertise backing you up every step. They'll help develop policies specifically for your needs, so you can avoid fines at all costs. Legal help is crucial in court. From contract disputes to infringement, lawyers can fight on your behalf and work towards a settlement that would otherwise be impossible. Their expertise gives you a fighting chance and could save the future of your business. The takeaway here is simple: seek legal help and stay informed. By always doing those two things, businesses can not only protect themselves but also position themselves for long-term success in today's fast-changing environment.

Chapter 8

Raising Capital and Financing

Raising capital involves acquiring funds for business operations, investments, or expansion projects. It is a complex process that demands meticulous planning, strategic decision-making, and efficient execution. By understanding the differing sources of material resources with which they might finance their companies' growth, entrepreneurs can effectively navigate the financial intermediary systems and position themselves in successful enterprises.

To raise capital effectively, you must have knowledge of the different types of financing options available. Entrepreneurs may choose from various sources, such as bank loans and equity finance, to fund their new ventures. Every alternative has its own merits and demerits; hence, it is incumbent upon an entrepreneur to carefully analyze their requirements before making any decision.

Many entrepreneurs opt for bootstrapping to commence their initiatives. This strategy involves self-funding a business using personal savings, operating revenues, or borrowing from friends and family members. Although bootstrapping allows more control and flexibility over one's business venture, it can also constrain growth prospects.

Another standard option among entrepreneurs looking for additional capital beyond personal resources includes applying for bank loans and credit. Outlets such as banks provide lending services tailored expressly to businesses; hence, they offer various products, including term loans, lines of credit, and Small Business Administration (SBA) loans to meet these entities' varied needs. Therefore, understanding the loan application process, eligibility criteria and repayment terms is crucial.

Equity financing involves selling partial ownership, often to venture capitalists (VCs), angel investors, or even private equity groups looking forward to share risk on an investment basis with young firms having high potential for scalability. Entrepreneurs have always needed help to raise equity capital since they need to effectively sell their business ideas and negotiate favorable terms with investors.

In recent years, crowdfunding, and microfinance platforms have arisen as other practical sources of entrepreneurial capital. With these platforms, companies can conduct online campaigns that attract funds from large numbers of individuals, also called backers. Crowdfunding provides a unique opportunity for validating one's business concept and generating pre-sales.

Apart from traditional financing options, entrepreneurs may consider grants and subsidies provided by government agencies, nonprofits, and industry associations. These funding sources can provide valuable support for research and development initiatives, innovation projects, and community-based initiatives. Grants usually involve competitive processes, where applicants must ensure that they meet specific eligibility criteria.

When planning fundraising activities, entrepreneurs must produce comprehensive business plans, financial projections, and investment pitch materials. Prospective investors or editors require you as the entrepreneur to demonstrate your vision about the enterprise, the size of the market, how the product(s) will be differentiated from those of others in the same line, and the means through which revenue can be made.

After getting ready, entrepreneurs can start fundraising by locating suitable funding channels, interacting with investors, and presenting their business proposals. The fundraising process often involves several steps, from preliminary contact with potential investors, due diligence, and negotiation, to closing. Entrepreneurs can increase their chances of obtaining investment for business growth if they approach it systematically and use available resources.

This chapter serves as a comprehensive handbook to guide entrepreneurs who are embracing the task of raising capital for financing their ventures. It enlightens entrepreneurs about the different opportunities and challenges they face in financial matters so they can make informed decisions toward continued growth over time.

8.1 Introduction to Raising Capital

At its center, capital is a significant force for promoting the growth of any enterprise. From starting new businesses to scaling existing operations or expanding research and development functions, access to sufficient financial resources allows entrepreneurs to exploit opportunities, negotiate challenges, and meet goals efficiently. To this effect, capital is an enabler for innovation. It will enable companies to invest in technology and human resources, including the best infrastructure that will help them gain a competitive advantage in the marketplace.

Entrepreneurs can use an outline of funding stages and sources to navigate the complex world of accessing funds for their businesses. At each stage, from seed funding up to Series A, B, etc., other investors have put different financing requirements in place. By appreciating these milestones, entrepreneurs can strategically plan their fundraising activities.

These options include traditional funding sources such as banks' credit lines, which provide long-term financial support for operations or short-term liquidity needs. More specifically, venture capitalists' funds give high-growth start-ups financial and strategic assistance, such as industry experience, whereas angel investors serve like equity firms that offer corporate finance services, including guidance throughout critical phases such as IPOs.

Similarly, crowdfunding platforms have emerged where entrepreneurs can obtain investments from large societies without the involvement of brokers. Through rewards-based campaigns, similar to equity financing campaign, and debt financing campaign mode, entrepreneurs can use a mass approach towards sourcing funds required during the start-up period until they prove their concepts are feasible and seek deeper investments. Grants from governments, subsidies, and tax incentives are another source of funds that maintain ownership and are thus preferred by firms focusing on research, innovation, and social impact.

Fundraising is a three-dimensional process involving strategic planning, networking, and efficient communication. Entrepreneurs who understand the role capital plays in business growth can comfortably navigate the stages of funding and know where they can get it. This will put them in good stead when they raise capital, so that their firms can become more successful in the world of entrepreneurship.

The Role of Capital in Business Growth

Capital acts as the bloodline of businesses, the primary energy that moves them toward growth, continuity, and prosperity. In every corner of an organization's operation, it enables innovation, growth, and ongoing competitiveness. A lack of adequate capital traps businesses, making them unable to take up opportunities or effectively address the same companies' challenges. For this reason, entrepreneurs and company heads must comprehend the multifaceted role of capital in driving business growth.

Capital empowers companies to support creative instincts, stimulate product and service development, and keep pace with ever-changing customer needs by allocating resources to research and development initiatives. Strategic investment aims to enhance competitiveness while positioning firms as leaders within their respective sectors, who can influence new trends and adapt to emerging technologies.

Capital also forms a cornerstone for scaling businesses, providing finances to venture into new markets, diversify products, or establish additional operations. Gaining access to financial resources through organic approaches or acquiring other companies within their industry allows businesses to extend all dimensions of their revenues, as they can thus tap into new customer bases. Through such an expansionist approach, many companies achieve revenue generation coupled with increased market presence and brand awareness, leading to long-term sustainability and steady growth.

Capital is a prerequisite for acquiring the talent you need. A high level of talent retention should be maintained by firms seeking breakthroughs in this fiercely competitive labor marketplace. Bear in mind that skilled personnel can make employment choices based on the total compensation packages offered by firms, so you need sufficient resources for employee training and a good working environment.

Capital cushions against economic uncertainty, since it guards enterprises against unforeseen events that may disrupt their operations. Sufficient liquidity and financial reserves also allow companies to withstand market downturns and adapt to changing regulations. This ensures continuity for the firm and protects shareholders' value.

Capital plays diverse roles in business growth that cannot be ignored. Entrepreneurs and business executives have no choice but to prioritize sound capital allocation techniques and financial management so that opportunities can be grabbed.

Overview of Funding Stages and Sources

The first stage of funding, the seed stage, is where a business idea or concept starts. Entrepreneurs usually employ personal savings, contributions from family and friends, or bootstrapping to pay for initial expenses such as market research, product development, and proof of concept during this phase. Seed funding is a basis for startups to validate their business model, build prototypes, or attract early adopters or investors.

Startups may require additional financing to expand their operations and scale up once they have gone through the seed stage and demonstrated some traction in the market. At this point, known as the early-stage or startup stage, angel investors, venture capitalists, or early-stage venture funds are often involved in fundraising activities. Individual investors' equity participation in these firms enhances speedy product development by startups, who can thus extend their customer base using a go-to-market strategy.

Once a company has attained substantial growth, with proven revenue-generating capabilities, it may move into the growth or expansion phase. Firms at this level may seek several types of capitalization methods, including Venture Capital Financing (VCF), Private Equity (PE) investment, and strategic partnerships, among others. Through the provision of funds, these sources enable firms to scale their operations by entering other markets, thus dominating other players in those markets.

Besides traditional equity financing mechanisms, debt financing can be considered as a potential option. Debt financing practice is about borrowing money from financial institutions like banks, alternative lenders, or even loan programs supported by governments, which need to be paid back within some time frame, usually with interest rates charged on the outstanding amount due plus interest accrued over a specified payment period. Bank loans, revolving credit lines, and Small Business Administration (SBA) loans are some common types of debt financing that are mainly tailored to cater for different business needs and risks.

Crowdfunding has become famous for startups and small businesses looking to attract capital from various investors or backers. Platforms like Kickstarter, Indiegogo, or GoFundMe allow entrepreneurs to present their projects or products to the global population with an opportunity to get funding in return for rewards, pre-orders, or equity.

In addition to external funding sources, nondilutive funding can help businesses finance specific projects through grants, subsidies, or government incentives. Government departments, industry organizations, and philanthropic bodies provide these types of financial assistance to support specific activities or projects without diluting ownership interests or increasing liabilities on the balance sheet.

8.2 Understanding Financing Options

In this section, we will investigate the basic mechanics of debt and equity financing, unraveling the complexities that go with each path and giving you a view on how to determine the right mix for your unique business needs.

A wide range of financing options are available to entrepreneurs and business leaders. First, let's look at debt financing and equity financing. Debt financing is simply borrowing money from external sources with an obligation to pay back principal amounts plus interest over a certain period. This type of funding allows instant access to capital without giving up ownership or control; thus, it is attractive for businesses that are planning to use their existing resources or implementing strategic objectives. It mandates a repayment schedule, which can negatively affect cash flow, and creates financial constraints, particularly during uncertainties of economic performance.

Equity financing means investors inject funds into the company by buying part-ownership in its shares. By selling shares of ownership, a business can raise funds without being indebted, creating a more flexible approach to capital acquisition. It also provides a pool of stakeholders who can contribute the expertise, networks, and resources necessary for driving the business's growth trajectory over time.

The decision between equity and debt financing is influenced by several factors, including the company's financial health, profitability outlook, risk appetite, and long-term goals. Other external factors such as market conditions and regulatory environments, including investor sentiment, influence firms' decisions regarding financial strategies, necessitating proactive and adaptive approaches toward capital management.

Finding the perfect balance between debt and equity financing is like walking a thin line that maximizes benefits while minimizing risks. Too much reliance on borrowing may create an excessive financial burden, whereas over-dependence on equity capital might water down the ownership structure, besides bringing issues of control. Consequently, it is essential to understand how debt and equity financing interact and tailor financial strategies towards specific business circumstances for sustainable growth and resilience.

Debt vs. Equity Financing

Debt and equity financing are two primary means businesses adopt to raise funds, each with benefits, concerns, and implications. Entrepreneurs and business leaders who have to maneuver capital acquisition and allocation in a complex environment must be able to distinguish between financing alternatives.

One significant advantage that debt financing has over equity financing is that it can be predicted. While equity financiers enjoy being shareholders in a business, entitled to the profits (and the losses), those opting for debt financing charge them fixed repayment terms, including the interest rate and repayment schedule. This allows organizations to plan their cash flows effectively, which allows for correct money management and decision-making.

Companies can take advantage of debt financing if they have steady streams of income or can pledge any assets they own as security. Firms might get lower rates while borrowing on favorable terms if they use current assets this way. Paying interest on debts may also help cut annual expenditures tax-wise, thus lowering costs for firms. There are certain risks and considerations attached to debt-financing options. For one thing, there will always be a requirement that should be fulfilled first; the obligation to repay the borrowed sum. Companies must keep servicing creditors' accounts, which will undoubtedly affect running cash flows, especially during recessions or times when sales fall.

If businesses rely too heavily on borrowing, they are exposed to more risk of insolvency and bankruptcy when they fail to honor their debt obligations. High debt levels can also reduce financial flexibility, thus limiting growth opportunities, since a large part of the proceeds will be allocated to servicing such debts.

Equity financing is characterized by more flexibility than debt financing. Rather than providing loans and other forms of repayment like interest charges, investors offer capital and become joint risk-takers with management. In such situations, liabilities for sales are avoided, especially when short-term cash flow is likely to be volatile or uncertain.

On the other hand, equity funding may attract stakeholders with good financial sources backed up by broad experience networks, among many different inputs. These investors are called venture capitalists or angel investors because they can mentor firms during the strategic planning process and access clients faster due to their wide contacts, speeding up the promotion of organizations' growth rate.

Equity financing is only appropriate for some companies, especially those with ambitious growth plans and future exit strategies. Selling ownership stakes can reduce opportunities for raising capital or controlling the firm's destiny. Equity finance is generally more expensive over time since shareholders typically demand a higher rate of return as compensation for the risks inherent in equity investments.

Choosing between debt and equity financing involves weighing various factors, such as the company's financial condition, growth prospects, risk appetite, and long-term goals. This means that there is no one-size-fits-all solution since the optimum mix of debt and equity financing will depend on the specific situations faced by individual businesses.

Companies must balance the advantages and considerations of each option, starting with the cost of capital and financial flexibility within parameters such as personal control levels or risk appetite. Some organizations may employ a hybrid method to take advantage of the advantages of either type while avoiding the negative aspects.

Market conditions, regulatory frameworks, and investor sentiments are external variables that affect the viability and attractiveness of different funding options. Therefore, businesses must remain watchful while flexible enough to review their financing strategies continually to suit changing dynamics, thus taking advantage of increasing value through growth opportunities.

Determining the Right Mix for Your Business

Different organizations have different financial backgrounds, objectives of growth, and risk attitudes, so determining the best combination of financing options requires a contemplative and strategic approach, taking into consideration various aspects and factors. In some instances, start-ups or early-stage businesses may lack the track record or collateral to access traditional debt financing. Consequently, equity financing may prove to be an effective alternative, enabling such firms to raise funds without incurring additional debts.

Established companies with secure assets and cash flow could find debt financing a more attractive option. By leveraging existing assets or revenue streams, these entities can offer their loans at a better rate, reducing the costs associated with capital borrowing. Businesses also enjoy predictability regarding repaying their debts since they know how much they need to pay back and within what time frame.

Another aspect that needs attention is risk aversion levels. Some companies are willing to take on larger debts for higher returns, while others prefer minimizing debt levels to mitigate financial risks. One cannot determine which mix of finances is appropriate without understanding the business's risk tolerance level and whether it suits their long-term aims.

Businesses must consider how their decisions on funding will affect their ownership and control. Equity finance comprises selling company ownership shares, thereby diluting ownership rights and control over management. Though offering a practical, well-experienced knowledge base for a business entity's decision-making process coupled with resources, this type comes with certain drawbacks, such as loss of autonomy against benefits entailed from raising outside capital.

If an enterprise utilizes debt finance, it has full authority over management because lenders do not have any say in policy-making processes within such firms. Nonetheless, too much reliance on borrowing can increase the level of financial leverage and curtail future growth prospects, since a large proportion of earnings will go to debt servicing.

Firms also need to consider how their financing decisions affect their overall capital structure. Capital structure refers to a company's mix of finance sources, such as debt, equity, and retained earnings. A company's capital structure must remain balanced to maintain financial stability and flexibility and maximize shareholders' value.

In determining which funding option is appropriate for your firm, you should also consider the cost of capital. The cost of capital is generally referred to as the overall cost that is incurred by an organization when it borrows money or uses other forms of finance, such as issuing shares, to raise funds needed for investment purposes. Entrepreneurs should compare the costs associated with each source of finance before making any decision.

Businesses must consider financing decisions' potential effects on long-term growth and survival. Despite its advantage in terms of immediate access to capital, firms have to consider the future implications of incurring extra debt. While equity financing can enable a business to obtain additional valuable resources and expertise, entrepreneurs need to consider the ramifications of diluting their ownership stakes.

A suitable blend of funding options must be determined after considering different factors, such as risk aversion. Making wise decisions about funds that will be used to support growth and sustainability should be based on the company's stages of development, risk preference levels towards financial stakeholders' objectives for control and ownership, capital structures, and milestones for long-term growth plans.

8.3 Bootstrapping Your Start-Up

Welcome to the bootstrapping section of your start-up journey into entrepreneurship marked by independence, perseverance, and inventiveness. This chapter delves into the art and science behind starting and growing a business with minimal external capital by using personal funds, early sales revenue generation, and creative strategies for lowering initial capital needs.

At its heart, bootstrapping means turning away from conventional approaches to obtaining funds. Instead, it lets founders use their resources and ingenuity to achieve their dreams. By applying personal savings, liquidating assets, or using personal lines of credit, founders have often shown their dedication to the idea of their business and retained 100% ownership as well as control over the development trajectory of their enterprise.

Frugality must be at the forefront of one's mind when bootstrapping rather than waiting for external investments. This is a different situation to other start-ups that rely on external finance, since they do not focus so much on the value proposition to clients; instead, they sell products quickly after launching them. When you are doing this, an income stream becomes crucial; first is a proof-of-concept regarding this start-up idea, plus it acts as a source of the cash flows necessary for maintaining operations, supporting growth initiatives, and refining product features based on market feedback.

Bootstrapping goes beyond using one's savings and building on early revenues: it implies an overall approach that seeks to minimize initial capital outlay, while maximizing resource use efficiency. It involves various methods, including the adoption of lean methodologies and production of minimum viable products (MVPs), reliance on open-source software, and outsourcing non-core activities. Those who bootstrap businesses are adept at stretching limited resources, thus optimizing every part of their company.

Bootstrapped companies can achieve excellent results, despite having little money, by embracing frugality, resourcefulness, and agility. Through the resilience and determination needed to adapt during trying business moments, bootstrap entrepreneurs often emerge stronger from the hardships of entrepreneurship. They create sustainable and robust businesses from scratch, unburdened by the demands or constraints that usually come with external investors.

Leveraging Personal Funds and Revenue

For people who want financial stability and growth, it is essential to understand the complexities of leveraging personal finance and earnings. One of the critical aspects of the effective use of funds is prudence in financial management. Potential risks and returns should be assessed through extensive research and analysis before committing personal funds to any venture. This includes knowledge of market dynamics, industry trends, and attributes related to specific investments or business opportunities.

Diversification has become a vital strategy when it comes to maximizing the effectiveness of personal finances. Spreading resources across several assets or opportunities rather than concentrating on one investment or business venture helps reduce risks while enhancing portfolio resilience. In addition, diversification brings about some level of protection from potential losses but also opens up new ways for tapping into diverse sources of income. By diversifying their portfolios, individuals can limit exposure to the volatility associated with any sector or market, improving general financial stability.

The other thing to consider when leveraging personal funds is balancing risk and reward. On one hand, high-risk investments may provide substantial returns on investments; they come with more significant uncertainty and increased vulnerability to market fluctuations. On the other hand, conservative investment strategies provide stability but may result in lower long-term returns over time.

Sustainable growth in finance is highly dependent on strategic re-investment derived from personal earnings. Instead of withdrawing profits passively, reinvesting them into the business or investment portfolio can accelerate wealth accumulation, thus creating room for expansion. This cyclical re-investment of funds enables them to tap into their existing resources for additional revenue and assets, fostering a self-sustaining growth trajectory.

Maintaining liquidity reserves to navigate unexpected expenses or exploit time-bound opportunities is also essential. While allocating all available funds to investments or business ventures might be tempting, a cash buffer ensures financial agility and resilience. Liquidity reserves serve as a cushion during economic recessions or emergencies, preventing you from having to borrow at exorbitant interest rates or sell long-term investments before maturity.

For financial success in the long run, it is crucial to create a solid base for finance, such as setting clear financial goals, making out budgets, managing debt responsibly, and prioritizing savings and investments. By providing a solid basis for financial safety, you can sail through hard economic times without losing your dreams. Embracing a mindset of resilience and adaptability is vital in navigating the unknowns on the horizon. Resilience comes from having constructive attitudes about setbacks and challenges, making people more robust.

Creative Ways to Reduce Initial Capital Requirements

Understanding how to creatively decrease initial capital requirements can be instrumental to individuals or businesses who want to start new ventures or expand their current ones. One of the creative ways is by exploring partnerships and joint ventures with other complementary companies or persons. Such alliances pool resources and expertise, thus sharing the financial burden and reducing the risks involved in starting a new venture. These partnerships create synergistic potential for cross-promotion, allowing partners to leverage networks and clientele bases for mutual benefits.

Another creative way to decrease initial capital needs is by efficiently using existing assets and resources. Instead of wholly depending on external finance, people can identify underutilized resources to generate additional income. This may involve leasing out unoccupied office space, machinery, or patents, creating other streams of income that don't require a heavy initial investment.

Crowdfunding has emerged as a popular alternative financing option for entrepreneurs seeking to raise capital without traditional loans or investments. Crowdfunding websites such as Kickstarter, Indiegogo, or GoFundMe allow people to present their projects before many potential sponsors who give small donations in exchange for some rewards or even equity shares. For instance, it enables start-ups to obtain funding before launching any product, thus market-proofing them.

Another way of minimizing primary expenditures is looking at non-conventional sources like P2P lending/micro-lending. Unlike typical bank loans, P2P lending online platforms directly link borrowers with individual lenders offering competitive rates. Meanwhile, microloans cater for small loans disbursed to entrepreneurs and small firms who are unable or reluctant to access mainstream banking products. Improvised options are more inclusive and flexible, implying that an individual can get money without going through the lender's strict criteria.

Bootstrapping techniques provide an excellent means of lowering start-up capital costs for small and young business entities. This involves utilizing the bare minimum available while reducing costs through frugality and resourcefulness. For instance, one can work from home, use open-source software products, trade goods or services, or even negotiate with suppliers and vendors for better terms. By taking a lean approach to business operations, entrepreneurs can use their limited resources to do more things.

Pre-selling products or services ahead of their full development and launch is a way of generating cash flow and testing demand. Early bird discounts or exclusive offers can encourage pre-orders so that there is enough money to finance production and development. This guarantees immediate profits while reducing potential financial risks related to unverified items or services investments.

Creative financing methods, such as revenue-sharing agreements, are another option for reducing initial capital requirements. Instead of upfront payments or investments, entrepreneurs can negotiate deals with suppliers, contractors, or investors based on a percentage of future revenues or profits. This aligns the interests of all parties involved and provides an incentive for performance and success while minimizing the need for significant upfront capital investments.

Another way to reduce initial capital requirements for eligible individuals or businesses is by exploring government grants or incentives to support entrepreneurship and innovation. Besides, many governments provide grants, subsidies, or tax credits to encourage research and development, job creation, or investment in specific industries or sectors. It is also possible for entrepreneurs to use such programs to acquire non-dilutive funding that can be used to launch their start-ups or offset the costs of capital acquisition.

To minimize waste and optimize resources, a lean start-up approach needs to be embraced; this entails testing and iterating on ideas quickly and cost-effectively. Using agile methodologies like rapid prototyping, customer feedback loops, and iterative product development, will enable entrepreneurs to validate refined offerings as well as reducing the risk of costly failures. Such an iterative strategy allows entrepreneurs to preserve capital while pivoting strategies in response to real-time market feedback, thereby raising chances for success while minimizing initial capital requirements.

8.4 Seeking Loans and Credit

Considering both the personal and business aspects of finance, amassing capital is an ongoing process involving significant decision-making and strategic thinking. The search for loans and credit forms the core of the process, and is instrumental in fueling growth, leveraging opportunities, and overcoming financial hurdles for individuals and businesses, respectively. This section provides a comprehensive guide to maneuvering through the complex world of loan-seeking, delving into various financing options and their implications for borrowers.

Traditional bank loans can give the borrower access to huge lump sums with fixed terms and conditions. Established financial institutions offer these, often to help facilitate long-term investments such as land purchases or business expansion. You can only successfully secure a traditional bank loan if you meet tough qualifying criteria, such as a sound credit history, stable incomes, and valuable assets that could serve as collateral securities.

Lines of credit and other short-term borrowing options are available to address immediate cash flow requirements while offering flexible funding solutions. Borrowers may utilize lines of credit up to a specific limit where interest charges are only applied on borrowed amounts. For instance, revolving credit is convenient because it helps people manage fluctuations in their cash flows, enabling them to deal with unforeseen expenses promptly. Conversely, short-term borrowing options like overdrawing or payday loans may be costly, so careful thinking concerning their appropriateness or sustainability is required.

Government-supported financing programs, including Small Business Administration (SBA) loans, offer significant opportunities for small businesses and entrepreneurs who wish to raise funds for growth. SBA loan packages have favorable terms, which include reduced interest rates, more extended repayment periods, plus lower collateral demands that make them accessible even when entrepreneurs cannot approach conventional lenders. As well as those linked to SBA lending activities, several others are run by the federal, state, and local governments, all aimed at boosting economic development, creating jobs, or encouraging innovations. These programs may offer grants, subsidies, and loan guarantees, among other benefits, to different individuals or business entities as per eligibility.

Apart from traditional bank loans and government-backed financing programs, alternative sources of finance like peer-to-peer lending platforms and asset-based financing give borrowers several options for raising funds. Peer-to-peer lending platforms directly match borrowers with individual investors who are willing borrowers, offering more flexible and accessible lending options than traditional banks. While asset-based financing relies on using assets such as real estate or inventory as collateral, it is helpful for companies with valuable assets but low liquidity.

The factors that need to be weighed include eligibility criteria, loan terms and conditions, and repayment obligations involved before seeking loans or credit. You must know the details of different traditional bank loans, lines of credit, short-term borrowing options, SBA loans, and financing avenues.

Traditional Bank Loans

Standard bank loans have been a pillar of financing for people and businesses for quite some time. These loans are given by well-established financial institutions like banks and credit unions to enable borrowers to access money for various purposes, such as buying a home, starting a business, or paying for unforeseen expenses. Traditional bank loans differ from other funding methods, such as peer-to-peer lending or crowdfunding, as they generally follow established lending practices and regulatory guidelines.

Another defining characteristic of this type of loan is collateralization. Banks usually ask borrowers to pledge collateral. This collateral acts as proof to lenders that they can retrieve their assets if the repayments default. Secured loans tend to have lower rates compared to unsecured ones, because they are less risky on the part of the lender.

When applying for traditional bank loans, one must undergo rigorous scrutiny, including financial history, credit score, and ability to pay the requested loan amount. Financial institutions assess whether you are creditworthy based on your stable income sources, level of debts compared with what you earn each month, employment background, and former credit involvement information. Bankers make these assessments based on information provided in credit reports obtained from any significant national CRBs (credit reference bureaus).

After approval, the borrower will receive cash, which needs to be paid back according to an agreed-upon schedule. Banks offer different kinds of traditional loans that suit various needs of borrowers, including mortgage loans for real estate investment, auto loans financing the purchase of a car, and business loans, which are explicitly meant for entrepreneurial activities. Every type of loan has its own set of criteria, terms of borrowing, and conditions.

Although traditional bank loans have many advantages, like affordable interest rates, structured repayment schedules, and more significant lending limits, they also come with limitations and risks. Strict qualifying standards can make it impossible for some to get these benefits. The process of applying for and receiving confirmation of such credits from traditional banks is usually long due to the various formalities involved so it may not work where quick funding is needed.

Lines of Credit and Short-term Borrowing Options

Banks offer a wide range of financial products that cater to the short-term funding needs of businesses and individuals. These include lines of credit and short-term borrowing options, which can be flexible in assisting with cash flow fluctuations, financing unplanned expenses, or taking advantage of immediate opportunities. This makes it essential for borrowers to comprehend these tools to find effective and convenient solutions.

Lines of credit are credit limits already preapproved by financial institutions to allow borrowers to draw down funds up to the agreed limit when needed. Compared to traditional loans, where borrowers receive their lump sum upfront and then repay it over a definite period, lines of credit are more elastic when it comes to borrowing and repayment. Borrowers can withdraw money when necessary and pay interest only on what is borrowed; therefore, they are helpful in managing fluctuating cash flows.

One key benefit of lines of credit is that they are revolving, which means that, as borrowers pay off the amounts they owe, the available limits get refreshed, thus allowing continued access to funds. This feature enables lines of credit to become valuable, especially for businesses whose cash flow depends on seasonal changes or irregular incomes. Lines of credit allow companies to use available funds for growth opportunities, operating costs, or emergency situations without disrupting normal operations.

Lines of credit often come with highly competitive interest rates, particularly for those with a good credit history. Financial institutions may offer secure lines of credit; requiring collateral such as real estate or inventory, or unsecure; backed solely by the borrower's credibility, lines of credit, among other types. Secured types generally attract low charges since lenders' risk exposure decreases, while unsecured ones come with a slight increase in interest rate.

Apart from that, banks equally provide more diverse short-term borrowing choices oriented towards specific needs; for instance, overdrafts allow account holders to go into negative balances subject to certain charge levies and interest. While this facility is a quick source of money in emergencies, it is essential to control the extent of overdraft usage to avoid huge charges or even damaging your credit record.

Another short-term borrowing option involves using business credit cards that offer revolving lines of credit similar to traditional lines of credit, but which can be used to make purchases directly using the card. Business credit cards are commonly equipped with reward programs, expense tracking tools, and more, so they are preferred by small businesses and entrepreneurs seeking flexible ways to manage costs.

Banks may also provide specialized short-term loans or advances, such as invoice financing, merchant cash advance, or equipment financing, whose primary purpose is addressing specific funding requirements. Such alternatives could benefit businesses that require short-term capital against assets and revenue sources because they expedite access to finance by utilizing existing assets.

SBA Loans and Other Government-Supported Financing

Government-assisted financing, such as Small Business Administration (SBA) loans, is a crucial resource for businesses to access and find cheap financing options. These programs provide incentives through more accessible terms and loan guarantees to stimulate economic growth, support entrepreneurship, and facilitate job creation. The Small Business Administration is a federal agency that supports small businesses through various programs, including loan guarantees. Unlike direct loans from the government, SBA loans guarantee portions of loans provided by participating lenders such as banks or credit unions. This guarantee reduces lenders' risk, making them more willing to provide credit to small businesses that do not qualify for traditional loans.

One of the best-known SBA loan programs is 7(a), which funds things like working capital, equipment acquisition, real estate purchase, and debt refinancing. Compared with conventional loans, this offers flexible terms at affordable interest rates over longer repayment periods, making it attractive to start-ups looking for additional funding as they grow their operations. Another important SBA lending program is CDC/504, which finances fixed assets such as property or equipment. In collaboration with lenders, certified Development Companies (CDCs) administer this program, which provides long-term fixed-rate finance requiring a smaller down payment and better terms for small firms seeking to buy or rehabilitate property or acquire significant machinery.

Other forms of government-supported financial assistance may consist of grants or tax credits targeting specific industries or addressing economic disparities. These may be run by different federal agencies besides state or local governments, providing research and development grants, export promotion funding, training workforce needs, and funding for community-based projects.

Government-supported financing initiatives often target underprivileged communities, such as women-owned ventures, minority-owned enterprises, veteran-owned companies, and rural corporations. The aim of these programs is to ensure equal access to the resources and capital essential for enabling these entities to prosper in the marketplace. Under government-supported financing schemes, disaster relief assistance might be available. This aids firms in bouncing back from natural catastrophes, economic recessions, or other negative occurrences, using low-interest loans, grants, and other forms of aid

SBA loan programs, like others supported by the government, serve as significant means of accessing affordable finance for enterprises across different sizes and industries. This way, entrepreneurs and small business proprietors not only stay above the poverty line but also contribute to GDP growth, create jobs, and improve the community through various social responsibility projects.

8.5 Equity Funding Sources

Securing ample finances is usually an anchor to success in the entrepreneurship journey. Among the myriad funding options available, equity funding is a sturdy platform for startups and well-established companies. This section thoroughly examines three pivotal equity financing sources: angel investors, venture capital, and private equity.

Angel investors are early supporters of entrepreneurial projects; they bring more than money on board. Their extensive experience in various fields, industry contacts, and strategic direction can influence young corporations' paths. Conversely, venture capital enterprises represent the lifeblood of the startup ecosystem, since they provide substantial investment and strategic partnerships, thus promoting innovation and growth. Through them, startups can get funds and other resources necessary for scaling up, including invaluable counsel on technology issues.

As firms mature and explore possibilities for expansion or restructuring, private equity from the capital markets becomes an option. Private equity firms invest in established businesses, with the aim of injecting capital that will drive operational efficiencies, improve profitability levels, and unlock latent value, among other things. The approach through which these entities make their interventions is always planned out, involving rigorous execution aimed at maximizing returns for stakeholders as well as investors.

Angel Investors: Finding Them and Pitching Your Idea

Getting funding from angel investors can be a game-changer in moving a start-up business forward. Unlike conventional sources of financing, angel investors have the capital to offer invaluable experience and connection. Attracting the appropriate angel investors and effectively delivering your ideas will require strategic planning, targeted outreach, and compelling narratives.

One of the most efficient ways of connecting with angel investors is through networking. Get involved in industry events, start-up meetups, and entrepreneurship conferences where you can find angel investors. Have meaningful conversations about your vision and interest in their insights by sharing them on social media platforms such as LinkedIn or Twitter. Trust-building is essential for credibility.

Online platforms for entrepreneurs seeking potential investors, like AngelList, Gust, or SeedInvest, are helpful. By developing profiles on such websites, start-ups can demonstrate their business ideas and connect with potential angels who share similar industry alignment characteristics with their own company stage and investment criteria.

Find out whether there are any networks or groups involving angel investors from your area and the industries of interest. This type of group often attracts money from wealthy individuals interested in finding business projects in which they can invest together. It is an arena where start-ups engage many people at once. Research local communities of business angels near you and participate in their gatherings, while using them to showcase what you have made.

Establishing relationships with accomplished professionals, including former industry players or successful businesspeople, may also result in them becoming an angel investor, because it increases your stature and makes you more visible among fellow financiers. You need to think about your pitch and language. Begin by creating an exciting introductory sentence that will capture any investor's mind. Follow this with a short summary introducing your product or service, target market, competitors, and pricing model. Discuss what makes you different from the rest and why your business will succeed.

Demonstrate traction by showcasing key metrics like customer acquisition cost, revenue growth rate, product development milestones, and strategic partnerships that prove business scalability.' Showing concrete evidence of progress builds trust among investors, thus reducing perceived risks.

Ensure that the investment opportunity is articulated well, including how much money you need, how much equity you are willing to part with for it, and what your strategic plan will depend on once these funds are received. State your funding timeline, expected milestones, and possible exit routes to manage investor expectations while showing them a way to return.

Build relationships and proactively follow up after your initial pitch, addressing any questions or concerns, and providing updates on your progress. Personalized follow-up emails, meetings, or event invitations can deepen connections and keep investors engaged throughout the fundraising process.

Venture Capital: How It Works and What VCs Look For

Venture capital is a critical factor in the growth of innovation, funding high-potential start-ups with equity. To secure funds to expand their businesses, entrepreneurs must understand how venture capital works and what venture capitalists are looking for. The venture capital process usually encompasses several phases, each with distinct sets of criteria and objectives:

Fundraising: Venture capitalists raise money from institutional investors such as insurance companies, foundations, and wealthy individuals to start a fund that backs start-ups. These funds are commonly structured as limited partnerships, with the VC firm acting as the general partner in charge of managing the funds.

Deal Sourcing: VCs look for possible investment deals by networking with entrepreneurs, attending industry events, or using existing relationships within the start-up community. They may also be referred to other investors by incubators, accelerators, or industry insiders.

Due Diligence: After identifying a potential investment opportunity, venture capitalists conduct due diligence checks to assess the feasibility and viability of the target start-up. This includes evaluating the team, market size, product and technology competition, business model, and financial projection scalability.

Investment Decision: Venture capitalists review their findings after conducting due diligence before making an investment decision. Suppose they find that the opportunity matches their firm's investment thesis and criteria well. In that case, they will negotiate deal terms such as the amount of funding, valuation, ownership percentage stake, and governance rights.

Portfolio Management: Venture capitalists continue to support and actively monitor their portfolio companies by providing strategic direction operational aid access network contacts as required. They may also be members of the Board of Directors. As chairs they oversee some aspects of these firms, while their advisory boards provide guidance and oversight activities.

Exit: Venture capitalists generally seek an exit strategy through IPOs, Initial Public Offerings, mergers, acquisition activities, M&A, or secondary sales. Timing and the manner of exit are determined by various factors, such as market condition, trajectory growth, and investor preferences.

Venture capitalists consider several key factors when evaluating potential investment opportunities:

Team: VCs value the founding team's experience, expertise, and track record, which significantly affect investment decisions. They look for founders with domain knowledge, relevant industry experience, strong leadership skills, and a clear vision for the company's growth.

Market Opportunity: The VC evaluates the market size, growth rates, and competitors before investing in such start-ups. They would look at start-ups addressing huge underserved markets with innovative solutions that could disrupt existing industries or even create new ones.

Product or Technology: VCs will analyze a start-up's product uniqueness, scalability, and defensibility. They will evaluate whether any offering from it will have the best value proposition, competitive advantage, and high potential for widespread adoption.

Traction and Milestones: VCs want some evidence of traction and progress, including customer adoption rate, revenue development partnerships or alliances, and balance sheet strength. This means that investors give preference to those businesses that have reached certain milestones or demonstrated traction.

Business Model: Venture capitalists analyze financial information, including revenue streams, pricing strategies, and path profitability, to assess business sustainability levels, ability to scale through expansion, long-term growth, capacity, and profit-making plans.

They also evaluate the potential exit possibilities for their investments, including the probability of an IPO or acquisition by a strategic acquirer. They seek start-ups that will give investors significantly high returns in a reasonable period. Venture capital contributes to innovation and growth through financing, providing capital and strategic guidance mainly for high-potential start-up enterprises. Entrepreneurs who are trying to raise funds to grow their businesses need to comprehend how venture capitalists operate and what they consider when selecting investment opportunities.

Private Equity: When it's an Option and the Trade-offs

Private equity (PE) is a route through which established businesses can obtain financing and be reconstituted. Early-stage start-ups are generally the preserve of venture capitalists, unlike private equity companies who front mature firms that have reliable incomes or growth potential. Business owners must understand when to consider private equity and what they may give up in return.

Specific situations or strategic support could make PE an alternative for many firms. Growth initiatives, new market entries, or strategic acquisitions are reasons businesses decide to get private equity for their capital requirements and expertise to expand. Private equity firms provide extensive financial resources and advisory services. There are also management buyouts (MBOs), family succession planning, or other situations where private equity can easily facilitate ownership transitions. The essence of such partnerships lies in the fact that their enterprise will continue growing after they retire from it because continuity will remain assured after their retirement.

Private equity can also fund turnaround strategies or restructuring exercises to save distressed or underperforming businesses with operational challenges or financial problems. Further, liquidity for owners wishing to monetize their investments can be obtained through private equity. Attractive as it may appear, this investment option has several trade-offs and is not suitable for every entrepreneur.

It is common practice among most institutions to invest in private equities, and they will seek substantial ownership stakes by buying into such organizations. Consequently, entrepreneurs may lose control over decision-making processes and daily operations as the investor becomes actively involved in governance issues. Investors who commit funds to this model expect attractive returns within a specific time—typically five to seven years. If PE investment is selected over other options, the company will be under increased scrutiny to achieve ambitious growth targets, operational efficiencies, and improved financial performance.

Private equity firms are known to use some financial engineering tricks, such as leverage or capital restructuring, to maximize returns for their shareholders, especially when it comes to value additions. While these can yield short-term growth, they may also heighten a firm's exposure to finance-related risks and debt load. Private equity investors aim to gain capital through sale, IPO, or secondary offering. An entrepreneur must carefully consider whether partnering with a private equity firm is worth the potential implications.

While private equity brings in capital and expertise for growth and transformational purposes, control may be lost, and there may be pressure to perform financial engineering and align exit objectives. The decision to pursue PE investments should be guided by the organization's strategic goals and long-term business vision for its success. Early-stage start-ups are generally the preserve of venture capitalists, rather than private equity companies, who front mature firms that have reliable incomes or any growth potential. Business owners must understand when it makes sense to consider private equity as an option and what they may give up in return.

8.6 Crowdfunding and Microfinancing

In today's world characterized by hyper-connectivity and digitalization, these alternative financing models have changed how individuals and enterprises raise funds by doing away with traditional obstacles to credit. This section aims to explore the ins and outs of crowdfunding and microfinance, thereby determining their relevance for funding small businesses or startups.

Crowdfunding has given democratic power to individuals, artists, inventors, and writers who can use it to get financial support for their projects. For instance, a person wishing to launch a new product may appeal to crowdfunding platforms to make their ideas visible to members of the public, who will provide monetary aid in the form of donations if they want to do so. Launching a successful crowdfunding campaign requires careful planning, strategic execution, and effective engagement with backers. Several factors contributing to success in raising funds through crowdfunding are setting clear objectives, constructing appealing narratives, and utilizing social proof while engaging with investors via transparent talkbacks or updates.

Microfinancing, especially in the mode of microloans, has become the only savior for small businesses and entrepreneurs living in poor communities all over the globe. Unlike conventional banking institutions that often require collateral or installment loans as lending criteria, MFIs offer unsecured loans without demanding securities like land titles, and with only some minimal documentation. These small-scale loans allow those excluded from mainstream finance opportunities due to poverty levels to establish or expand business operations, making income for them and improving their living conditions. Such micro-loans can promote entrepreneurship, cause poverty alleviation, and foster inclusion into formal economic systems.

Crowdfunding is an innovative way of generating funds for small businesses and startups. By providing access to capital for all and promoting entrepreneurship at the grassroots level, crowdfunding and microfinancing can enable economic growth, job creation, and social impact. Entrepreneurs, investors, and policymakers who wish to foster positive change in the world through crowdfunding campaigns and microfinance initiatives should understand how it works.

How to Launch a Successful Crowdfunding Campaign

One of the most important things a person can do to have a successful crowdfunding campaign is to plan correctly, tell a good story, and get involved in attracting potential funders and supporters. Your campaign's goals and objectives should be defined; this is essential. Know how much money you need, how it will be used, and the desired results. Specific, measurable targets will help you concentrate efforts and effectively communicate your project's vision to the prospective backers.

Crafting an appealing story will help catch the attention of your audience. Share the background of your project, which should state what problem it solves, its impact, and why it matters. Personal stories combined with passion and inspiration can make people emotionally attached to your project, prompting them to support you.

Your fundraising page on crowdfunding serves as the central hub for all your fundraising efforts. Please make sure you spend enough time creating an appealing page that thoroughly explains what your project is about, its objectives, and rewards. You should also use high-quality visuals to show off your projects better and lure visitors into becoming funders.

Giving valuable incentives attracts more backers to any funding drive. Various rewards should be provided at different prices so that other groups of people can be attracted by them. You need to ensure that all these incentives are pertinent and rewarding and can serve the interests of those who might back you.

Realistic funding targets must be set for a campaign's success. Avoid setting high goals that may be achievable or realistic, given the scope of your project or its target audience. Breaking down a goal into smaller achievable milestones might create momentum as well as encouraging contributors. For purposes of reaching fundraising goals effectively, one requires effective promotion strategies in place. Utilize present networks, social media platforms, and email listings to educate more people about this initiative, while driving traffic toward your page. By collaborating with influencers or bloggers, you will be able to amplify your message to reach a wider audience.

Regular communication is essential in keeping backers involved and informed. Provide updates about the campaign's progress, milestones, and achievements. Transparency and open communication build trust and credibility with your backers, thus creating a sense of community around your project. Respond promptly to comments or questions from contributors. Encourage conversations where people can give feedback or appreciation for the support provided. The more valued supporters feel, the stronger their connection to a particular project becomes.

Sticking to what one has said is essential in maintaining trustworthiness with those who have already supported you. Backers should be kept updated on how rewards and other deliverables that need fulfillment are going. If there is anything wrong, address it openly. Several things may enable a person to have a successful crowdfunding campaign: proper planning, good storytelling, and engaging with potential funders. Your campaigns should have clear goals. You should know how much money you require, how it will be used, and the intended results. Setting up specific, measurable targets helps you concentrate your efforts and effectively communicate with prospective sponsors about the vision of your project.

Storytelling helps create a narrative that will catch the attention of your listeners. Share with them the background of this project, such as what problem it solves, its impact, and why it matters. With personal anecdotes laced with passion and inspiration, one can build an emotional attachment between oneself and one's audience. As such, your fundraising page represents a central hub upon which these fundraising activities will rely until funding is achieved successfully. Ensure you create an interesting webpage that talks more about what your project is all about, including its aims and rewards.

There is a need for valuable incentives that reward people for backing a funding drive. These incentives should be relevant and rewarding and must appeal to the interests of target backers. Campaign success requires setting realistic funding targets. Avoid overly ambitious, unattainable goals, given your project's scope and audience. Achievable milestones can be created after breaking down your funding goal, leading to momentum building and enticing supporters.

Effective promotion is essential. People can use their email lists, social media platforms, or even existing networks to promote this campaign, while also aiming at driving traffic back to their pages.

8.7 Preparing for Fundraising

Preparing for fundraising is a vital milestone in any startup or entrepreneur's journey. A good business plan, financial model, persuasive pitch, and investor presentation are essential building blocks in this preparation. These foundational elements prepare your company for success in a difficult funding environment by adequately communicating your vision, value proposition, and growth prospects to potential investors. A sound business plan acts as a roadmap for your venture, delineating what you aim to achieve in the market, who your competitors are, where you find clients, what components may be sold at what price, and how the business can grow.

Concurrently with having a business plan, you must develop an impressive financial model that proves whether your enterprise is economically viable or even scalable. This should show revenue forecast and expense projections, especially cash flow estimates over a three-to-five-year period. You need to include assumptions such as market size pricing strategy, customer acquisition costs, growth rates, and sensitivity analysis of various scenarios affecting a firm's performance financially within your financial model. An elaborate but pragmatic financial model assures investors about sustainable ROI generation and effective management of financial risks.

Crafting a Compelling Pitch and Investor Presentation

To effectively communicate your business concept, value proposition, and growth potential to potential investors, you must create a compelling pitch and investor presentation. This requires an understanding of who your audience is; this can be done by researching their investment focus, industry expertise, and investment criteria to tailor your message to meet their interests, preferences, and expectations. In this way, you customize your pitch to talk about their interests and specific concerns.

Your introduction should start with a punchy hook, which enables one to capture the attention of his or her audience right from the beginning. Using storytelling techniques, create an emotional connection with the audience, drawing them into your narrative. Use provocative questions, statistics, or memorable anecdotes to arouse curiosity and set up the stage for your pitch.

Articulate what distinguishes your venture's value from those of rivals and why customers would prefer purchasing your products or services. Emphasize your solution's unique advantages and benefits to illustrate how you will address critical market needs or pain points. To convince investors about your venture's successful prospects, show them facts regarding market validation and traction in a relevant industry. Highlight critical milestones achieved and significant customer testimonials validating demand for the product or service. Confidence in commercial viability can be obtained through demonstrating interest in markets, client adoption, income increase, and partnering activities.

Outline features and functionality benefits while presenting a clear solution involving specific examples such as demos, screenshots, and prototypes. Visualizations help display how valuable solutions are. Describe how revenue is earned, generated, sourced, and captured. Specify pricing strategy distribution channels and customer acquisition approaches. Make projections that support this revenue model in terms of scalability and profitability.

Emphasize strengths, qualities, and accomplishments that make an individual suitable for joining the group. Outline relevant industry experience, domain knowledge, and past successes, showing the team's ability to execute and deliver results. Say how much capital you need and what this money will be spent on. You should include a persuasive explanation of why investors should invest in your venture and the potential returns they can expect from it.

Practice your pitch thoroughly to refine the delivery, timing, and messaging. Learn the weakest aspects of your speech and work on them. Ask about tone and body language. Presenters should make their speeches precise, to inspire confidence and trust among audience members.

8.8 The Fundraising Process

Networking and identifying potential investors are the most essential aspects of fundraising. Entrepreneurs must have strong connections within the investment community to access valuable resources and opportunities. Potential investors can be met through industrial events, conferences, or even mutual friends who know them, thus enabling one to create a stronger relationship by discussing various issues concerning investments available in the market.

The critical phase here is due diligence, where investors examine a business plan's feasibility, associated risks, or attractiveness as an investment option. Investors consider many factors, such as the business model, size of market opportunity, and other factors. Entrepreneurs should provide complete information on different points raised during this process, while being transparent.

When you sign an agreement that seals an investment made into you to understand investment documents, especially term sheets, which contain vital terms such as valuation, governance rights, the amount invested by a company during its establishment stage, and funding stages. Deal closure requires attention to detail, practical communication skills, and teamwork.

Networking and Identifying Potential Investors

Start-ups must network and identify potential investors as the first step in the fundraising process. Good relationships with resourceful people, insiders, and like-minded individuals within the investment industry are critical to an effective fundraising campaign. This section highlights some of the strategies that can help you improve your networking skills and identify prospective investors.

Participate in Trade Fairs and Conferences: Businesspeople can use trade fairs or conference meetings to meet investors and discuss their business ideas. Look for specific events, seminars, and workshops where there are chances of meeting such people. These forms of exchange conversations are usually facilitated through panel discussions that allow an entrepreneur to meet these potential partners.

Employ Online Platforms and Networking Groups: Aspiring businesspeople may join online platforms such as LinkedIn and AngelList and be part of a start-up community to widen their network across possible investor groups. In addition, it is also essential to join industry groups, which should offer an opportunity to participate in discussions while taking advantage of social media networks, to show how knowledgeable one is regarding these topics and connect with willing sponsors.

Ask Mutual Connections for Introductions: It's beneficial if they have mutual connections that would introduce you to potential investors during the business period. Entrepreneurs could strategically use existing links from peer group members at the workplace, mentors, or advisers, including alums, to contact possible funders around their area friends. The personal references they give you will increase your credibility in securing investor meetings.

Attend Pitch Events and Demo Days: Entrepreneurial students can participate in pitch competitions or demo days organized by incubators like accelerators or start-up contests, where many capitalists are in the invited audience. You might also want to consider joining any accelerator programs or demo days where you could present your business venture, get feedback on it, and mingle with angel investor teams.

Engage in Investor Pitch Meetings: Another way to get a meeting with a potential investor is by participating in investors' pitch meetings or arranging one-on-one talks. Find those venture capitalists who have previously invested in similar ideas to yours and arrange for meetings with them.

Cultivate Authentic Relationships: Entrepreneurs should concentrate more on establishing solid and genuine relationships with investors rather than on immediate funding opportunities alone. An entrepreneur needs significant time and energy to develop a personal rapport with prospective sponsors, learn about their investment policies, and adjust the start-up specifics to fit the investors` requirements. Gaining foundational trust from these investors will enable future discussions about finances and a business partnership.

Follow Up and Stay Connected: Whenever you meet someone interested in your enterprise during meetings or after the initial conversations, it is necessary to email them as soon as possible, thanking them for their time and offering additional information where needed. The businessperson should keep in touch with these supporters through newsletters communicating any development made so far, as well as issuing reports based on milestones reached over a certain period. Constant communication indicates that a founder is serious enough about their product while ensuring steady growth before taking money from any angel.

Through active networking and identification of possible sources of financing, entrepreneurs get better chances to reach many customers, secure the funds needed for day-to-day operations, and create strategic alliances that can facilitate further progress of such ventures. Although it does take time, effort, and persistence to build up a reliable network of financiers, it ensures access to the capital required to achieve rapid sales growth.

The Due Diligence Process Explained

The fundraising journey includes the critical due diligence process, where potential investors evaluate an entrepreneur's business ideas and their feasibility and riskiness. This stage confirms the entrepreneur's story, reveals profit opportunities, and signals possible danger. To facilitate the due diligence process, investors typically ask entrepreneurs to provide a range of documents and materials. These could include, but are not limited to, business plans, financial statements, revenue projections, customer contracts, legal agreements, intellectual property filings, or regulatory filings. Entrepreneurs need to have all hands-on deck to provide comprehensive and accurate information within the stipulated timeframe for smooth running.

During the due diligence process, meetings or interviews may be held between investors and critical members of the entrepreneur's team, such as founders, executives, or advisors. Such sessions can help an investor learn more about the founder's thoughts on vision-making strategies. Investors may also wish for more information about aspects connected with a particular business idea or its potential risks.

They will need to determine market opportunity and the competitive landscape to know if there is enough demand and growth prospects for an entrepreneur's product or service. It is important for an investor to validate assumptions and projections made by an entrepreneur through market research, competitor analysis, and customer interviews, and even industry benchmarking.

During financial due diligence, a thorough examination of entrepreneurs' financial statements, including revenue projections, cash flow forecasts, and accounting practices, is performed. Revenue sources are scrutinized, and cost structures are dissected along with profit margins plus other essential financial indicators that say something about the sustainability of the venture in question. Historical performance and future growth prospects will also be evaluated here alongside any other possible risks and contingencies.

Some investors want to know any legal or regulatory risks that may impact the venture's operations or prospects as part of their due diligence checks on entrepreneurs' companies. These include, but are not limited to, assessments of corporate governance practices, contractual obligations, employment agreements, and intellectual property rights. While carrying out due diligence, entrepreneurs should confirm that their firm is operating in line with the existing laws and regulations while addressing legal matters emanating from the process.

Throughout the due diligence process, there will be an evaluation of risk and uncertainty connected with this investment and the entrepreneur's plan for reducing these risks. Such discussions involve reviewing strategies for managing risk, contingency plans, and other mitigating factors that could affect the success of such initiatives. Investors are always ready to listen to those entrepreneurs who can respond convincingly while reassuring them about their ability to manage risk effectively.

The due diligence process usually has an agreed-upon timeline with specific milestones and deadlines for different steps. The final outcome of due diligence determines whether investors make an offer for investment, negotiate new terms, or withdraw from investing altogether.

Closing the Deal: Understanding Term Sheets and Investment Documents

A deal closure is a huge milestone in the fundraising journey. It is when entrepreneurs and investors put down their investment agreement and legalize the terms of the deal. Key to this process is understanding term sheets and investment documents, which set out the terms that define an investment. Term sheets are not binding contracts; instead, they spell out basic conditions for an investment between entrepreneurs and investors. Though they are not legally enforceable, term sheets serve as a basis for bargaining and provide a guide to structuring the transaction. A typical term sheet will include items such as the amount invested, valuation, governance rights, liquidation preferences, ownership interest, anti-dilution clauses, and exit strategies.

Once the parties to this agreement have agreed on all the terms stated in the term sheet, they can draft it as a legally binding investment document. These could be agreements like subscription agreements, shareholder agreements, or any other legal papers needed to finalize business deals. The amount of money invested in a venture capital firm is one crucial aspect that must be outlined in every good term sheet and its valuation. The former refers to how much cash has been committed by those taking the risk, while the latter details before and after valuations made during negotiations with potential investors. To secure sufficient control over their venture, founders should strive to meet investors' return expectations through fair valuations reflecting their potential.

Ownership stake is the percentage of equity an investor gets from their investment, thereby giving them some control over company decisions. Besides ownership stakes in term sheets, you need to define whether board seats belong to venture capitalists or founders. Management roles shared with owners of these shares should be highlighted here. Before doing so, entrepreneurs should evaluate whether this action will allow them to maintain control over their venture, and if not, they should negotiate for better terms.

Shortly after the term sheet is agreed upon by both parties, it is embodied in legally binding investment agreements. These include investment agreements, subscription agreements, shareholder agreements, and other legal documents that may be required to consummate the transaction. The document protects entrepreneurs' rights in their ownership structures while investors benefit from legal security.

The figures will determine the percentage of equity an investor buys into, along with a pre-valuation expressed as an amount or a ratio. Every startup founder should seek the most favorable valuation through fair negotiations that are based on true business potential and are still able to provide reasonable returns in terms of the percentage ownership expected by capitalists. They also indicate how funds from liquidation events like sales or winding up shall be shared among shareholders, depending on their hierarchy. For example, vesting rights may prioritize money being returned to a venture capitalist(s) before any other person. There are anti-dilution clauses aimed at protecting initial investors from having their common stock interest diluted due to later issues.

Exit strategies can also be covered in term sheets, which outline how an investor will recover their money plus profits, resulting in gains on investments made. The typical exit routes involve IPOs, M&As, or even repurchase arrangements, singly or combined. It is typically necessary for business owners and financiers to agree on the preferred method of quitting and fix terms that can maximize payback across all parties involved.

Careful consideration and legal scrutiny by both parties are needed when negotiating term sheet provisions and investing documents. Entrepreneurs should engage attorneys who will help them understand the implications of such legalities within that agreement and review whether they are acting smartly enough; this includes advising founders about the jargon used in legal circles as well as what might trigger disputes between contracting parties otherwise ignored during finalization stages, where better offers could otherwise be secured.

The deal will only be completed if the terms of the investment transaction are settled and reflected in legally enforceable investment documents. Executing the investment agreements, transferring money, and issuing shares to investors are all part of closing the deal. Entrepreneurs must comply with all legal and regulatory requirements relating to the transaction, as outlined in the term sheet and other investment documents.

Chapter 9

Branding and Marketing Essentials

At the heart of every successful organization is a strong brand that resonates with its consumers. Appreciating what branding means necessitates recognizing how brands can stir emotions, impact customers' minds, and serve as a value proposition in the market. A powerful brand helps differentiate an organization from other players in the industry, shapes consumer attitudes toward it, drives purchase decisions, and encourages loyalty.

A well-developed branding plan provides the basis for creating a compelling brand identity and guiding all marketing activities. This entails outlining the business's mission, vision, values, and position within the market while also defining who the target audience is, along with their needs and preferences. An integrated approach toward branding complements overall enterprise goals by providing direction for consistent messaging about brand image, visual look, and customer experience.

The brand identity encompasses all visual elements associated with a company, such as logos, color schemes, fonts or typescripts, and imagery used during communications. Developing an identity involves creating aesthetically pleasing assets that will help engrave into consumers' mindsets the personality of this logo and values, among other things. A strong brand concept captures attention, thus influencing sales volumes through repeat purchase behavior.

Building an increased level of brand awareness (how customers perceive your company) requires significant investments across multiple platforms, including advertising campaigns, public relations, social networks, and content creation.

Well-targeted distribution begins with deep knowledge of the market, competitors, and target group. Marketing research and analysis involves collecting and analyzing data to gain insights into consumer behavior, market trends, and industry dynamics. This helps us to make decisions based on facts that are available in real-time, which will lead to identifying growth opportunities and developing marketing strategies that resonate. A well-crafted promotion plan defines goals, strategies, and tactics for reaching and involving target customers successfully. Market segmentation, targeting, positioning, pricing, distribution, and advertising are some of the components included in a good marketing plan. It directs marketing activities, hence its importance in evaluating the effectiveness of the business's programs.

The traditional four Ps (product, price, place, and promotion) constitute the marketing mix, an essential tool for developing a company's marketing strategies or plans. Contemporary marketing extends this framework to address more aspects, such as people processes, physical presence, and partnerships. Each element is essential when shaping overall marketing strategies to benefit customers. Companies create and share valuable, relevant, and consistent content in content marketing to engage their target audience. Storytelling is a critical component of content marketing strategy that allows companies to connect with people, stimulate emotions, and effectively express the narrative of their brand. Companies can gain new customers by creating stories that are meaningful to them.

Building strong customer relationships and fostering loyalty is vital for long-term business success. Companies must interact with customers at every touch point using retention strategies, while addressing any question or concern swiftly and exceptionally. This leads to a satisfied customer who remains loyal through repeat purchases. Every company should be focused on satisfying its consumers, since this will entail positive publicity and repeat buying, which will be rewarding in terms of revenue generation.

To navigate the complex world of branding and marketing, businesses need a strategic approach integrating these critical principles and strategies. For instance, understanding branding, establishing a unified brand strategy, developing an attractive brand identity, and raising brand awareness and customer relations are the ultimate keys to high ROI in a competitive market. A strong bond between a company and its customers can only be created through various initiatives such as discussions about goals for future products or services, providing unique experiences that increase product recognition so that the communication doesn't get lost in the noise, and building processes around existing clients.

9.1 Understanding the Power of Branding

A strong brand lies at the heart of every successful business. It is not just about good looks; it involves building emotional ties with customers so they can trust you, be loyal to your product or service, and speak positively about it. Such brands distinguish themselves from other players by creating an exclusive identity. Branding is thus strategic capital that enables businesses to move onward while accelerating growth, profitability, and sustainability.

To understand what branding is, we must first look at three essential components: Identity, Image, and Equity. Brand identity means everything that your company stands for; including values, beliefs, and personality. The tangible and intangible elements such as logos, colors, or what you say, carry out the mission constitute an organization or company's brand voice. In addition, brand messages contribute to building an image in consumers' minds. By establishing consumer willingness to pay premiums over time, brand equity helps build market resilience.

By investigating the impact of branding on businesses, one can understand how deeply it influences business achievements and the intricate dynamics of branding. This entails developing a clear sense of brand identity, cultivating an attractive and positive brand image, and nurturing customer loyalty through investing in long-term positional advantages, namely brand equity. These corporate attributes help cultivate strong bonds between manufacturers, businesses, and buyers, thus leading them into sustainable development through loyalty within the market context.

The Role of Branding in Business Success

Branding is more than logos, colors, or eye-catching phrases; it's a vital strategic asset that can significantly impact a company's success in the marketplace. At its core, branding represents a business's soul—its values, mission, personality, and promise to customers. It forms the basis upon which businesses build customer relationships, differentiate themselves from competitors, and generate growth and profitability.

One of the critical roles of branding in business success is creating identity and differentiation in the marketplace. In an era where consumers are bombarded with options, a clearly defined brand image enables companies to have an exclusive place within the market, making it easier for their customers to identify with your company. By communicating a clear and compelling brand identity, businesses can attract their desired audience, create trust, and foster loyalty over time.

Branding plays a massive role in shaping customer perceptions and influencing buying behavior. A strong brand creates good feelings and associations among buyers, making them more likely to choose one brand over others. Branding thus helps establish emotional ties with consumers, promoting trustfulness, dependability, and credibility. Such an emotional tie can lead to repetitive purchases and advocacy.

Branding allows companies to command premium prices, increasing profitability. Well-established brands with a solid reputation among loyal customers can justify higher price points for their products or services. In many cases, consumers are willing to pay extra for trusted brands offering perceived value compared to the competition's level of performance.

Branding ensures consistent messaging across all touchpoints, guaranteeing congruence throughout the entire consumer journey so that clients enjoy a unified experience through different contact points within a given brand sphere. Each interaction with the brand, from advertising communications to product design, encompasses how consumers understand the brand.

In today's digital era, branding has gone beyond traditional marketing channels to include online platforms such as social media. Social media platforms offer businesses opportunities to interact with their target audience directly, amplify the brand message, and establish a community of loyal followers. Effective social media branding can humanize your brand, increase awareness, and promote engagement and conversion.

The role of branding in business success cannot be exaggerated. A strong brand is an invaluable asset that creates differentiation, influences customer perception, fosters loyalty, and ultimately contributes to long-term growth and profitability. By investing in branding efforts and continuously delivering on their brand promises, companies position themselves for success within the competitive marketplace today.

Defining a Brand: Identity, Image, and Equity

Brand Identity is the bedrock upon which a brand's story is built. It embodies those fundamental beliefs, values, and aspirations that define a company's identity or purpose. Branding identity comes out through physical features such as logos, color palettes, typography, design elements, and intangible qualities like the tone of voice used in messaging or the overall personality of this product.

Brand Image refers to the perceptual landscape that consumers move in when they come across a brand. This encapsulates clients' perceptions, affiliations, or feelings towards an item. Not only does it exist as part of marketing communications or advertising, but every point at which consumers get in touch with brands, starting from customer service encounters, word-of-mouth recommendations, social media interactions, and even product experiences. This all affects how people view your company's name. A positive image forms a strong emotional connection with buyers, giving them trust and loyalty. In contrast, a negative image can lead to reduced consumer confidence, causing a decline in sales.

Brand Equity reflects how much numerical value and influence one's name has over buyers' mindsets. It represents collective goodwill developed over time. Substantial brand equity allows an organization to dominate the market, compete successfully, and sustain growth and income.

Defining a brand requires an inclusive comprehension and combination of identity, image, and equity. By creating a unique identity for itself, managing its reputation, and nurturing its value in the marketplace, a good brand can maintain its existence in the minds of consumers. Such is a robust measure that results in meaningful consumer relationships, increasing chances of success.

9.2 Creating a Brand Strategy

Creating a brand strategy is an integral part of business growth; this is the guiding star in a brand's journey in the competing world. Setting your Brand Values and Mission helps define what a brand stands for and why it exists. By authenticating these values or writing down a concise mission statement that appeals to customers, brands can establish meaningful relationships with their target audience and align themselves with their aspirations and beliefs.

For an organization to differentiate itself from competitors and attract customers' attention, there must be a compelling Unique Selling Proposition (USP). The USP explains how customers will benefit from the use of the product or service, differentiating it from the competition and influencing customer perceptions.

Your Brand Positioning and Personality define how consumers see the brand. Positioning refers to marketers strategically positioning their brands against rival products, but personality makes consumers associate your company with human traits or qualities, thereby increasing their interactions.

We will discuss each separately, emphasizing its significance and offering solutions to develop compellingly branded strategies. Knowing how vital it is to have a brand strategy that speaks directly to the client's heart while keeping an eye on organizational goals is crucial today.

Establishing Brand Values and Mission

The basis for any prosperous brand is establishing your brand values and mission. At this stage, a brand's essence is defined by identifying its personality, hopes, dreams and guiding principles. Developing brand values and mission is not a task but an intense reflective journey where brands delve into their core beliefs, motivations, and anticipated impact on society.

Brand values serve as the brand's moral compass, which expresses the ideals and principles that guide actions and decisions. The brand's identity is built on these foundations, ideally reflecting a commitment to integrity, authenticity, and social responsibility. Clear and authentic articulation of brand values make them more than mere words on a page; they become the force behind every brand action that influences business strategies, including product development or customer service. Companies that remain true to their values consistently build credibility with their audience, fostering long-term customer loyalty.

A brand's mission serves as its North Star. It communicates what the company stands for and the desired changes it seeks to cause in the world. A vital mission inspires internal stakeholders while resonating with external audiences, so that people from different walks of life can rally around it together and create purposeful objectives within their shared visions. When companies have clear missions beyond profit-making, they unite their stakeholders behind initiatives to bring about positive change or societal good.

In order to craft these brand values and missions, collaborative reflection is required among key stakeholders such as employees, customers, and the executive management team. There should be open dialogue so that diverse voices are respected in such conversations. In interviews, workshops, or feedback sessions, brands can discover what beliefs guide them and define who they are.

Once established, brand values and mission will dictate various aspects of strategy formulation. They determine positioning strategies, messages, and communication, which should be designed so that they align with the brand's identity and aspirations.

It has never been more critical than today for brands to establish brand values and missions, given the current dynamic marketplace where consumers seek authenticity, purpose, and meaning from the brands they support. Truly embracing such values, not paying lip service to them, is what makes a brand stand out, allowing it to resonate deeply with its audience. A company that genuinely lives its values and embodies a clear mission stands on better foundations.

Developing a Unique Selling Proposition

A unique selling proposition (USP) is one of the most effective ways to differentiate a brand and catch consumers' attention in a crowded marketplace. The USP sums up how a brand is different to and better than its competitors.

A great USP must be founded on knowing the target audience and their needs, wants, and pain points. To identify unmet needs or untapped market segments that can be used for differentiation, brands should do extensive market research and consumer analysis. Understanding what sets this target apart from others and drives their buying behavior will enable brands to develop a focused USP that resonates with them and effectively addresses their specific needs.

A compelling USP has to go beyond product features or benefits. Whether it's superior quality, innovative technology, excellent customer service, or a one-of-a-kind experience, the USP should communicate something real in addition to intangible benefits. It should answer the bottom-line question: 'Why should consumers choose our brand over others?'

Creativity, innovation, and questioning conventional wisdom are critical requirements for USP development. Brands must think outside conventional boxes to uncover distinctive angles or viewpoints that differentiate them from business rivals. This might involve utilizing proprietary technology, giving exclusive advantages, rewarding loyalty programs, or delivering customer service that astounds clients by exceeding expectations. A compelling USP is established on credibility and authenticity. Brands must always keep the promises made in their USPs. Companies can enhance their USPs and create long-term loyalty and advocacy by developing trust and reliability.

Brands must continually assess and refine their USP to respond to market movements, changing consumer demands, and competitive pressures. They must be able to adapt while innovating to stay competitive in the face of evolving marketplaces and emerging competitors. This would involve revisiting their target audience, re-evaluating their value proposition, or exploring new opportunities for differentiation. By knowing their target audience, discovering unmet needs, and making a compelling value offer, brands can establish strong USPs that set them apart from the competition and drive success in markets.

Brand Positioning and Personality

Branding is not just about brand positioning and personality; it is what the brand is all about, its identity, and how it stands out from the crowd. Brand positioning involves deciding how consumers should perceive a company's product relative to what exists in the market. It consists of finding the sweet spot where a brand's unique features, benefits, and values meet the needs and wants of the people it targets. This process relies on deep diving into marketing insights and understanding competitors' strategies and consumer characteristics, to identify those untapped areas with potential that brands can occupy. The success of this strategic art depends on a clear comprehension of who the brand is targeting, what motivates them, and what their aspirations are. Brands must put themselves in customers' shoes to understand what truly matters to them.

Meanwhile, personality gives human-like attributes to brands through emotional traits and characteristics that lead to a bond between them and consumers. Like people, each brand has its personality, which forms part of how they are perceived or remembered. Some examples include being reliable, like an old friend you've known for years; innovative, like someone who thinks ahead; or even playful, like an easy-going partner. This way, companies can enhance their image by having a bond with customers.

Developing a brand personality entail picking out essential character qualities that reflect their identity and values. This may include being true, inventive, dependable, or empathetic, among other things. By maintaining uniformity across different platforms, including customer service experience and advertising communication messages, brands can build strong identities capable of evoking meaning at a home level between themselves and individual clients.

Adherence to the desired positioning and brand personality is essential. Brands' messages, visuals, and actions must correspond with how they desire to be seen and how they would like their clientele to perceive them. Thus, businesses will maintain their identities while at the same time gaining stronger links over the long term.

9.3 Designing Your Brand Identity

A brand's visual identity goes beyond having a logo or color scheme. It is like its soul taking tangible form by encapsulating everything it believes in, its personality, and its aspirations. In this context, the logo acts as an anchor around which everything revolves, thereby symbolizing what the company stands for. A good logo isn't about beauty but the emotional attachment between customers and the company. Colors are also essential since they tell a story about a brand. The choice of each hue evokes certain feelings or ideas, giving depth to communication about a particular product or service associated with it. When it comes to user perception, though, it is essential to note that colors significantly affect consumer behavior.

In addition, typography also plays an integral part in expressing brands through font types and letterforms, which can speak volumes about their identities. Typical styles vary from bold ones demanding attention to elegant ones suggesting sophistication, creating room for various shades of meaning and amplifying some messages while connecting with the target audience at deep levels. Regarding consistency within branding materials, typographical features can provide coherence across all other channels. Typography should remain consistent so that every time people see any text-related stuff, they subconsciously think: 'This brand never changes.'

A strong brand identity's real power lies in consistency across all touchpoints and interactions. For instance, whether it is a digital advert, product packaging, or a storefront display, every meeting with the brand should represent its values and character. In the long run, cohesive branding elements create an integrated brand experience that engenders consumer confidence and loyalty while strengthening the business's position in the marketplace.

In designing a brand identity, one must balance the artistic aspect with strategic thinking, since each element must be well thought out as part of a compelling narrative for consumers. By understanding the logo design, color schemes, and typography used, brands can make their visual identity more relatable to their audience, which will keep it relevant, even as time passes.

The Elements of Brand Identity: Logo, Colors, and Typography

Brand identity is not just a logo or a choice of colors; the essence separates it from the numerous competitors aiming for an attention share. The core elements at the heart of this identity comprise a triumvirate of symbols, including the logo, colors, and typography. Collectively, these constitute the bedrock upon which the visual story of any brand is built to create one compelling narrative with immense appeal that will engage audiences in their consciousness.

The logo is a flagship for the brand's identity—it visually represents its mission and ethos, reduced into a single symbol. It is one of the first things consumers come into contact with, drawing them in to explore the brand's world more. A good design goes beyond mere aesthetics—it captures something about a brand that can be easily seen. From McDonald's golden arches to Nike's tick mark, iconic logos have come to mean trustworthiness, authenticity, and quality.

Every color carries specific symbolism and meaning, and thus conveys unique messages calling for distinct responses in customers. Red indicates energy and passion as well as excitement, while blue demonstrates dependability, trustworthiness, and professionalism. Color selection plays a vital role in shaping the overall personality of a brand and determines how people perceive, communicate, experience, interact, and feel about it.

Uniformity in color throughout branding materials ensures a consistent brand experience, reinforces identity, and promotes familiarity and confidence. Coca-Cola has vibrant red, while Starbucks has a soothing green appearance that makes it easy for consumers to engage with the brand at an emotional level.

Strong typography can give a more refined approach and voice to a brand's communications. Different fonts have different emotional implications, from bold sans serifs to elegant serifs, all contributing to the company's unique tone of voice and look. Good typography is one way that brands can deliver their messages in a way that doesn't require too much deliberation but will convince you they are not fake.

The most essential element of a successful brand identity is consistency. Brands must consistently use logos, colors, and typographies across all touchpoints, including websites, social media, packaging, or advertising. Developing a consistent and cohesive approach to all these elements can result in a robust and long-lasting brand.

Consistency across Branding Materials

The prime thing in brand identity design relating to consistency is the logo, which sums up whatever a brand stands for at one look. Using it consistently on all branding tools, such as business cards, letterheads, packaging material, and digital platforms, is vital because it helps maintain instant recognition and re-emphasizes brand visibility in consumers' minds. Whether it is presented in full color, black and white, or grayscale format, the logo should be consistent with its original form throughout other applications to maintain uniformity and strengthen your brand's identity.

Colors are essential in determining how people perceive a particular visual feature of a company's image. Properly using colors across different branding materials creates a unified view throughout the business, ensuring that regardless of who looks at them, they will understand what kind of business it represents, which helps keep up with its personality and sets the tone for communication. Whether this implies primary corporate colors or secondary accent hues being introduced into advertisement layouts, maintaining consistency when applying shades will maintain the uniformity of the visual language used by the company in advertisements.

Typography contributes towards brand identity by presenting a uniform voice and tone over the various channels through which the message gets disseminated. Whether these are headlines, texts, or call-to-action elements, we need our typography to be consistent since it is here that we can establish clarity and readability, thus supporting the brand's overall image and style, thus enhancing the general brand integrity.

Even when it comes to branding materials such as layouts, images, and graphics, you have to maintain similar design perspectives to facilitate customers' harmonized experience of a brand. Be it elegant, minimalistic, or a bold, bright look, consistency in design re-emphasizes what a company stands for.

Consumers are more likely to perceive the brand as reliable, professional, and trustworthy when they encounter consistent branding materials across various touchpoints and interactions. It brings about confidence among clients while strengthening their belief in the genuineness and reliability of a company being branded.

Consistency across branding materials is critical to designing robust, memorable brands. Organizations tend to create a campaign that speaks to them individually while separating them from other players within the same field by maintaining consistency in elements such as logo designs, colors, typography patterns, and overall brand language. Consistency builds brand recognition, fosters trust, and strengthens the relationships between the audience and us over time, guaranteeing sustainable market growth.

9.4 Building Brand Awareness

Building brand awareness is a blend between science and art, with strategic moves that ensure improvements in the visibility of a brand. Brands can employ traditional marketing techniques or digital innovations to gain interest from target customers.

One of the key elements to focus on here is increasing brand visibility, ensuring that the name, logo, and messaging are easily recognizable and accessible to the target audience. To increase the number of potential customers who become aware of the brand, other channels that could be used for promoting them include television, radio, and print media; websites, social networks, or search engines are also instances of these communication channels in digital forms such as e-commerce sites like Amazon.com and Alibaba.com. All these channels can be strategically employed by brands to significantly impact on new markets they venture into, by leaving lasting footprints on their customers' minds.

Today's market is characterized by digital interconnectivity and social engagement; social media has created a platform upon which brands can interact with their audience, creating meaningful relations while sharing great content. Thought leadership may be realized through creating content, and thought leadership, related to the relevant industry, where companies drive the conversation towards action-oriented practices. For example, they might do this through blog posts, then cultivate massive following across all platforms within which they maintain an active presence.

Brand partnerships are another avenue for collaborations between businesses because they help expand exposure while reaching new audiences at scale. Working together with similar-minded businesses or influential persons can extend the network and increase exposure in a more targeted way. Collaborations and partnerships allow brands to make the most of social proof and endorsement through co-branded initiatives, sponsored content, or influencer endorsements to drive brand awareness and form brand affinity among customers.

Strategies for Increasing Brand Visibility

Increasing brand visibility is a complex process that demands a well-planned internet and offline strategy. Another essential thing to note is that having a commanding web presence is critical for enhancing the brand's visibility. In this modern digital era, an official website is the basis of any brand's online identity. It serves as a virtual store where customers can obtain information about various aspects of the company, such as products, values, the services they offer, and more. Website optimization (SEO) is essential in improving visibility on SERPs by search engines.

Apart from websites, brands must also be active participants in social media platforms. Platforms such as Facebook, Twitter, Instagram, and LinkedIn provide unprecedented opportunities for brands to interact with their target market through posts or tweets. By posting relevant and engaging content constantly, companies can expand their market share and increase customer engagement.

Search engine optimization (SEO) is another powerful tool for boosting online brand visibility. Through SEO techniques implemented in website content, meta tags, and backlinks, companies can increase their chances of attaining improved rankings on search engine results pages, thus attracting organic traffic to the site.

Pay-per-click advertising (PPC) represents another targeted mechanism to boost brand visibility on the internet. Google Ads and social media advertising allow for focused ad campaigns based on demographics, interests, or online habits. PPC methods are used so that businesses will appear prominently both in search results and social media feeds, with the result being more visitors visiting their sites.

Valued content creation is pivotal in improving brand recognition by offering helpful information to intended readership groupings. To more directly suit their audiences' needs and wants, brands can create various types of content, such as infographics, videos, podcasts, and blog posts. By offering high-quality and informative content that can educate, inspire, or entertain them, brands can attract and retain potential clients' attention. This ultimately brings about brand visibility and engagement.

Engaging in guest blogging and thought leadership activities can also enhance a brand's visibility. For instance, if brands publish insightful articles on well-established websites in the industry, they can build their trust and reach new audiences. Similarly, thought leadership platforms such as LinkedIn Pulse and Medium provide opportunities to showcase industry knowledge and expertise, further enhancing brand visibility.

Attending industry events and conferences allows established businesses to increase their presence while meeting potential clients or partners. By sponsoring or exhibiting at relevant events, companies can display their wares and talk with attendees to generate leads. At these forums, businesses have an opportunity to present themselves as experts in their respective fields, in order to be recognized by other people in the industry.

Leveraging Social Media and Content Marketing

Social media and content marketing are crucial tools for creating a strong brand presence and reaching their target audience effectively. If brands use social media platforms efficiently and create engaging content, they can increase their outreach, acquire meaningful contacts, and align with their marketing strategies to form a unique brand voice.

Social media platforms offer countless chances for brands to interact with consumers individually, grow customer loyalty to the company, and promote engagement. Billions of active users exist on popular social networking sites, including Facebook, Instagram, Twitter, LinkedIn, and even TikTok. This allows these brands to access diverse audiences. By utilizing social media channels, brands can tell their stories and display their products or services, while getting feedback from consumers in real time, thus making the process more interactive and fostering trust.

Brands can achieve considerable leverage for distribution by deploying social media platforms during campaigns for content generation. Promotional blog posts, video cases, and other assets may be shared via social networks to increase consumer coverage measured through likes, shares, comments, reposts, etc. Since algorithms prioritize engaging content over non-engaging ones, this ensures that any brand needs its audience-resonating content, ensuring interactions.

Organic content-paid advertising on social networks allows brands to reach their customers in a targeted, cheap way. Such websites include Facebook Ads, Instagram ads, and LinkedIn ads, which enable brands to create precise ad campaigns according to demographic characteristics, interests and behavioral patterns. Using customized messaging for specific targeting of audience segments by these brands helps drive website traffic, thus leading to lead generation and increased brand awareness.

Social media listening tools allow companies to track real-time conversations about their products, industry, and competitors. Mentions, comments, and hashtags will offer companies crucial knowledge of consumers' feelings, likes, or trends in different markets, thereby allowing marketers to adjust their plans accordingly. Therefore, it is possible for a company's social media listening to enable further interactions with its customer base, whereby it can also answer questions and engage them through digital platforms to become loyal brand followers.

Collaborations and Influencer Partnerships

Collaborations and influencer partnerships are vital tactics in branding and marketing that offer dynamic opportunities for brands to extend their reach, establish a bond with different people, and create a unique brand. In the hyperconnected digital environment, consumers are exposed to a barrage of ads and promotional materials, so aligning strategically with influencers or like-minded brands is seen as innovative, as this helps businesses rise above the cluttered advertising space and engage more deeply with customers.

One critical benefit of collaborations and influencer partnerships is that they increase brand visibility and enable companies to explore untapped segments of their target audience. By partnering with relevant influencers or complementary brands, organizations can take advantage of existing networks and enter new markets that were previously inaccessible. This increases the brand's visibility while expanding its customer base.

Such alliances bolster trustworthiness, an important attribute among today's discerning shoppers. Associating with respected influencers or reputed brands allows companies to rely on the trust built by them among their followers or customers. This way, customers will be more likely to see the company positively, establishing a good ground for trust and loyalty.

Collaborations and influencer partnerships go beyond mere credibility building, allowing marketers to create impactful campaigns that resonate well with target audiences. Brands can develop emotional advertising campaigns by collating creative ideas from all parties involved, in contravention of conventional marketing practices. These endeavors may include co-branded product launches, events, or interactive social media activities.

Collaborations and influencer partnerships provide beneficial insights into markets upon which strategic decisions are made. Organizations can obtain real-time information on preferences, trends, and competitive factors shaping consumer behavior in joint projects with other entities operating within a similar industry niche or opinion leaders and celebrities. Such information is crucial for designing future marketing campaigns and new product development.

Collaborations and influencer partnerships are an active approach to branding and marketing that results in increased visibility, credibility, memorable advertisements, and access to invaluable knowledge for brands. As brands navigate the complexities of the digital age, these strategic alliances will prove to be vital resources for achieving brand growth, consumer engagement, and loyalty within a noisy market.

9.5 Marketing Research and Analysis

Marketing research and analysis are the foundation of any successful marketing strategy. Today's business world is characterized by dynamic market conditions and shifting consumer tastes; organizations need to get usable insights from extensive research and analytical processes to stay competitive.

Effective marketing strategies start with extensive market research. Market research entails numerous methodologies and techniques aimed at obtaining and analyzing information about consumer behavior, market trends, and competitive dynamics. Businesses can obtain useful details about their customers' needs, preferences, and behaviors through methods such as surveys, focus groups, interviews, or observational studies. By getting into the minds of its customers, companies can find hidden opportunities, identify emerging trends and anticipate shifts in demand, supporting strategic decision-making while developing marketing initiatives.

Market segmentation is crucial to effective marketing research and analysis since it assists businesses in identifying target customers. Marketers segment the main markets into different groups based on similar traits such as demographics, psychographics (personality, lifestyles values, opinions attitudes, interests, favorite activities), geographic location (city, region, county, state, country, continent, global) or behavioral traits. Companies customize their products or services according to each segment; ensuring that the message used is relevant to individual segments' requirements, therefore creating deeper connections with target audiences.

Leveraging data for marketing strategies has become increasingly important. Businesses can access various data sources, including website analytics figures, social media metrics, sales data, and customer feedback. This data pool enables organizations to make better decisions because they can see what works and what does not. By examining this information, businesses can identify patterns, trends, and relationships that inform marketing strategies, optimize campaign performance, and drive measurable outcomes. As a result, companies engaging in such campaigns can improve their messaging by reaching the right segments and delivering personalized experiences that engage customers.

This process enables the company to focus its efforts only on specific groups of clients who are likely to be interested in its products, thus reducing costs for promotions while forming strong relationships with target consumers that subsequently help businesses grow stronger.

Conducting Market Research to Understand Your Audience

Understanding the complexity of market research provides a more profound comprehension of customers' attitudes, allowing shaping products, services, or marketing activities. One method that is widely used in market research is surveys. These direct channels allow enterprises to have feedback from their audience on the products they produce. It could be done online, by phoning or physically where it involves collecting numbers on different issues concerning a target population. By scrutinizing survey answers, companies get more insights that may inform their strategic planning processes.

Focus groups also rank highly among market research methods. These involve bringing together representatives of the target audience to discuss specific subjects or products. In an open forum and group discussions, businesses can collect more information about attitudes, motivations, and preferred choices from participants. Focus groups provide qualitative insights into the target audience's emotions, motivations, and behaviors, offering nuanced perspectives that may not be captured through quantitative surveys alone.

Another practical approach to understanding one's audience better involves using observational research methods. This entails watching how consumers behave in real-life environments like retail stores, websites, and social media networks. Businesses can gain insights on preferences, pain points, and purchase drivers, by studying consumer interaction with products offered, navigation around websites, and even brand engagements on social media platforms.

Secondary sources can also be used to assist primary research. These include industry reports, market studies, and academic publications, which have already been done and published by someone else. Using information already available, together with in-house analysis, business leaders can get insights into trends that shape market dynamics regarding competition and customer tastes. Secondary research gives a broader context for the companies' findings; thus, it serves as a backup for their primary data.

Market research is necessary for enterprises that want to understand consumers deeply before making marketing decisions. Utilizing a mix of these methods provides an array of perspectives on demographics, preferences, and behavior. This knowledge empowers marketing departments to develop promotions uniquely designed for distinct segments of customers, and the company to redefine products through strategic decision-making.

9.6 Crafting a Marketing Plan

In the present-day business world, organizations must develop an all-inclusive marketing plan. This process involves three things: SMART marketing goals, budgeting for marketing initiatives, and selecting the proper marketing channels.

A structured approach can be created to define clear and attainable objectives through the SMART (specific, measurable, achievable, relevant, and time-bound) goals-setting system. Specific goals are designed with clarity about what needs to be achieved; measurable goals enable you to track progress and measure success. Achievable goals ensure that objectives are realistic and within reach, while relevant goals align with the broader strategic objectives of the business. Time-bound goals establish deadlines for achievement, providing a sense of urgency and focus. Using the best criteria for companies will help organizations develop meaningful targets to enhance their business performance.

Another critical step in creating an effective marketing plan is budget allocation. This includes determining the financial resources required to achieve predetermined marketing goals while ensuring that returns are maximized on investments made in this area. You need to consider various expenses, including advertising costs incurred within each quarter or year, campaign development costs incurred once, and ongoing marketing activities' expenses, which occur regularly, such as content creation for websites or brochure printing. By linking budget allocations to strategic priorities and revenue projections, businesses can optimize their spending on advertising by allocating money. Regular supervision and updating of advertising expenditures will enable managers to allocate funds accurately based on prevailing customer trends and market conditions.

Proper marketing channel selection is also critical in effectively reaching target markets. Nowadays, there are many platforms for marketers, especially digital ones such as social media. There are also the traditional media vehicles like radio, T.V. as well as newspapers. Identifying the appropriate platform requires understanding consumer behavior patterns, market trends, and channel effectiveness. Through market research, organizations also track sales by knowing where their customers are most active and responsive to promotional messages. This, in turn, allows for customized marketing efforts, which maximizes the success of the campaigns being undertaken, increasing engagement and conversion ratios.

Setting SMART Marketing Goals

Nothing is more critical to any marketing strategy than setting SMART (Specific, Measurable, Achievable, Relevant, Time-bound) marketing goals. This framework will give you a good foundation for defining objectives and directing efforts toward meaningful outcomes.

To provide clarity and focus, specific goals should state what needs to be achieved, in no uncertain terms. Rather than vague statements like 'increase sales,' one could have goals such as increasing online sales by a significant percentage within a defined timeframe or generating new leads to a specified number every month. These kinds of goals are explicit and give the direction for effective marketing strategies consistent with broader corporate objectives.

Measurable goals help track progress and assess effectiveness. When marketers establish quantifiable metrics for success like website traffic, conversion rates, or social media engagement, it helps them to quantify their performance while identifying the areas that need improvement. Measurable goals offer feedback on the impact of marketing campaigns and facilitate data-based decision-making.

Realistic targets ensure that business objectives can be realized within the organization's resources and constraints. Although ambitious targets that promote growth must be set, they also have to be attainable. Unrealistic goals may lead to frustration and demotivate staff, while attainable ones build confidence among employees.

Such goals should contribute directly to an organization's overall mission and vision. Ensuring these are related to other strategic objectives at the management level is crucial for marketing purposes. If you want to open a new market, then some of the marketing-oriented objectives would involve market research, audience targeting, and brand campaigns carried out in those regions.

Time-bound goals create deadlines, which enable the accomplishment of objectives; this gives urgency and focuses people on achieving them. Marketers will generate a sense of accountability and momentum if they specify exactly when everyone should meet the target set or achieve the desired result. Time-bound goals will prevent procrastination and ensure consistent progress towards milestones and targets.

When setting intelligent marketing goals, consider these factors:

Marketing Analysis: Thoroughly analyze the market landscape, including competitors' movements, consumer trends, and industry insights. This information will assist in setting realistic and actionable goals suited to specific needs and challenges.

Consumer Insights: Understanding the target audience's preferences, behaviors, and pain points is essential. By aligning marketing goals with customer needs and desires, businesses can develop strategies that resonate with their target market and drive engagement and loyalty.

Internal Resources: Available resources within an organization, such as budget and manpower, have to be taken into account. For marketing initiatives to make any sense, achievable goals must be set based on a realistic assessment of existing resources necessary for this purpose.

Benchmarks & KPIs: Establish benchmarks and key performance indicators (KPIs) against which you can measure your progress towards your goals. These metrics allow marketers to track performance over time.

Flexibility & Adaptability: SMART is good, but it is also crucial that you remain flexible enough and ready with all needed answers concerning changing market conditions or other unforeseen obstacles. Therefore, business strategies and environmental dynamics should be regularly reviewed to ensure that they still fit prevailing business goals.

You should set sensible marketing goals before formulating a company's strategic plan. In this case, the business can integrate its marketing into the general objectives of the whole business to improve performance and get important results. Marketers can create realistic, actionable, and long-term business ambitions by incorporating market analysis, customer insights, internal resources, benchmarks, and flexibility.

Budgeting for Marketing Initiatives

Are you looking for ideas on how to budget your marketing initiatives? You are not alone. Most businesses allocate the most time in their strategic planning process to this topic. Getting this right is crucial because it helps determine the financial resources required while maximizing return on investment.

Evaluate your current financial health and available marketing resources. You do this by looking at current revenue streams, profit margins, and cash flow projections. By understanding where you are, you can establish realistic budgets that align with what you have and want to achieve.

The next step is allocating funds to specific marketing activities. If you have a large budget, high-impact activities, such as a new product launch or major advertising campaigns, should receive larger chunks of your money. If your budget is more modest, lower-priority activities should receive less funding.

When determining which areas to allocate most of your funds, consider the potential return on investment (ROI) by estimating revenue or other key performance indicators (KPIs) associated with each activity. This ensures that funding decisions are strategic and aligned with the company's growth objectives.

After considering ROI, all costs associated with each activity must be accounted for, including advertising costs, production costs, and agency fees. By doing this accurately, businesses can avoid overspending and ensure they are realistic with their budget allocations.

It doesn't stop there. You must continually monitor these allocations after implementation, as things may change rapidly. Businesses must also keep track of actual expenditures against budgeted amounts and adjust when needed. Be flexible and adaptable. Responding accordingly to changes in market conditions can help optimize your spending; this is better than making an educated guess without reevaluating budgets frequently enough.

Selecting the Right Marketing Channels

Choosing the perfect marketing channels is a critical decision. It can have a significant effect on the success of your marketing strategy. There are many platforms to choose from today, and consumer preferences keep changing. How do you find the right one for your target audience?

Knowing who you're targeting is the first step in finding your golden channel. Businesses can determine which channels will resonate with their audience by identifying critical demographic characteristics, preferences, and behaviors. For example, if the target audience consists primarily of active millennials on social media, then Instagram or TikTok may be particularly effective.

Market research is essential for understanding where your target audiences are most active and ready to listen. Analyzing industry trends, competitor strategies, and consumer behavior patterns will provide insights into which channels are most relevant and influential within your niche. This should give you a good foundation for making informed decisions about channel selection.

Consideration should also be given to each marketing channel's unique strengths. Each platform has its own set of capabilities that distinguish it from others. For example, while Facebook and Twitter are excellent for engaging with customers on a personal level, email marketing may be more effective at generating leads that convert into sales.

It's important to consider how competitive each channel is—and how noisy it is. Some channels might already be oversaturated with competitors shouting over one another for attention, in which case it could be more beneficial to explore less cluttered platforms elsewhere. Different channels come with different price tags, ranging from paid advertising on social media platforms to content marketing initiatives and search engine optimization (SEO) efforts. Take some time to evaluate what you can do before committing yourself to anything.

It would help if you considered whether each channel aligns with your brand identity. Consistent messaging across all platforms builds trust among consumers. Select those that allow cohesive messaging and branding across all touchpoints. It's essential to remain flexible, both in the channels you choose and how much time you spend on them. As consumer preferences and technology continue to evolve, businesses must be willing to experiment with new channels and adapt their strategies accordingly. This involves reallocating resources from underperforming channels to those that show more significant potential for success or exploring emerging platforms that offer unique opportunities for engagement.

Take a data-driven approach when selecting your marketing channels. After gaining an understanding of your target audience demographics, market research insights, channel strengths and limitations, competition, budget constraints, and brand alignment, you'll be able to find the perfect fit for your business.

9.7 The Marketing Mix: 4 P's and Beyond

Comprehending and ultimately mastering the marketing mix is crucial for businesses that want to succeed in today's dynamic marketplace. At the center of it all are the four Ps: product, price, place, and promotion. These elements make up any marketing strategy and play a major role in shaping the overall customer experience and driving business growth.

The first element, product, refers to the goods or services offered by a business. Creating offerings that meet customers' needs is essential. This involves developing high-quality products or services and understanding what customers prefer or dislike. By focusing on creating value for customers and addressing their needs effectively, businesses can differentiate themselves from competitors and build strong customer relationships.

The second element, price, directly impacts profitability and perceived value. Businesses must carefully consider various factors, such as production costs and competitor pricing when developing pricing strategies. Depending on your overall objectives and who you're targeting, determine whether you should use a premium pricing strategy or a penetration pricing strategy to gain more market share.

Place is another essential component of this mix; it is about distributing your products or services through different channels to serve enough people to get noticed. As they say, 'out of sight, out of mind.' Depending on your target audience's preferences, this may include direct sales, retailers, wholesalers, or online marketplaces.

Developing an integrated promotional strategy that uses multiple channels will help businesses effectively broadcast their value proposition across different touchpoints. There are some other elements, such as people, processes, physical evidence, and partnerships, that companies might want to analyze, if they want to take things up a notch.

Product: Creating Offerings That Meet Customer Needs

Establishing services that meet customers' needs is at the core of successful marketing. In modern-day markets, businesses need to go further than selling products or services; they need to leave their customers feeling satisfied and valued. This means businesses have to fully understand what their customers need, want, and dislike, as well as always looking for ways to do things better.

When it comes to making a product, being customer-centered is critical. Businesses must prioritize what people want throughout the entire development process. Companies can identify this through market research and customer feedback. One way to find those specific needs is to segment the market into smaller parts based on demographics, psychographics, or behavioral characteristics. By understanding these consumer groups, a business can tailor its offerings to more effectively meet those needs.

Another key thing companies must consider when making an offering is the value proposition. Companies must communicate why their offerings are unique and the best option. This can be done by understanding what sets their products apart from others in the market.

While innovation gets you ahead of your competition, only quality will keep you there. Customers expect top-tier service from the business's employees and will only return if they get it. In addition to quality control, businesses must also focus on reliability in their selling. If a product doesn't work as promised, the customer will not trust that company again. Businesses should consider how every step of making an offering affects the customer experience. From the first time someone hears about your brand until they purchase something and beyond, every interaction could easily make them jump ship if they are appropriately handled.

A business must always be ready to change its offerings. They need to stay on top of customer satisfaction and wants and look for anything they can improve. A company that creates products that meet customer needs is destined for success. By putting customers first, your business can see long-term growth and profit.

Price: Strategies for Pricing Your Product or Service

Developing pricing strategies is crucial for businesses. Good strategies allow you to maximize profitability and maintain a competitive edge—prices can change the game. One strategy that businesses often use is cost-based pricing. This involves setting prices based on production and operation costs associated with the product. If you do this right, you'll ensure your prices cover all expenses while generating profit. Other factors must be considered though, such as customer demand and competitor pricing.

Another approach is value-based pricing, which homes in on what customers think the good and services' value is. Aligning price with what customers believe they're getting out of it will make your product easier to sell at higher prices. Dynamic pricing is another strategy that involves adjusting prices in real-time based on conditions. This allows businesses to make exact decisions from one moment to the next, considering things like demand and competitor prices.

Price skimming is a popular way of introducing new products or innovating existing ones. It involves initially setting high prices, when only early adopters are likely to buy them. Over time, once the development costs have been covered, the price slowly falls so that a typical customer can afford to buy them.

Putting a low initial price tag on your new item isn't always the worst idea, if done correctly—penetration pricing might work wonders in quickly gaining market share for yourself. Pricing psychology takes things up a notch: You may want to target consumer psychology specifically through numbers that appear more affordable than they are, like $19.95 instead of $20.

Bundle pricing combines multiple products together, usually at discounted costs. The goal here isn't just for customers to purchase more items, but also to increase the overall value of their purchase, allowing upselling and cross-selling opportunities. Price discrimination is a sneaky way of charging different prices to different customers for the same product based on factors like location and purchase history. This lets you attract extra revenue from price-sensitive customers while also making money from people willing to spend more.

Businesses must be able to adapt their pricing strategies based on external factors like regulation changes, competition, and the economy in general. With constant change outside your company, you don't want to be caught slipping—so always stay informed.

Place: Distribution Channels and Market Coverage

Distribution channels are the roads that businesses can take to deliver their products or services to consumers. A marketing strategy's success depends on the careful selection of these channels and the ensuring of market coverage. Deciding which channel to distribute your product through is an aspect of place strategy. This distribution channel depends on the kind of product you're offering, who your target audience is, and industry trends. There are many distribution channel options, such as direct sales, retailers, wholesalers, distributors, and online marketplaces.

Direct selling allows you to sell directly to customers without any third-party involvement in the transaction process. This approach allows companies to have more control over their sales process and customer interaction but may require significant investment.

Retailers are companies selling products directly to consumers through online or physical stores. Partnering with retail stores gives your business access to a larger audience since they've already established a solid customer base and brand recognition. Businesses must consider factors such as shelf space, competition, and retailer fees when selecting retail distribution channels.

Wholesalers and distributors are intermediaries between businesses like yours and other retailers or resellers. They purchase merchandise from you at wholesale prices and then resell it at a markup from the manufacturer's suggested retail price (MSRP). Working with these middlemen gives you a more significant geographic range than if you had a one-on-one distribution agreement with a retailer.

Online marketplaces such as Amazon give small businesses an additional platform for selling products, where they can potentially reach millions of users worldwide. These platforms come with tools that can help businesses manage their online presence effectively, including setting up professional store pages and listings.

Apart from selecting which channel to use, companies must also consider the extent of their coverage in different regions or markets. The extent of this coverage will change depending on company size, competition strength, and overall business goal. The primary goal of the intensive distribution strategy is to make products available in as many retail outlets as possible. This strategy is best for businesses whose products are in high demand with low prices, like fast food shops or dollar stores. This approach helps companies maximize exposure and ensure their products are easy to find.

Selective distribution strategy limits the number of outlets a company sells its product through. This strategy is mostly used by luxury brands since it conveys a sense of scarcity and quality, which can drive up demand. By not allowing many retailers to sell their products, businesses have more control over the distribution process and ensure that products are sold in an environment that aligns with their brand image.

An exclusive distribution strategy gives only one retailer or distributor exclusive rights to sell your product in a specific geographic area or market segment. The most common example is the iPhone, which is sold in an exclusive deal to Verizon, AT&T, or T-Mobile. This method helps companies establish a sense of scarcity around their product, driving up demand and enhancing brand perception.

Finding the right places to distribute a product and guaranteeing enough coverage in the market are essential parts of any good marketing strategy. By knowing what each channel is good at and not so good at, thinking about things like competition and target market size, and ensuring distribution strategies align with business goals, companies can reach their intended customers, boost sales, and find success.

Promotion: Advertising, Sales Promotion, and Public Relations

Promotion is a crucial part of marketing because it helps spread the word, generate excitement, and drive sales of products or services. It entails various activities that aim to communicate with target audiences and persuade them to purchase. The three main promotion components are advertising, sales promotion, and public relations.

Advertising involves paid communication promoting products, services, or brands to a specific group. It can take many forms, including print ads, TV commercials, radio spots, online ads, and social media promotions.

Advertising allows businesses to reach many people quickly and effectively and build brand awareness. The best ad campaigns are creative and memorable and specifically tailored to the preferences and interests of the intended audience.

Sales promotion offers short-term incentives to convince consumers to take immediate action toward purchasing. Examples include discounts, coupons, rebates, contests, and giveaways. Sales promotions are commonly used to increase demand and sales volume or create buzz around a product or service. While they can be effective in the short term, businesses must be careful to use them sparingly, as this may dilute their brand value or reduce profit margins.

Public relations (PR) are about managing customer, employee, and investor relationships through communication efforts. PR activities aim to create positive perceptions of your business and build trust among all who encounter your brand. Media relations, planning events, responding efficiently during crisis situations, and community relations initiatives can improve your brand's reputation and credibility, ultimately contributing to long-term success.

Integrated marketing communications (IMC) combines various promotional elements into one cohesive strategy so that you deliver a consistent message across all platforms, including both offline & online media—which is more impactful on the target audience than using one channel only once or twice per month. Businesses can create a unified image and maximize impact by coordinating advertising, sales promotion, public relations, and other promotional activities. IMC will ensure each activity is there to help you achieve your marketing goals and drive desired outcomes.

One of the hardest things for businesses to do when promoting their brand is to measure ROI effectively. For example, some promotional strategies like advertising are direct and can easily be measured by how many people see it, how many engage, and how many buy from you. Other strategies, such as public relations, may have more intangible results—but by setting clear objectives, tracking relevant metrics, and analyzing what happens, businesses will eventually find a way to optimize future campaigns and make data-driven decisions.

In this modern era, we have many tools that can allow us to reach the target audience quickly and effectively. Social media marketing content, email partnerships, and influencers are a few examples of these types of promotions. Businesses who know they have the right demographics can create ads or content that will grab attention and drive brand awareness and sales of their products or services. This approach requires creative planning, strategic thinking, and a deep understanding of market dynamics for long-term success.

. . .

Chapter 10

Final Word

Coming to the end of our journey, "The Start of All Things Good: A Complete Guide to Building Your Business'" has been an eye-opening experience. As you go through this book, you will have encountered loads of knowledge and strategies that will guide you as you navigate the world of entrepreneurship. From forming a mindset for business to understanding how to get your product out there, every chapter should have served its own unique purpose.

I want you to know that entrepreneurship is not just about building a successful business, but also about growing, learning and adapting. I believe that, with all the tools and frameworks that have been provided in this guide, aspiring entrepreneurs such as yourself can make your dreams of innovation and prosperity become a reality.

As you proceed on your entrepreneurial path, I hope that the information featured in this book inspires you to think outside the box and be daring enough to take risks. Always remember; success is not determined by how much money you make or how successful your business gets—it is more so about what difference your product or service makes in people's lives.

Before you let go of this guide for good, I encourage you to continue carrying the spirit of entrepreneurship within yourself. Don't forget that it takes audacity, courage, and perseverance to truly succeed. Create an impact! Go out and set things in motion because, once innovation starts taking place, it propels boundless opportunity.

So long until next time, my friend. Let curiosity lead your way as well as determination. The start of all things good is just that—the start. Now go forth and build something extraordinary.

Printed in the USA
CPSIA information can be obtained
at www.ICGtesting.com
LVHW010338170924
791230LV00008B/60/J